Blood in Their Eyes

Books by Grif Stockley

Expert Testimony
Probable Cause
Religious Conviction
Illegal Motion
Blind Judgment
Salted with Fire

BLOOD

The Elaine

IN THEIR

Race Massacres

EYES

of 1919

GRIF STOCKLEY

The University of Arkansas Press
Fayetteville
2001

Designer: John Coghlan

∞ The paper used in this publication meets the minimum requirements
of the American National Standard for Permanence of Paper for Printed
Library Materials Z39.48-1984.

The Library of Congress has cataloged the hardcover edition as follows:

Stockley, Grif.
    Blood in their eyes : the Elaine race massacres of 1919 / Grif Stockley.
        p. cm.
Includes bibliographical references and index.
    ISBN 1-55728-717-1 (cloth : alk. paper)
    1. Phillips County (Ark.)—Race relations. 2. Elaine Region
(Ark.)—Race relations. 3. Riots—Arkansas—Elaine Region—
History—20th century. 4. Massacres—Arkansas—Elaine Region—
History—20th century. 5. Sharecroppers—Arkansas—Phillips
County—Social conditions—20th century. 6. African Americans—
Arkansas—Phillips County—Social conditions—20th century.
7. African Americans—Legal status, laws, etc.—Arkansas—Phillips
County—History—20th century. 8. Trials (Murder)—Arkansas—
Phillips County—History—20th century. 9. Camp Pike (Ark.)—
History—20th century. 10. United States. Army—Civic
action—History—20th century.
I. Title.
    F417.P45 S76 2001
        305.896'073076788—dc21

                                                                2001003852

To Lynn Pence

Acknowledgments

There are many people and institutions to acknowledge. First, I wish to thank Lynn Pence for her unwavering belief in the validity of this book. Tom Dillard and his staff at the Butler Center for Arkansas Studies, including Tim Nutt, Cary Cox, Linda McDowell, and Rel Corbin, patiently shared their expertise in Arkansas history on many occasions. As Tom Dillard was the first historian to rediscover the contributions of Scipio Africanus Jones and other Arkansas African Americans, his close reading of the manuscript and his enthusiasm for this project were helpful beyond words. Though we disagree about the role of the U.S. military in the slaughter of African Americans in Phillips County, Jeannie Whayne holds wide knowledge of the subject, and her suggestions and corrections of an initial draft of the manuscript were also invaluable. The ultimate focus of Dick Cortner's work *A Mob Intent on Death: The NAACP and the Arkansas Riot Cases* is the significance of the U.S. Supreme Court case of *Moore v. Dempsey,* but his exhaustive research of the events in Arkansas during this period is indeed impressive. As the number of citations to his work indicates, his research on this subject has set the curve for those who follow.

Many of those who initially provided information to me will be surprised that this book is not the historical novel I originally intended it to be. It is the person of Scipio Africanus Jones who caused me to abandon the idea of this book as a novel. Though a draft of a novel survives, I felt increasingly uncomfortable with the idea of this complex human being as a character in any fiction I might render. Ms. Hazel Adams of Chicago, Jones's granddaughter, reports that a diary kept by her mother (also named Hazel) exists but has been lost. Should it be found, historians may be given some clue as to the inner life of this amazing individual.

Fascinated by the character of Ulysses Simpson Bratton, I was finally able to track down the granddaughter of Ocier Bratton, Ms. Virginia Lee "Thea" Crossier, who lives in Florida. In many American families, someone keeps track of the ancestors, and Ms. Crossier shared with me her lore of the Brattons. David Bratton in Michigan and Sally Wilson in Arkansas were also of considerable assistance.

Price Roark, an Arkansas resident and nephew of Anne Roark Brough, shared with me information about his aunt and Charles Hillman Brough. My interpretation of Governor Brough's actions and motives and his place in history, is, of course, my own and not Mr. Roark's.

Though employees of libraries and repositories of historical documents modestly tell you they are merely doing their jobs, their professionalism and commitment to their work are a matter of life and death to a writer. Within the state of Arkansas I wish to especially thank Kathryn Fitzhugh, reference and special collections librarian at the University of Arkansas at Little Rock, William H. Bowen School of Law. During the writing of this book, Ms. Fitzhugh acquired for the library a number of legal documents from *Moore v. Dempsey* from the federal archives, thus allowing future researchers to almost completely trace the complicated legal odyssey of the Elaine defendants in one venue. I also wish to thank Russell Baker and his staff at the Arkansas History Commission; Ethel Simpson, Todd Lewis, Cassandra McGraw, and Andrea Cantrell of the University of Arkansas, Fayetteville, Mullins Library, Special Collections; Linda Pine and her staff at the University of Arkansas at Little Rock, Ottenheimer Library, Archives and Special Collections; the Phillips County Library; the Quapaw Quarter Association; the Arkansas Department of Corrections; and Hendrix College.

I also acknowledge the assistance of the staffs of the Wisconsin State Historical Society, the Library of Congress, the National Archives, the Mississippi Department of Archives and History, and the Memphis Public Library.

In addition, I thank Judith Kilpatrick, Eric Freedman, Brian Greer, Gerry Crabb, Nashid Madyun, Frances Keesee, Judge James Mixon, Marshall Trieber, Vincent Vinikas, Mark Schneider, Michael Dougan, Toney Brasuell, Michele Barger, Gailon McHaney, Lynn Foster, Joseph Solomon, Cal Ledbetter, Foy Lisenby, Richard Wormser, Ken Storey, Representative Vic Snyder and his staff, Curtis Sykes, Conie Reamey, Kirk Reamey, Jim Lilly, Richard C. Butler Sr., Ernie Dumas, Hal Hubener, Starr Mitchell, Judge Annabelle Clinton, John Crow, Constance Sarto, Seetha Srinivasan, J. E. Bush IV, Alice Saville Bush, Ann Clements, James Lilly, James Lilly Jr., Ronnie Nichols, John Graves, Bill Clements, and Nan Woodruff.

Finally, I wish to express my appreciation to the University of Arkansas Press, to its editor and director, Larry Malley, and to Brian King, its managing editor. Not least I thank Carol Sickman-Garner, my superb editor on this project. All errors, alas, are the author's.

Contents

Acknowledgments   vii

Preface   xi

Introduction   xiii

Chronology of Events   xxiii

Chapter 1. Charles Hillman Brough's Midnight Train Ride   3

Chapter 2. The Law of the Delta   19

Chapter 3. The Boys from Camp Pike   34

Chapter 4. A Committee of Seven   61

Chapter 5. More Than One Version   80

Chapter 6. Little Rock and New York: An Uneasy Alliance   92

Chapter 7. The Trials Begin   106

Chapter 8. Colonel Murphy for the Defense   138

Chapter 9. The Retrials of the Ware Defendants   151

Chapter 10. The Changing of the Guard   176

Chapter 11. Affidavits from Unlikely Sources   192

Chapter 12. *Moore v. Dempsey:* A Supreme Victory   208

Chapter 13. Scipio Jones Takes Charge   223

Notes   235

A Note on Sources   257

Index   259

Preface

Arkansas history is a quilt of many colors—but it is also a fabric with an ugly hole in it. The Elaine massacres of 1919 are far more than a mere historical blemish; they are the single most bloody racial confrontation in Arkansas history. Adding insult to injury, the massacres have never received the kind of historical analysis that is needed to bring the event to some appropriate historical closure. In this book Grif Stockley provides a strong tonic to cure these historical ills.

Mr. Stockley is a lawyer, not a historian, and that background is a useful one from which to undertake a new analysis of the massacre and its aftermath. Also, Stockley is tireless, and this energy allows him to delve into the Elaine episode with a determination never brought to this subject previously. He uses sources that have never been used or that have been misinterpreted. He looks into the personalities of both the white and black participants, and his findings are sometimes surprising. For example, one of the white defense attorneys has traditionally been depicted as having had a far greater interest in collecting his fees than in providing a meaningful defense. Stockley concludes, however, that he was actually an astute strategist who deserves much credit for the defense's eventual success. Another white participant, a civil judge in Little Rock, was willing to put his reputation on the line by issuing a ruling on the case when it was clear he did not have jurisdiction; this action bought time at a critical stage, when the executioner was suiting-up to do his work.

The author possesses two skills that allow him to go beyond the norm: he sees beyond the surface level, and he really writes well. His analysis of black defense lawyer Scipio A. Jones is exceptionally strong, and it reminds us that Jones is a central figure in Arkansas legal history.

Amazingly, some white residents of Phillips County still defend the actions of the white community in using force to suppress a supposed black "insurrection." And many of these residents are not happy to see the subject brought up again. At least they cannot charge the author with being an outside agitator, for Mr. Stockley grew up in Lee County, next door to Phillips County, in the heart of the Delta.

Like an Old Testament prophet, Stockley does not hesitate to take unpopular stands. For example, traditionally historians have believed that the regular U.S. Army troops from Camp Pike were instrumental in restoring peace to Phillips County. Stockley, after a long and careful consideration of the evidence, concludes that at least some of the soldiers participated in the butchery.

Certain aspects of our history cry out for remembrance. The Elaine massacres will not go away. The uncounted dead still lie in their unmarked graves. While we might never know how many people were murdered during the massacre—much less who they were—we can consider this book as a belated memorial for them. And for the perpetrators, this book serves to remind us that while they might have avoided detection during their lives, there is no historical statute of limitations.

Arkansas history—and indeed the history of the nation—demands and deserves this book.

Tom W. Dillard
Curator
Butler Center for Arkansas Studies

Introduction

*DESPERATE FIGHTING BETWEEN WHITES AND NEGROES OCCURS IN SOUTHERN SEC-
TION OF PHILLIPS COUNTY*
       *—Headline across entire front page of Arkansas Gazette,
       October 2, 1919*

In the morning hours of October 1, 1919, urgent calls went up and down the Mississippi River from the heart of the Arkansas Delta: *blacks in Phillips County are rioting.* No one seemed to be clear about what had touched them off, but a shoot-out at a church in a hamlet called Hoop Spur in the southern part of the county had left one white man dead and others wounded. A white posse from the county seat, Helena, drove the twenty-odd miles to Hoop Spur, three miles north of the town of Elaine, but instead of surrendering, some blacks fought back. By two in the afternoon two members of the posse were dead. Help was needed immediately because, as in much of the Delta, blacks in this area of the county were overwhelmingly in the majority. Planters and their families were in danger, and women and children were being sent to Elaine for protection, though Elaine itself was believed to be under attack.

Frantic telegrams, three in number that day, began to arrive at the governor's office in Little Rock requesting that five hundred troops be rushed to Phillips County to restore order. Governor Charles Hillman Brough called the War Department in Washington, but the response was agonizingly slow. Unencumbered by military bureaucracy, an estimated one thousand white males, primarily from neighboring Arkansas Delta communities but also from across the river in Mississippi and Tennessee, had by nightfall heeded the alarm and descended on Elaine. After midnight, a troop train bearing Brough and 583 soldiers—including battle-hardened veterans of the Second Battle of the Marne in France, armed with machine guns—rolled out from Union Station, across from the state capitol in Little Rock, heading south and then east for the eight-hour journey to Elaine.

What occurred on October 1 and over the following week in Phillips County, Arkansas, has been the subject of intense debate among historians,

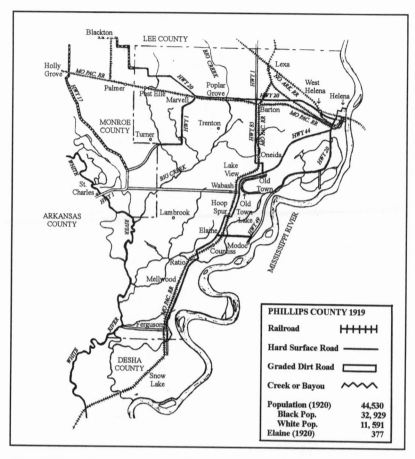

Map of Phillips County at the time of the massacres. *Courtesy of Butler Center for Arkansas Studies, Central Arkansas Library System.*

students of race relations, and of course residents of the area. It is documented that five whites, including a soldier, died at Elaine, but estimates of African American deaths, made by individuals writing about the Elaine affair between 1919 and 1925, range from 20 to 856; if accurate, these numbers would make it by far the most deadly racial conflict in the history of the United States.

It is my belief that the United States military participated in the massacres along with white civilians from Arkansas, Mississippi, and Tennessee. Yet there has never been an admission from the government of the United States or from the state of Arkansas that any massacres took place. The cover-up of the activities of the military and white civilians began on October 1, 1919, and was so effective that the dimensions of this American tragedy will never be known.

In February 2000, historians and the general public met in Helena for a conference about the 1919 events in the Arkansas Delta. No effort was made to determine the number of African Americans killed. The historical truth is that it is too late now to ever know the total. The tragedy of the Elaine massacres is not only that they occurred but also that we are ignorant of them today.

The fear and terror that were the daily staples of the African American psychological state during that era have never been adequately communicated by the term "Jim Crow." Until recently in Arkansas, historians have concentrated on the segregation and political exclusion of the era and have neglected the harder-to-document white-on-black violence that was an indivisible component of "Jim Crow" and that has long been covered up as part of a pattern that began with slavery.

In the state of Arkansas there are many monuments to the state's Civil War dead. There are none to the victims of slavery or segregation. The question of why this is so is related to the phenomenon of the incredible disparity in the estimates relating to the number of African Americans who lost their lives in Phillips County in 1919. As early as the second day of the Elaine massacres, the white power structure in the Delta, including the media, began to formulate an explanation of the events that was psychologically irresistible to almost everyone, including the governor and the black elite of the state. Though the details would continually be refined, one theme was constant: *there had been no lynchings.* Over the years, as evidence began to mount that something horrible had indeed occurred in Phillips County, a fallback position would emerge and be adopted by future investigators: *what happened in Phillips County in the fall of 1919 depends on what version one believes—the black account or the white account.* Or as Jeannie M. Whayne, professor of history at the University of Arkansas, diplomatically puts it, "Historians, struggling with a mass of rich but contradictory and even tainted evidence, have failed to arrive at a common narrative of events."[1]

In fact, the evidence shows that blacks were murdered by white mobs and U.S. soldiers from Camp Pike and that a sustained and largely successful effort was made to convince the public and future historians that only blacks who had resisted lawful authority were killed. In its exploration of the Elaine massacres, it is the underlying thesis of this book that few Southerners, white or black, have personally come to grips with the intense anguish that would be brought about by a frank discussion with each other of the Jim Crow period or slavery. Southern whites have buried shame and guilt about the pain of slavery and apartheid beneath a mound of rationalizations about historical context. In fact, the contradictions between the ideals expressed in the Declaration of Independence and the practice of slavery were apparent to all from the beginning. Only a monumental conflict could have ended the practice. The continuing failure of white Southerners after the Civil War to acknowledge the devastating personal corruption that accompanied ownership of other human beings skewers our view of race relations and history even today. Though by 1919 the practice of slavery was over, the massacres in Elaine and their denial predicted the future just as surely as they replicated the past.

In 1998, I planned to try to write a novel about the events of 1919. From Little Rock in the center of the state I drove east to the town of Elaine in the Delta and was told that I should see a woman by the name of Mary Louise Demoret Fiser, the leading citizen of the town and owner of the Delta State Bank. Mrs. Fiser's father and grandfather owned a general store in Elaine in 1919. She had written a number of articles on Elaine for the *Phillips County Historical Review*. Though I told her that I had read it, she insisted on giving me a copy of an *Arkansas Historical Quarterly* article published in 1961 entitled, "The Underlying Causes of the Elaine Riot of 1919." It would tell me what had occurred in the Elaine area during that troubled time. The article—written by two whites, J. W. Butts and Dorothy James, who describe themselves as lifelong residents of Helena, the county seat of Phillips County—is an effort to refute point by point an article published in the *Arkansas Historical Quarterly* the preceding year by O. A. Rogers Jr., then president of Arkansas Baptist College, a small black school in Little Rock.

Relying primarily on documents published at the time by the NAACP and on a pamphlet written by the antilynching crusader Ida B. Wells-Barnett, Rogers argues that blacks had formed a union of sharecroppers whose purpose it was to gain fair settlements on their cotton crops: "The chief plan [of the Hoop Spur lodge] included withholding all cotton, thereby forcing their landlords to make equitable settlements."[2]

Blacks had contended that after whites broke up the meeting at Hoop Spur, the members returned fire, killing one white man, Will Adkins. The next day a posse from Helena came to the area "and began to search and ransack the Negroes' homes, arresting men and women indiscriminately. . . ."[3] Blacks continued to resist, prompting the whites to ask Governor Charles Hillman Brough to request federal troops to restore order. Rogers mentions that the troops' arrival did end the fighting and that twelve blacks were convicted of first-degree murder and sentenced to death but were eventually released. Rogers's nine-page account neither makes an estimate of the numbers killed nor mentions the activities of the estimated six hundred to a thousand white men from surrounding towns on both sides of the Mississippi who came into the area when given the news that blacks were armed with weapons and fighting back. Nor does it mention the behavior of the white troops when they arrived in Elaine on October 2. Rogers's article is aimed primarily at the modest goal of showing that the blacks by forming a union had been seeking peaceful redress of their grievances.

To refute Rogers, Butts and James interviewed white sources primarily from the Elaine area. They conclude, in part, the following:

> There is no evidence to show primary aggression on the part of the whites. . . . Many of the casualties of the Negroes [sic] sustained by the Negroes occurred in this battle [with the federal troops on the morning of October 1]. . . . The whole Elaine affair lasted only two days. . . . After that there was no disorder. . . . A majority of the Negroes had nothing to do with the union. . . . Certainly, no peaceful attempts were made to correct any real or fancied grievances. . . . All those accused of complicity in the Elaine Riot were given fair trials. . . . No mob violence was attempted. . . .[4]

For different reasons neither article deals with the actual scope of the black carnage or with the six-year struggle that pitted the state of Arkansas against the outside world. The fact that Mrs. Fiser kept a collection of copies of the Butts-James article on hand to give to visitors in 1998 indicates that two different versions of the events of 1919 still lay smoldering beneath the surface. But by the time of the Elaine conference, Mrs. Fiser was no longer willing to talk about it. "Nothing we can do can go back and change what's happened," she told an Associated Press reporter less than two weeks before the historians gathered. "It's part of the past. We have to look forward."[5] Perhaps suspecting that historians were about to pick apart the Butts-James article, she pointed out that no one knows for sure what happened.

Mrs. Fiser was correct. We do not know all the particulars of what happened in Elaine. In his book *Vital Lies, Simple Truths: The Psychology of Self-Deception,* the psychologist and writer Daniel Goleman states that "there are, it seems, vital parts of our lives which are, in a sense, missing— blanks in experience hidden by holes in vocabulary. That we do not experience them is a fact which we know only vaguely, if at all."[6]

Goleman tells us that the blanks in our experience are centered around those moments that generate intolerable anxiety, including emotions of fear and shame. Our avoidance of intolerable anxiety comes at a price, he observes. The price, of course, is that we do not see events as they are. Goleman's observations fit the collective experience of race relations in the South and the experience of both whites and blacks during 1919. The Elaine massacres provoked extreme anxiety among Arkansans both white and black. The efforts to avoid confronting that anxiety continue into the present.

It appears that both whites and blacks who lived in Arkansas during the Elaine affair often failed to *notice* what was happening around them. Neither whites nor blacks, of course, existed in a vacuum in the Arkansas Delta. During all phases of the massacres, the psychology of the group dominated the individual. Goleman argues that the "we" that composes a group "is as vulnerable as the self to self-deceptions. The motivating force behind the forming of shared illusions in a group is identical to that in the self: to minimize anxiety."[7]

Those of us old enough to have lived during the days of segregation in the Arkansas Delta can easily confirm the feeling of what it meant to be a part of a group, much more easily than our children can articulate their feelings about their identities today. In analyzing the psychological implications of what happened in Arkansas and the Delta in 1919, it will be crucial to keep in mind the obvious—that at all times the actors in the Elaine massacres saw themselves as part of specific racial groups. Jeannie Whayne has pointed out that the racial conflict in Elaine was an isolated instance of Delta whites coming together to transcend the class conflicts that existed between members of the planter class and the rural white poor, who were often sharecroppers competing with blacks for contracts.[8] For our purposes, however, more important than this temporary alliance are the well-known psychological dynamics that operate in groups generally. In order to reduce anxiety, "Much of what group members say to each other to justify a shaky course of action is rationalization, a story line they pool their efforts to concoct and believe. Rationalizations serve to build confidence and reassure the group about the morality, safety, wisdom, or other validity of their decisions."[9] Goleman shows that the "group" invariably makes assumptions about the rightness of its cause: "These ethical blinders help the group avoid feeling ashamed or guilty about what otherwise might be questionable means or goals."[10]

Though our historians have begun to acknowledge the horror and violence of slavery and segregation, our understanding of ourselves in the South has rarely included a grasp of just how deeply imbedded groupthink has been as a part of our culture. Indeed, the effort to avoid the truth of the shame of slavery and the Jim Crow era has been so pervasive that at the height of both institutions it defined our very existence. To ignore the power of group-think would be to hinder our understanding of what proved to be a titanic struggle between the state of Arkansas and outside forces. One of the hallmarks of the Elaine massacres was the degree to which Governor Charles Hillman Brough was able to rally people in the state, including whites and middle-class blacks, in support of his action in requesting that troops be sent to Elaine—troops whose actions are in dispute to this day. Nothing characterizes the Elaine massacres more than the psychology of the group. Defending the state against outside criticism became a litmus test of one's loyalty. Those who dared attack the planter-sharecropper system publicly inside the state were literally persecuted. Ulysses Bratton, a white attorney who had agreed to represent the members of the sharecropper union, received death threats and moved himself and his family to Detroit within months of the massacres.

Thus, it will not be enough to make the case that what occurred in Phillips County had to do with economics and power. That explanation alone will not tell us why accounts of the events vary so widely. This is not to say that standard historical interpretations should or can be ignored, but by casting a wider net, we hope to learn something more fundamental about the events in 1919. To say that blacks and whites did not always *notice* their experiences of slavery and segregation is, of course, to use a metaphor that points to the familiar defense mechanisms of denial and reversal (reaction formation), repression, rationalization, intellectualization, and projection. That we all engage in these coping devices on a daily basis is beyond dispute. What is most characteristic of these behaviors, psychologists tell us, is that we are not consciously aware that we are, for example, "projecting" our own behavior and feelings onto others.

As a white male growing up in the 1950s in Lee County, which borders Phillips County (I was born in 1944), I had ample opportunity to hear about Elaine. My grandmother, who in her day was the unofficial historian of Lee County and wrote numerous historical articles for the local paper, was from Marvell in Phillips County. She never mentioned Elaine to me, so far as I remember. I have a vague recollection of hearing at least once as a teenager from a friend that some "niggers" had been killed during a riot back then, but that is all. At the conference in Helena, a black woman in her thirties said from the audience that she had lived in the area all her life and had never heard of the events in Elaine in 1919 until recently. Though scholarly interest and occasional stories in the press have sporadically drawn attention to the subject, for eighty-two years within Phillips County it has been an affair more whispered about than publicly dissected.

My own experiences as a child in the Delta in the 1950s provide a psychological context for thinking about what happened in Elaine in 1919. My father, Griffin Jasper Stockley Sr.—"Jake," as he was known—owned a series of small businesses in Marianna, the county seat of Lee County, and though financially he was not as well off as at an earlier part of his life, he was able to provide us a comfortable existence. On a typical summer's day when I was ten, in 1954, I would come downstairs to where my mother, Temple Wall Stockley (her father had been a doctor in Lee County), had laid out for me a breakfast that invariably consisted of hot tea, toast and jelly, and a strip of bacon. Beside the plate would be the sports pages of the Memphis *Commercial Appeal.* I had become that year a fan of the Cleveland Indians, and they were to go on under their manager Al Lopez to beat the hated Yankees and win the American League pennant, though losing four straight to the Giants in the World Series. After breakfast I would go outside to see Buttons and Bows, our two beagles, and once a week would encounter the black men who took care of our yard. I would greet them by calling them by their first names, Andrew and Newt (I didn't know their last names). They called me "Mr. Grif" though I was ten years old. *My* memory is that they seemed as comfortable as I did. I sensed no indication they were seething with resentment at having to call a child "Mister" while being called by their first names. Interpreting our exchange now, I can see that each of us knew what we could notice and could *not* notice without inducing severe anxiety.

As a child, I knew that at one time my father had been a farmer and had black people working for him. Though it may seem unbelievable to the reader, I never consciously realized that he was part of the planter-sharecropper system that is at the heart of this book until I was in my fifties.

In the late 1960s, when the Civil Rights Movement finally picked up steam in Arkansas (the Student Nonviolent Coordinating Committee had established a couple of beachheads in the Arkansas Delta earlier before being basically killed off by the Black Power Movement), whites often expressed genuine consternation at what was occurring. In Forrest City, seventeen miles from Marianna, the editor of the local paper was quoted as saying, "There is no reason . . . no logic in this type of action. It's one of those awful things that has always happened somewhere else . . . never here at home . . . not in Forrest City where race relations have always been so good."[11]

If ordinary Germans can begin to undertake the process of understanding the evils of the Nazi era, surely the South can at least begin the process of comprehending what it has forced black people to endure. The mechanisms whereby we have been able to evade this responsibility provide useful explanations of how we have been able not to *notice* our history. However, though they are a part of our human makeup, our defense mechanisms may explain us but do not absolve us.

Not only are we doomed to repeat our history by not knowing it, we *are* repeating it. Phillips County today is rife with racial tension as African Americans finally come to power, just as, indeed, the entire Delta and to a greater or lesser degree the rest of Arkansas, the South, and the nation continue to be confronted by the seemingly endless dilemma of race in America.

One thing is certain. The entire truth of the Jim Crow era and segregation will never be known until both blacks and whites summon the courage to battle the emotional anxiety that will accompany the discussion of these times. The present era in the United States is marked by such a slavish devotion to political correctness that we seem increasingly unable to express our deepest feelings about we have done to one another and why, no matter what is at stake. In Arkansas, for example, few historians have made use of the slave narratives, the collection of thousands of interviews with former slaves conducted by WPA workers during the 1930s. One of the reasons given is the age of ex-slaves at the time the interviews were conducted. How could their memories be trusted when so much time had passed? Our history and our capacity to understand fully the slave era are vanishing before our very eyes. Of course, the same problems exist today as historians and the public ask what really happened in Phillips County in 1919.

Chronology of Events

September 30, 1919. Approximately 11:00 P.M. Firefight outside Hoop Spur church between members of the Progressive Farmers and Household Union and Phillips County law enforcement officers. Will Adkins is killed.

October 1, 1919. 2:00 A.M. Phillips County law enforcement sends nine individuals from Helena in two cars to Hoop Spur church to investigate shooting.

October 1, 1919. Morning. Helena American Legion Post sends volunteers, including World War I veterans, to Hoop Spur area. Calls go out all over the Delta on both sides of the Mississippi River reporting that blacks are fighting back. Throughout the day, six hundred to one thousand armed men from outside Phillips County arrive to hunt down blacks.

October 1, 1919. Morning. Governor Charles Hillman Brough, who is at the state capitol in Little Rock, receives the first of three telegrams asking that troops be sent to Phillips County. He begins the process of asking the War Department in Washington for troops to be sent from Camp Pike, which is composed of World War I veterans, some of whom had fought in the Second Battle of the Marne.

October 1, 1919. Though a sheriff's deputy sends a report that the town of Elaine, three miles south of Hoop Spur, is under attack by a force of blacks, no white casualties in the town are reported. The *Arkansas Gazette* reports the next day that bodies of "at least fifteen negroes were lying in the streets and outskirts of the town and that more would probably be found in the woods." A *Memphis Press* reporter notes corpses of blacks on the road outside of Helena: "Enraged citizens fired at the dead bodies of the negroes, as they rode out of Helena toward Elaine."

October 1, 1919. From a master's thesis by Bessie Ferguson from neighboring Lee County, published in 1927: "Barberism [*sic*]such as cutting off the ears or toes of dead negroes for souvenirs and the dragging of their bodies through the streets of Elaine are told by witnesses."

October 1, 1919. Whites ransack the homes of black union members in the Hoop Spur area and steal their personal possessions. Blacks flee into the dense canebrakes and woods in the area.

October 1, 1919. Morning. Ocier Bratton, eldest son of Little Rock lawyer

Ulysses Bratton, arrives by train at Ratio, five miles south of Elaine. Unaware of the shoot-out at Hoop Spur, he and Robert Hill, founder of the union, meet with members of the Ratio lodge. Black sharecroppers pay fees and sign retainer agreements in order for the Bratton law firm to represent them in their dispute with planters. Bratton is taken into custody by a group of whites, driven to Elaine, and placed in a store where whites are expecting an attack by blacks. Robert Hill escapes before he can be arrested.

October 1, 1919. A group of blacks from the Hoop Spur lodge, some of whom have military experience, decide to defend themselves and march in formation until they see whites. A shot is fired, killing Clinton Lee, a member of the Helena American Legion Post posse. James Tappan, also part of the same posse, is killed while searching for blacks in the dense canebrakes.

October 1, 1919. D. A. E. Johnston and his three brothers, members of a prominent black family in Helena, are shot to death while they are being transported to Helena by local posses and law enforcement. Their bodies are thrown out into the road. O. R. Lilly, a member of the white posse and a Helena resident who was in the same vehicle, is killed, allegedly by D. A. E. Johnston. Other stories say that Lilly was killed by the posse.

October 1, 1919. Probably alerted by black couriers, a group of armed blacks rides from the Lambrook plantation west of Elaine toward Hoop Spur. They inflict no casualties.

October 1, 1919. Panicked by fears of a black uprising, whites in the Hoop Spur area seek safety in Elaine. Women and children are taken by train into Helena. Fearing that Ocier Bratton is about to be lynched, Phillips County Circuit Judge J. M. Jackson arranges for him to be taken to Helena and put in jail. No white farmers and their families report attacks by blacks. Ocier Bratton observes no attack on the town of Elaine.

October 2, 1919. Because of bureaucratic delays, the Camp Pike troop train, which carries over five hundred men and twelve machine guns, does not leave Little Rock until shortly after midnight on October 1. Governor Brough is permitted to accompany the troops, who are under the command of Col. Issac Jenks, a West Point graduate. Brough tells reporters he is going to Elaine so that he can make an accurate assessment of what is occurring.

October 2, 1919. Morning. The troop train arrives in Elaine. Colonel Jenks secures the town and orders that everyone, black and white, be disarmed. A detachment is sent in to Helena to guard the jail to prevent lynchings. Accompanied by Governor Brough, Jenks sets out with a company of men that includes two machine guns for Hoop Spur, where there is fighting reported. In his official report of the encounter, Jenks fails to mention that his troops fired even a single shot. He reports the death of one of his men and the wounding of another. The newspapers report that three shots were fired over the governor's head. The troops return to Elaine. No other whites, civilian or soldier, will be reported killed by blacks, though Jenks accepts the whites' explanation that blacks were attempting an "insurrection."

October 2, 1919. The white mobs depart. The soldiers assist whites in interrogating blacks, some of whom are tortured. Hundreds of blacks are confined in makeshift stockades until their employers vouch for their innocence. Military intelligence reports claim that blacks have confessed to planning an insurrection, though no names of individuals are given. Blacks are taken to the jail in Helena where the torture continues.

October 2, 1919. Afternoon. Governor Brough travels to Helena and marches at the head of the troops. He meets with the "Committee of Seven," a group composed of city and county officials and planters who propose to Brough that this group lead an investigation of the disturbances. Though the group has no legal authority, Brough gives them his blessing and returns to Little Rock the next day. Brough receives the promise that there will be "no lynchings" in Phillips County.

October 3, 1919. The *Helena World* headlines announce that the Committee of Seven is now in charge. Brough holds a press conference in Little Rock and praises the valor of the five whites who have been killed. He does not mention the activities of the white mobs.

October 2–9, 1919. Troops from Camp Pike remain in the Elaine area. In 1925, a book appears in Little Rock entitled, *What a Preacher Saw Through a Keyhole in Arkansas,* which alleges that 856 blacks were killed in Phillips County, mostly by troops from Camp Pike. Written by a white reporter for the *Arkansas Gazette,* Louis Sharpe Dunaway, the book contains little documentation. Jenks's official report mentions that only two blacks were killed. Military intelligence reports place the total of black deaths, at most, at twenty.

October 7, 1919. The Committee of Seven announces its findings: the fight at the Hoop Spur church prematurely set off an insurrection by blacks planned for October 6. Planters were marked for death; Robert Hill, still at large, was the union's mastermind and had organized the union for purely personal gain. Told to expect support by the federal government, blacks had expected to take over the planters' lands.

October 7, 1919. A circular is passed out to blacks advising them to get back to work and to act as if nothing has happened.

October 7–19, 1919. Editorials in Arkansas, Tennessee, and Mississippi warn blacks against further agitation, pointing out that it will only result in more black deaths.

October 8, 1919. Walter White, a black assistant field secretary for the NAACP in New York whose skin is white, deceives Governor Brough into thinking he is an open-minded journalist from the North and gains an interview with him. White also meets with Scipio Jones, the leading black attorney in Little Rock, who introduces him to Ulysses Bratton, who gives him information on peonage in Arkansas. White then travels to Helena but only remains for a few hours before he is nearly lynched.

October 2–30, 1919. Attempts by Ulysses Bratton to get his son Ocier released from jail fail. Edgar McHaney, a well-connected attorney with the Little Rock firm of Murphy, McHaney and Dunaway, travels to Helena but is told that Ocier would not be guaranteed safe passage out of Phillips County even if he were released.

October 11, 1919. The NAACP holds a press conference in New York, decrying the events in Phillips County. The first of several articles by Walter White about conditions in Arkansas appears in the Northern press. Governor Brough is furious and tries to prevent the *Crisis,* an NAACP magazine, and the *Chicago Defender,* a black-owned newspaper, from being distributed in Arkansas.

October 19, 1919. A letter signed by Scipio Jones and other members of the black elite—including Philander College president, James Monroe Cox; Arkansas Baptist College president, Joseph A. Booker; and Bishop J. M. Conner of the African Methodist Episcopal Church—appears in the *Arkansas Gazette,* praising the actions of Governor Brough and expressing support for him.

October 27–31, 1919. The Phillips County grand jury meets and charges 122 blacks with crimes ranging from murder to nightriding. The prosecuting attorney, John E. Miller, dismisses charges against twenty-one blacks for lack of evidence. Ocier Bratton is released by Judge Jackson, who personally sees to it that he gets out of Phillips County alive.

November 3, 1919. Judge Jackson begins the first trials against blacks charged by the grand jury. Outside the courthouse, troops stand guard to insure that no lynchings occur. Jackson appoints local white attorneys, who go through the motions of acting as defense counsel. They neither interview nor call witnesses, they strike no jury members for bias, and in general they put on no defense. In the first case, Frank Hicks is convicted of the murder of Clinton Lee. The jury is out eight minutes. The penalty is death.

November 3, 1919. Jackson empanels a new jury and begins the trial of Frank

Moore, Ed Hicks (brother of Frank Hicks), Joe Knox, Ed "Sweat" Coleman, and Paul Hall for aiding and abetting in the murder of Clinton Lee. Though there is no evidence that Coleman or Hall had anything to do with Lee's death, all are convicted. The penalty is death. Executions are set for late December and early January.

November 4, 1919. Alf Banks Jr. and John Martin, two of the guards outside the church at Hoop Spur, are convicted for the murder of Will Adkins. The jury is out for nine minutes and returns a verdict of guilty.

November 4, 1919. Albert Giles and Joe Fox are tried for the murder of James Tappan. These two defendants fled into the dense canebrakes near Hoop Spur and were hunted by the posse from Phillips County. They are convicted and sentenced to death.

November 4, 1919. William Wardlow, a guard outside the Hoop Spur church, is convicted for the crime of aiding and abetting in the death of Adkins. The jury is out two minutes. The penalty is death.

November 5, 1919. Ulysses Bratton arrives in New York and begins meeting with the staff of the NAACP and its supporters. He describes the peonage system in Arkansas and helps the NAACP raise funds to defend the men in Arkansas. He suggests the law firm of Murphy, McHaney and Dunaway to represent them.

November 5–6, 1919. Dozens of the defendants enter into hurried plea-bargains to escape the electric chair. The *Helena World* reports that sixty-five men have been convicted of crimes ranging from second-degree murder (twenty-one years) to nightriding (one year). Other cases are continued; some are dismissed for lack of evidence.

November 17, 1919. Ed Ware, the secretary of the Hoop Spur lodge, is captured and put on trial for the murder of Will Adkins. Suggs Bondsman, who says he has lived in Elaine for three years, testifies that he was at a meeting of the Elaine lodge and overheard Ware and others naming planters who were to be killed. This is the only evidence the prosecution introduces in any of these trials of a plot to kill planters. There is no cross-examination. Ware is the last of Elaine Twelve to be convicted and sentenced to die.

November 24, 1919. Murphy and his firm are hired by the NAACP to represent the Elaine Twelve for three thousand dollars and incidental expenses. The deal does not include representation if the cases go to the United States Supreme Court. During this same time, blacks in Little Rock begin to raise money for the Elaine Twelve and hire Scipio Jones, who begins to work with the Murphy firm on the cases. Other black attorneys, including Thomas Price, John Hibbler, and J. R. Booker, will assist Jones. Thomas Price, partner of Scipio Jones, appears to have previously represented the Progressive Farmers and Household Union of America.

November 24, 1919. Brough convenes a statewide biracial panel in Little Rock. He names a number of the black elite of Arkansas to the panel. The black members once again endorse the actions of the governor, who calls the events in Phillips County a "damnable insurrection."

Late November 1919. Bratton informs the NAACP that Scipio Jones has met with Governor Brough, who has told him that he will commute all the sentences except one.

December 20, 1919. Murphy and Jones file motions for new trials that are denied by Judge Jackson the same day. Brough issues a stay of the executions to allow the cases to be appealed.

January 20, 1920. Robert Hill, the leader of the union, is arrested in Kansas, setting off a protracted battle to have him extradited to Arkansas to stand trial.

February 2, 1920. Black elite of Arkansas, including Cox, Conner, and Booker, write a public letter to the governor of Kansas saying that Hill will get a fair trial if he is returned. They are denounced by the Northern black press and praised by Brough. Ulysses Bratton, who feels he has been run out of Arkansas and eventually moves his entire family, including his adult sons, to Detroit, meets with Governor Allen of Kansas to persuade him not to extradite Hill. Bratton too is highly critical of the black elite's position.

March 23, 1920. After a hearing in which Arkansas is represented by its own attorney general, Governor Allen of Kansas announces he will not extradite Robert Hill, incensing Brough and embarrassing the state.

March 29, 1920. The Arkansas Supreme Court announces its decisions and affirms six of the convictions and reverses and remands the other six for new trials on a technicality. From this day forward, the cases are severed into two distinct groups. The group that will receive new trials will be known as the Ware defendants and will include Ed Ware, William Wardlow, Albert Giles, Joe Fox, John Martin, and Alf Banks Jr. The group whose convictions are affirmed will be known as the Moore defendants and will include Frank Moore, Joe Knox, Frank Hall, Ed "Sweat" Coleman, Frank Hicks, and Ed Hicks.

May 3–11, 1920. The Ware defendants are retried in Helena and again receive death sentences. However, Murphy and Jones are able to raise the issue that no blacks are on the petit or grand jury. Scipio Jones cross-examines Suggs Bondsman during the Ed Ware trial. Bondsman can't remember other persons at the meeting the night a plot was allegedly hatched to kill planters and testifies falsely that he wasn't arrested. Jones puts on rebuttal testimony that others were at the meeting but did not hear Ware name planters to be executed. The six defendants are to be executed on July 23. Though Brough contends that "absolute justice" has prevailed, he grants another stay to allow appeals.

October 11, 1920. Murphy, seventy-nine, dies. The same day Scipio Jones and Edgar McHaney, Murphy's partner, receive the news that their petition for a writ of certiorari, which had been filed on behalf of the Moore defendants, has been denied by the U.S. Supreme Court. Also on the same day they find out that Robert Hill, who had been kept in jail in Kansas on federal charges of impersonating a federal officer, has finally been released.

October 11, 1920. Debate continues over who will take Murphy's place. Ulysses Bratton argues that Edgar McHaney is only interested in the money he can make on the cases. The NAACP, however, decides that McHaney, who has already been paid, and Scipio Jones will continue to represent the defendants.

November 15, 1920. Brough, under pressure from both sides, decides not to commute the sentence of a single one of the Moore defendants. However, about to go out of office, he does not reset the execution dates, leaving that to his successor, Democrat Thomas McRae.

November 17, 1920. In the first sign that statewide opinion is no longer unified, the *Arkansas Democrat* advises that there is no hurry to execute the Moore defendants.

November 29, 1920. The mandate denying review by the U.S. Supreme Court in the Moore cases arrives in Arkansas, clearing the way for the executions.

December 6, 1920. The second Ware cases are decided by the Arkansas Supreme Court, which reverses Judge Jackson once again. The grounds for the reversal are discrimination against blacks because there were none on the grand or petit jury.

January 1921. Thomas McRae becomes governor and sets the Moore executions for June 10.

June 8, 1921. McRae announces that he will not interfere with the legal process and thus will not halt the executions of the Moore defendants.

June 8, 1921. Jones and McHaney, who planned to file a petition for a writ of habeas corpus in federal court, find out that no judge is available to hear it and in desperation file a writ of habeas corpus in state court in Little Rock. Judge John Martineau, who has been reversed on the same issue, signs the writ and sets a hearing on the petition.

June 9, 1921. The Arkansas attorney general files a writ of prohibition with the state supreme court, seeking to carry out the executions as scheduled. The court refuses to summarily overturn the writ of habeas corpus and schedules oral arguments on June 12, thus gaining the Moore defendants valuable time.

June 20, 1921. The Arkansas Supreme Court rules against the Moore defendants, and Jones and McHaney file a writ of error in the United States Supreme Court.

June 21, 1921. Judge Jackson grants a change of venue in the second Ware trial. The defendants are to be tried in neighboring Lee County in October.

August 4, 1921. As expected, the U.S. Supreme Court denies the writ of error, and McRae resets the executions of the Moore defendants for September 23.

August 30, 1921. McHaney writes the NAACP that he has found two new witnesses. They are H. F. Smiddy and T. K. Jones, who are now living in Memphis but who both testified for the prosecution in Helena. The sworn affidavits of these two individuals, which will be attached to the Moore defendants' petition in federal court for a writ of habeas corpus, will forever change the landscape in both the Moore and Ware cases. Both Smiddy and Jones admit to torturing blacks in the Helena jail to make them testify favorably for the prosecution. They also identify others by name who tortured blacks in the jail. The affidavits also contain other allegations that, if true, will make the prosecution of the cases more difficult. The affidavit of Smiddy verifies that a massacre of blacks took place on October 1, 1919.

August 30, 1921. McHaney requests permission to hire local white counsel in Marianna and in a neighboring town to represent the Ware defendants.

September 21, 1921. McRae again denies clemency and refuses to halt the executions of the Moore defendants. Jones and McHaney file a writ of habeas corpus in federal court. Judge Jacob Trieber, a Republican and the first Jewish federal district judge in the United States, grants a hearing that stays the executions but then recuses from the cases because he lived in Helena for many years before moving to Little Rock.

September 26, 1921. Trieber's replacement, J. H. Cotteral, from Oklahoma, holds a hearing and rules for the state of Arkansas on the law without holding an evidentiary hearing.

September 27, 1921. Judge Cotteral certifies that there is "probable cause" for an appeal to the U.S. Supreme Court.

October 1921. The prosecution in the Ware cases announces it is not ready for trial, and the cases are postponed until the spring of 1922.

November 1921. Two blacks are lynched in Phillips County.

February 10, 1922. Six hundred and fifty men gather outside of Little Rock for a Ku Klux Klan initiation.

April 1922. Again, the prosecution in the Ware cases asks for a continuance, which is granted.

October 1922. For the third time, the prosecution in the Ware cases gets permission to postpone the trials.

December 1922. Final preparations are made on the brief to go to the U.S. Supreme Court in the Moore cases. The NAACP has hired Moorfield Storey, a former NAACP board president and prominent Boston lawyer.

January 11, 1923. The case of *Moore v. Dempsey* is argued orally to the U.S. Supreme Court. Storey has selected Ulysses Bratton to help argue the case against the Arkansas attorney general. Scipio Jones, who was hired to prepare the papers in the case for the appeal, has been led to believe he would participate in the arguments. At the last moment Storey wires the NAACP that Jones is not needed.

February 19, 1923. The Supreme Court rules in favor of the Moore defendants. It is a great constitutional victory on due process grounds, reversing the decision in the Leo Frank case. The decision calls the Helena trial court proceeding in the Moore cases a sham that has gone uncorrected by the Arkansas appellate court. Though it is a great victory for the NAACP, the only relief afforded to the Moore defendants is that their cases are remanded back to the federal district court for an evidentiary hearing.

March 1923. Apparently without running his idea by the NAACP, Scipio Jones contacts John E. Miller, whose partner C. E. Yingling is now prosecutor, and asks if a deal is possible for the release of the men.

March 24, 1923. Miller responds that he thinks a deal is possible if the Moore defendants plead guilty to second-degree murder and accept sentences of five years from the date of their initial incarceration.

April 1923. Edgar McHaney argues before the Lee County Circuit Court on behalf of the Ware defendants that two terms of court have passed without a trial and that the Ware defendants must be released. Local counsel R. D. Smith and Burke Mann testify that the former Judge Jackson is mistaken in his testimony that they asked for a continuance. The "good ole boy" system in eastern Arkansas is no longer in effect. Though Judge Robertson rules against the Ware defendants, the case is appealed to the Arkansas Supreme Court.

June 25, 1923. The Arkansas Supreme Court rules in favor of the Ware defendants, finding that two terms of court have passed without a trial, and orders the men freed. To avoid the possibility of a lynching in

Marianna, Judge Robertson complies immediately with the order. At Robertson's direction, the sheriff of Marianna puts the men on a train to Little Rock and takes them to "the Walls," the penitentiary in Little Rock. The warden refuses to accept the men, and they are released in the middle of the night into the custody of Scipio Jones. The Ware defendants are free at last.

July 2, 1923. At the suggestion of Scipio Jones and with the blessing of the NAACP, Moorfield Storey contacts George B. Rose, perhaps the most prestigious lawyer in the state of Arkansas, to see if he will use his influence to free the Moore defendants. He writes John E. Miller, who responds positively to his letter.

November 3, 1923. Scipio Jones telegraphs the NAACP that he has received a concrete offer to settle the cases of the Moore defendants. Without waiting for further direction from the NAACP, Jones makes the following deal: the sentences of the Moore defendants will be commuted to twelve years in prison with the private assurance that within a year the men will be pardoned by the governor.

November 1924. Governor McRae has declined to run for a third term as governor, and a member of the Ku Klux Klan is elected governor, to take office in January. The month of November passes, and the Moore defendants are not released.

December 19, 1924. Scipio Jones secures the release of the last of the remaining Elaine prisoners with the exception of the Moore defendants.

December 20, 1924. The *Arkansas Gazette* runs an article that says the Moore defendants will not have their sentences commuted.

January 13, 1925. The day before McRae leaves office, Scipio Jones visits him. Afterward, Jones telegraphs the NAACP that the men will be released.

January 14, 1925. McRae signs indefinite furloughs for the Moore defendants, which although not pardons, free the six men.

May 4, 1927. Little Rock experiences its last lynching after the murder of a young white girl and a physical assault against a young woman and her daughter. Scipio Jones and other black leaders work to keep blacks off the streets and indoors while whites riot. John Martineau, now governor, calls out the National Guard to restore order.

March 28, 1943. Scipio Jones, his circumstances much reduced, dies at the age of eighty.

Blood in Their Eyes

CHAPTER 1

Charles Hillman Brough's Midnight Train Ride

He does not look upon the "Jim Crow" car as a humiliation—in fact, he infinitely prefers the freedom of his own car to one where the presence of the white race would be felt as a restraint.
—Charles Hillman Brough

October 1, 1919
Little Rock

When Democratic governor Charles Hillman Brough received the initial telegram from the mayor of Elaine, Sid Stokes, one of his earliest political allies in the Delta, requesting troops to quell "race riots in Elaine" on October 1, 1919, he was at the end of a special session of the Arkansas legislature. Part of it had not gone well, and he was angry. He had asked the legislature to pass an antiprofiteering bill, but businessmen from all over the state had come to Little Rock and killed it.[1]

Brough was taking this defeat hard. He had spent a good part of his time and energy in his second two-year term as governor helping President Woodrow Wilson win the "war to end all wars." He had made hundreds of speeches in Arkansas and all over the country in the effort to sell Liberty Loan Bonds and raise money for the Red Cross and other war-related causes. During the war he had been proud of the state's effort: everyone—business and labor, men and women, white and black—had come together in the name of patriotism. Brough would have remembered how astonished U.S. secretary of the treasury William Gibbs McAdoo had been when the Little Rock mulatto lawyer Scipio Africanus Jones, on the stage of the Kempner Theater, had presented him with a check for Liberty Loan Bonds for fifty thousand dollars from the Mosaic Templars, a Negro fraternal organization.[2] Jones, a black leader Brough had always been able to count on, had proudly told McAdoo that if that wasn't enough, he could raise another fifty thousand dollars if the country needed it. Then

Jones had gone out and done just that. Blacks like Scipio Jones were always helping to make the community better. When there had been trouble between colored and white soldiers based outside of Little Rock at Camp Pike, Scipio Jones and other black leaders had arranged for some of the colored clubs to be moved to lessen the chance for conflict.

Now the war might be over, but the world still wasn't safe for democracy—not overseas and not in this country. Bolsheviks seemed to be everywhere, in labor unions like the radical IWW and even in the halls of Congress. During the war Brough had told an audience in Saint Louis that there existed "no twilight zone in American patriotism. In this war we are either for the president and for the flag, or we are against the president and against the flag."[3] Not one to shy away from controversy when the security of the country was at stake, Brough, in a speech at Milwaukee, had called the Wisconsin antiwar senator Bob LaFollete a Bolshevik leader. He wouldn't be surprised now if the Bolsheviks were somehow behind the trouble in Elaine. There had been so many race riots in the country recently that surely they couldn't all be coincidental. A horrible race riot had just occurred last week in Omaha, Nebraska. The mayor, trying unsuccessfully to protect a black prisoner, had nearly been lynched himself. A rope had been placed around his neck, and he had been wounded as well. The Omaha courthouse had been burned. Thirteen hundred troops had been rushed to the scene. There had been other riots and race violence in the past few months in places like Washington, D.C., Chicago, Knoxville, and Indianapolis. In today's edition of the *Arkansas Gazette,* there was a front-page story out of Oklahoma City headlined, "Mob Seeks Negro." More than three hundred people had gathered at a police station after an African American had shot and killed a streetcar conductor. Right below that story was another about a posse in New Jersey that had finally caught a black man who had reportedly attacked a white woman.[4] There had been no warning out of Phillips County, and now a second telegram arrived, this one more alarming and specific than the first: "Circuit and county judges, sheriff, mayor and leading private citizens urgently request immediate dispatch of 500 troops with machine guns to Elaine. One hundred seventy-five negro prisoners are expected to arrive at any moment among white men. Two dead and from 5 to 25 wounded."[5]

If the president had not been so sick, Brough might well have called the White House. A fellow Southerner, Wilson had been scheduled to come to Little Rock on Saturday as part of a national tour to drum up support for America's entry into the League of Nations. The president had collapsed while on a podium in Colorado and now perhaps was dying. So instead, after the first telegram Brough called the secretary of the War Department, Newton D. Baker, who granted permission to use troops from Camp Pike, but this was going to take a bit longer than anyone wanted. With the war over and with a reduction in troop strength, Commanding General S. D. Sturgis had to cobble together a force from different units.

Then a third telegram came from the mayor of Helena, J. C. Knight, with news that would have been chilling: "Posse numbering at least 500 will be in Elaine neighborhood before 6 P.M. Considering situation it is absolutely necessary troops be in Elaine at earliest possible moment."[6]

With this telegram Brough would have known that a bloodbath was occurring in Phillips County. In 1902 he had published an article for the *Mississippi Historical Quarterly* about a race riot that had occurred in his hometown of Clinton, Mississippi. Three whites had been killed by blacks after a political rally in 1875, at the tail end of Reconstruction. White volunteers, Brough had written, had come from Vicksburg on a special train, "asking no questions and submitting to no commands." This group of former veterans "soon put the country-side in fear."[7] And not just fear. Brough wrote: "An arrangement was made with the citizen soldiery, now fully 200 strong, that if they would end the killing of the negroes, the United States officers would not assume command but leave matters in charge of the civil authorities."[8]

No one would ever know how many black lives had been taken. "No accurate estimate has been made, or can be made, of the number of negroes killed after the arrival of the troops," Brough wrote.[9] He reported that the number was variously estimated at between ten and fifty but that the Hinds County grand jury, which took testimony from over one hundred witnesses afterward, had reported that the number could not be determined.

After the killing had ended, Republican governor Adelbert Ames, who presided "as the Carpet-bag Charlatan of a mongrel governmental mixture," had urged President Grant to intervene, but the "laconic President advised the hot-headed Governor that the general public were tired of these annual autumnal outbreaks in the South, and announced a policy of non-intervention on the part of the Federal Government."[10]

In summing up, Brough wrote: "The return of the terrorized negroes to their homes after the riot was gradual, and their return to municipal, county and State politics was like that of the ship homeward bound, but which never reached its long looked for destination. This lesson of Anglo-Saxon supremacy, written in letters of blood, will ever remain the most important of the many lessons taught in the modest college town of Clinton to the rising young manhood of a proud and untrammeled Commonwealth."[11]

Not only did Brough know the history of his own state, but since moving to Arkansas in 1903, he would also have become conversant with his adopted state's record of violence against African Americans if he had done nothing but read the newspapers. Upon Brough's arrival in Arkansas, Jeff Davis was governor, and the state had reached its nadir in gubernatorial leadership—at least in the area of race relations. Davis, who served as governor from 1901 to 1907 before moving on to the United States Senate, promised in one of his most chilling campaign speeches that "we may have a lot of dead niggers in Arkansas, but we shall never have negro equality, and I want to say that I would rather tear, screaming from her mother's arms, my little daughter and bury her alive than to see her arm in arm with the best nigger on earth."[12] Campaigning in 1904, Davis told his audience "that 'nigger' dominion will never prevail in this beautiful Southland of ours, as long as shotguns and rifles lie around loose, and we are able to pull the trigger."[13]

Brough, who by then had a Ph.D. from Johns Hopkins University in "economics, history, and jurisprudence," would have known that this unusually savage disposition toward blacks from an Arkansas governor had been building in the state (and the South) since the early 1890s, when attitudes had begun to harden, resulting in increased violence, disfranchisement, and segregation. In 1892, a black Arkansas preacher reported, "some [blacks were] being strung up to telephone poles, others burnt at the stake and still others being shot like dogs. In the last 30 days there have been not less than eight colored persons lynched in the state."[14]

As a new arrival in the state, Brough could not have had any illusions about the actual practice of race relations in the Arkansas Delta, but if he did, they would have been quickly dispelled. On March 27, 1904, the statewide *Arkansas Gazette* printed on its front page a story reporting that the town of Saint Charles was now "quiet" after the last four days, during which eleven blacks had been lynched. Only twenty miles west of Elaine, Saint Charles blacks were reported to have been "organizing to defy law and order."[15] The lynchings had come about because of a fight between a white man and two blacks named Henry and Walker Griffin, who were then reported to have successfully resisted arrest by a white deputy sheriff. From that point on, it was open season on blacks in Saint Charles who seemed in any way hostile. Three blacks were shot by a vigilante group for "defy[ing] the posse."[16] Five more were taken out of a jail by a mob "who shot them to death."[17] By the time the dust had settled, thirteen blacks were dead, including the Griffin brothers. No whites were charged.

Lynchings of blacks continued, and violence and intimidation remained commonplace throughout Arkansas, not just in the Delta. Between 1900 and 1910 the black population of Harrison, a town of fifteen hundred residents just miles from the Missouri border, decreased from 115 to one through two instances of racial cleansing in 1905 and 1909, in which white mobs forced black persons out of their homes, giving them twenty-four hours to leave. As a professor in Fayetteville and then later a candidate campaigning for votes throughout the state, Brough would have noticed that "after 1910 few African Americans resided in extreme northwest Arkansas."[18] Like every other resident of Arkansas, he would have known that blacks were not supposed "to let the sun go down on their heads" in this part of the state.

By 1919, confident as he was in dealing with whatever problems blacks in the Delta might have been presenting him, Brough would have felt any governor's frustration in dealing with the federal government. General Sturgis was refusing to allow the actual deployment of the troops until he obtained a formal order from the War Department. All hell was breaking loose in the Arkansas Delta, and the Army was sitting on its confused bureaucratic behind. Brough got in touch with Arkansas senator W. S. Kirby, who complained in a telegram to the Army chief of staff that Sturgis was refusing to move without an order.[19]

Brough was confident that he could handle the crisis if he could just get the troops down to Elaine. After all, nobody in the history of the state had been better prepared to be governor. After coming back to his Clinton alma mater, Mississippi College, to teach, Brough had picked up a Master of Arts degree in psychology and ethics. Then he quit his teaching job and acquired a law degree from the University of Mississippi, completing a two-year course in twelve months and graduating with distinction.[20]

Brough would have stayed in Mississippi had he been hired as head of the new state department of archives and history. Losing that job by a five to four vote, in 1903 he applied for and received a new teaching job at the University of Arkansas in Fayetteville.[21] A popular professor on campus and widely known for his speechmaking, he first made an aborted run at the governor's office in 1913. He announced as a candidate to fill the unexpired term of Joe T. Robinson, who was appointed to fill a seat in the United States Senate. Brough withdrew when it became clear he didn't have the necessary support and bided his time.

By 1915 Brough felt that his adopted state would accept a professor as governor. Finally, the people were ready to be taught that Arkansas could only make progress if it were willing to invest in education. It had made a start under former governor George Donaghey. It could do more under Brough. But he had to be elected first.

In July 1915, at the age of thirty-nine, Brough submitted his resignation to the university and began to campaign in earnest, though the primary wasn't until the folllowing year. His phenomenal memory for faces and names helped make him a natural politician. Even though he didn't act like an egghead professor, he did look a bit like one. At five feet ten inches, he was quite bald on top and had a prominent Roman nose. Yet, despite his braininess, he wasn't stuffy. He liked people and with his friendly down-to-earth manner put them at their ease. In 1908 he had acquired a wife, Anne Roark, from Kentucky, who seemed born to occupy a governor's mansion. Talented, gracious, intelligent, and with strong likes and dislikes, Anne Roark was not particularly domestic. Her interests lay in helping her husband go as far in the world as he wanted to. In fact, she had served as his campaign manager and driver in his first full race.[22]

The 1916 Democratic primary (which was tantamount to election) came down to three candidates. Brough was only truly worried about one. Earle Hodges was associated with the immediate past governor, George Hays, who had run strong in the Delta. Though Brough was able to tag Hodges as the machine candidate, he had his own soft spots: for one thing, he could be made to seem weak on the Negro question—a Negrophile, in fact, the Hodges campaign charged.

How to combat this? Those closest to Brough knew he was a Southerner from head to toe. He liked to say that he was "to the manner born."[23] Yet he had a problem. As a professor at the University of Arkansas Brough had chaired the Southern Sociological Congress's University Race Commission, and his views had become a matter of public record. He had studied the "Negro problem" and was confident that he knew the solution. It was relatively simple. During slavery blacks had benefited from the experience of having been around whites. They had imitated their masters and had begun the process of becoming civilized. The Civil War had abruptly ended this teacher-student relationship, and neither race was better off as a result. Brough had written: "This close social contact of the races has now almost disappeared. Separate schools, separate churches, separate telephones, the 'Jim Crow' car, restrictions of the ballot, not to mention violent anti-negro political agitation in at least two of the states, have produced an alienation of the two races without parallel."[24]

Of course, a desperate opponent would deliberately misinterpret his meaning. In his speeches and writings during this period Brough had also said that economic improvement did not equate with social equality and that blacks should not vote. Naturally, Hodge would not call attention to Brough's views on miscegenation—to which, he said, the South was "unalterably opposed," viewing its increase with alarm. Brough had also said that mulattoes were difficult, an "incarnated protest against the color line," while pure-blooded Negroes "were naturally unambitious, tractable, and easily satisfied."[25] The pure-blooded Negro was uninterested in the ballot and generally satisfied with the status quo: "He does not look upon the 'Jim Crow' car as a humiliation—in fact, he infinitely prefers the freedom of his own car to one where the presence of the white race would be felt as a restraint." Thus separate coach laws were "wise," according to Brough.[26]

The "best Negroes," Brough believed, had applauded the work of his race commission. They understood that he was saying nothing about industrial education that their leader Booker T. Washington had not already said. Ever a supporter from his earliest days, Scipio Jones had written a letter in support of Brough's work as head of the commission.[27]

But now there must be no misunderstanding of Brough's position. He immediately took out advertisements in the papers which set forth his views: "I am not in favor of social equality. . . . I am not in favor of negroes serving on juries, I am not in favor of negroes holding political office in the South."[28] In a speech in Stuttgart, Arkansas, he was quoted as saying that the task of whites "was to make a better citizen of the negro and to cause him to render more efficient service to the white man."[29]

Brough got his point across. He was square on the Negro question. He won going away. Hodges finished third. During his first term in office, in 1917, Brough pushed through significant legislation in areas such as education and taxation by passing a compulsory attendance law and putting the state on a millage basis.[30] He easily won a second term. Republicans didn't even bother to field a candidate against him in 1918.

Now, from his window at the newly constructed state capitol, Brough had a view to the north of the Union train station and the Arkansas River. Thanks to the poor roads in the state, the only way a troop convoy could get to Elaine quickly was by train. And it wouldn't be that quick. It would take eight hours. Finally, the adjutant general of the Army, P. C. Harris, telephoned Camp Pike with orders to move out. The train would not leave until 12:20 A.M. on the morning of October 2.

Whatever was happening with the five-hundred-man posses, Brough was sympathetic to how isolated the whites must be feeling. Phillips County was overwhelmingly black, especially in the southern part of the county, where the fighting was said to be occurring. Out of a population of over forty-four thousand, there were only eleven thousand whites.

Studying a map of the area, Brough might have felt his old wariness in dealing with the politicians in eastern Arkansas. All they really wanted was to be allowed to carry on as they always had. During the race for his first term, he had thought—mistakenly, as it turned out—that campaigning in the Delta would be a complete waste of time. The machine politics of the area had always bothered him. His campaigning wasn't a total loss, however. After being elected to his first term, he had received a congratulatory note from Sid Stokes, the mayor of Elaine's four hundred citizens, who had signed one of the telegrams. "The enclosed will show that we did all we could to balance the Helena vote," Stokes had written. "Our little precinct giving you the biggest majority in the county."[31]

It was Helena, the county seat of Phillips County, that was booming, a town on the move, its lifeblood cotton. The sixth largest city in Arkansas, Helena—with its Business Men's League headed by a transplanted Yankee by the name of E. M. "Mort" Allen—was a model for the rest of the state. Actively soliciting industry, the league boasted of its bond issues for paved streets and its commitment to growth. As successful as he had been in Elaine, Brough would have known that Allen owned the townsite there, which was not yet incorporated but was being developed. Campaigning, he had gone through Elaine and would have been struck by the boast on its water tower: WIDE AWAKE, ELAINE, WATCH US GROW.[32] Not likely with its swamps, canebrakes, and impassable roads most of the year. Elaine was stuck off in the southern part of the county, above where the White River emptied into the Mississippi. Granted, the land was some of the most fertile in the county, producing on a single acre an entire bale of long-staple cotton. Yet few believed, despite the optimistic prediction on the water tower, that Allen would ever turn Elaine into a Helena. Still, who could know? The Lambrook logging and cotton enterprise that had begun in 1913 near Elaine was colossal. Twenty-one thousand acres worth of virgin hardwood timber—ash, oak, hickory, and gum—was shipped daily by rail out of the area, and once the timber was cleared the cotton came. And this enterprise had been started by a Yankee too—Gerard Lambert, whose father owned a pharmaceutical company in Saint Louis.[33] Carpetbaggers were still coming to Arkansas, but that was all right with Brough. These men had the kind of drive and enthusiasm for business that the state needed if it was going to catch up with the rest of the country. What the state did not need was a race war. An intellectual who had been on the public payroll for most of his life, Brough admired businessmen. He did not share their inclination or ability, but he was more than willing to praise them, unless they became unduly selfish, as they had proved to be in this most recent session of the legislature.

Besides the telegrams, the information coming in to the capitol about the riot would have been sketchy and contradictory. The riot had started the night before in a small church at a place called Hoop Spur, three miles north of Elaine. One version was that authorities were out looking for a bootlegger gang when their car broke down in front of the church. A Missouri-Pacific railroad security man by the name of Will Adkins was shot dead when gunfire erupted. A second white named Charlie Pratt was wounded, as well as a black trusty from the Phillips County jail called "Kid" Collins. But why would African Americans in a church open fire on three innocent men?

One of the strangest stories coming out of Elaine was that one of Ulysses Bratton's sons (there was confusion about which one) had been taken into custody for leading blacks into revolt. Ulysses S. Bratton was a well-known Republican lawyer in Little Rock. For years he had served as an assistant U.S. attorney and later as postmaster of Little Rock. He was now in law practice with his son Guy. He also had two other sons, Ocier and Ulysses Jr.[34]

As the hours stretched by, the news became worse. White women and children from the area had been brought into Elaine and placed in the brick schoolhouse for their protection. Word was that it could be overrun at any time. Oddly, the sheriff of Phillips County, Frank "Happy" Kitchens, had declared himself sick and appointed Sebastian Straub, a white furnishings merchant, as acting sheriff.

Brough at some point during the day decided to accompany the troops to Elaine. The *Arkansas Gazette* reported his reason the next day as follows: "The governor said that he is going to the scene because he thought that it would be best for him to be at the scene personally and obtain correct information on the situation."[35] He wouldn't have looked forward to telling this news to his wife, who may well have come to pick him up at the capitol that afternoon since he didn't drive. If her husband was "to the manner born," so was Anne Brough. Not only was her father a distinguished attorney and president of the Simpson County bank in Franklin, Kentucky, but he was also president of Franklin Woolen Mills. She could trace her ancestry to the Bullochs of Virginia, whose patriarch, Hugh, was a member of the Council of Williamsburg in 1631. After graduating from Franklin Female College, Anne Brough had attended Hollins in Virginia to further her musical education and then wintered for a season in New York, attending the opera and symphony. It seemed as if all her life she had been preparing to become a first lady. How strange that this should happen in Arkansas, which was such an odd state, bristling like a little boy at any slight, real or imagined, when in fact Little Rock, at least, was a real city and growing fast. The strangest part was that her husband—who was an intellectual, an academic, and perhaps a genius but not an Arkansas native—had become the state's biggest booster, defending its honor with a fierceness that might even be amusing to an outsider.

Anne Brough hated criticism of her husband. His opponents couldn't criticize his intelligence, so they pointed out that he was bald, an "egghead," as if he could do anything about it. As a boy he had been skinny (according to his pictures), but now he had filled out nicely.

Eleven years earlier the wedding columnist for her hometown newspaper had noted 'her slender girlish figure draped in a costly bridal gown of ivory marquisette, built on a foundation of ivory satin mescaline."[36] She had been an old maid at twenty-eight! So what? People were always watching them, as well they should have. Her face had not been unpleasant to look at on her wedding day, nor was it now. She was, as is said, a handsome woman. And if, in the eleven years since that happy day, her skin had begun to dry and coarsen, there was no help for it. Anne Brough didn't feel old, but when she looked at the amazing photograph of her husband surrounded by suffragettes and male supporters of women's right to vote, taken two years earlier on the steps of the state capitol, she may well have shuddered a bit at how much she had aged. And that would have made her angry, because the day that Arkansas permitted women to vote in primary elections had been one of the most thrilling days of her life. She had been so proud of Hillman and of the backward state he presided over. And for once the product of virtue had happily not been its own reward: women had given Hillman forty thousand votes in his last election.

There had been no children, but Anne and Hillman Brough seemed perfectly happy without them. It wasn't that they disliked young people. Far from it. When Hillman had been a professor at Fayetteville, their house had been overrun with students. Hillman had been wildly popular, no doubt in part, according to his biographer, because he couldn't bear to give students low grades.[37] Thus his courses were jammed, which led to criticism from other professors. Her husband was a pleaser. He trusted others when he shouldn't have, according to Anne Brough's nephew, Price Roark. That was his problem as a politician. People took advantage of his good nature. He gave away too much. Compromised when it wasn't always a good idea.[38]

Anne Brough was made of sterner stuff. She had a temper. Hillman Brough needed someone who did—someone who could keep all those people who weren't as idealistic as her husband in check. She surely must have been dismayed when she learned that her husband was going to Elaine that very night. What on earth could he do? He didn't even know how to drive a car.

Yet she would have known why he had to go. His father had been an officer in the Civil War—albeit a Yankee one, but as Hillman had pointed out during his political campaigns, he couldn't be blamed for that. Hillman himself had never had his war. He had been basically raised as an orphan by his aunt and uncle in Mississippi after his mother died. His father, off in Utah, had been too busy to take him in hand, even after he remarried. No wonder Hillman was a pleaser. How he loved to give speeches about the glories of the Old South. In his pleasant baritone voice, he would twine together a flowery rhapsody to golden memories of the Southern plantation with an optimistic view of the new booming age. People ate this up. The Old South was in vogue.

Anne Brough could have easily persuaded her husband to see *Birth of a Nation,* which had played in Little Rock in February.[39] With its glorification of Dixieland and the Ku Klux Klan as noble and necessary, *Birth of a Nation* would have been right down the governor's alley.

If we can imagine them driving home from the capitol in order for Anne to pack Hillman's bag (their car had been stolen in crime-ridden Little Rock in February and found stripped and abandoned), we can see

Hillman nervously imagining his military campaign and waving to the five o'clock crowd spilling out of the shops and office buildings along Capitol Avenue as if it were made up of the people of Phillips County he was going to save from slaughter.[40] Little Rock was bursting at the seams. The papers said that there was no place to build in the entire city, meaning only the central area of Little Rock. Ordinarily, Anne Brough would have enjoyed the daily drive from the capitol. She loved her husband, and when he was happy, so was she, generally—at least when he wasn't going off to play soldier.

At the mansion at Fourteenth and Scott, however, she could quit smiling and begin to worry in earnest. On any day but today, she would have been more than happy to be home on fashionable Scott Street with her husband, though she was hardly a homebody. Anne had resisted learning to cook, knowing that cooks begin and end their day in the kitchen. That was why one had servants, and on Hillman's yearly ten-thousand-dollar salary as governor, she could continue to live in a style to which she had become accustomed as a mill owner's daughter. The four-thousand-square-foot house—not including the upstairs and downstairs porches that surrounded it—had been built in 1873 by Augustus H. Garland, governor of the Redeemers, in the Italianate Victorian style.[41] The Broughs were renting it, along with the furniture from William Starr Mitchell, whose wife's father had been a wealthy carpetbagger.[42] Anne Brough's favorite room was next to their bedroom on the second floor, where she did her Red Cross work for the war. From this room she could open the gyb doors, raise the windows, step out onto the upstairs porch, and get a catty-cornered view across Scott Street of the lovely Victorian Second Empire mansion built in 1881 by a scandalous Italian named Angelo Marre. In 1902 it had been rented to Governor Jeff Davis, a scandal himself. With its circular stair, fourteen-foot-high ceilings with drop borders, and brass and crystal chandeliers, it even eclipsed their own mansion. The stories about Davis would have made Anne Brough sick. He had been an embarrassment to polite society. She was glad she hadn't lived in Arkansas when he was governor. He had said such horrible things about Negroes in public. Hillman—Anne never called him Charles—was too much of a gentleman to have gotten in the gutter with a man like Davis.

The public's favorite room, with thirteen-foot ceilings and two matched chairs with carved griffins for arm- and headrests, was directly beneath this room.[43] With no children and none expected, she and Hillman hardly needed so much space for themselves, but a man who owned six thousand books needed to put them someplace, and after dinner he could usually be found upstairs in his library, the mantle over its fireplace finished with bird's-eye maple.

All Anne could do now was pray that the commanding officer would have enough sense to keep Hillman out of harm's way and out of the danger of being shot by some crazy Negro. It took her breath away to think what might be happening to those poor innocent women and children in Phillips County, who had been forced to take refuge in a schoolhouse. She agreed with her husband that there were primitive urges in Africans that made them fundamentally different from Anglo-Saxons. It would take centuries to make them fully civilized. In truth, according to Hillman, the future of the Negro was a bit cloudy in the South. He had urged crop diversification so that the South could get away from its dependence on King cotton. Neither planters nor sharecroppers ultimately benefited from putting all their eggs in one basket, no matter how high prices might go in a single year. As governor, Hillman could only do so much for Negroes, and his opponents believed that he had already gone too far. There were actually more blacks in Pulaski County than in Phillips, hardly a comforting thought at the moment. However, they weren't in the majority, as they were in Phillips County, and they were certainly of a better class. In Little Rock there were a number of black lawyers, physicians, dentists, businessmen, and educators, all of whom thought her husband hung the moon, at least compared to the governors who had come before him. Rural Phillips County contained God-only-knew-what.

For his part, Hillman Brough could not fail to be impressed with the quality and enthusiasm of the soldiers he accompanied to Elaine. The troop train leaving Little Rock late that night was carrying four hundred men from the Third Infantry Division and one hundred fifty men from the Fifth Infantry Division, including a unit of twelve machine guns. These men were not members of the Arkansas National Guard, but many were seasoned veterans of the recent War for Democracy in Europe. Perhaps the governor heard the bloodcurdling stories of nineteen-year-old Roger C. Mears from Arkansas, who had been a hero in the Second Battle of the Marne.

Only a year before, Mears had been one of three men in Company K not to have been killed or wounded so badly as to be sent home from France. A handsome, strapping lad who looked as if he were about to burst out of his uniform, Mears seemed harmless enough in his train seat, but he could have told the governor the story of how he and twenty other men had kept an elite German regiment from crossing a pontoon bridge by firing at point-blank range from their dug-in position on the bank of the Marne River at Château-Thierry, fifty miles southeast of Paris. Mears had personally burned out seventeen Browning automatic rifles and had earned the coveted Crosier French Braid on his left arm in a battle the world would not soon forget. The Germans had sent the crown prince's special troops four abreast across the bridge into such withering fire that they broke off their advance. The Browning automatic rifle fired clips of twenty rounds, and so many German bodies had washed into barbed wire below the fighting that the Marne had soon overflowed its banks. Mears, who had enlisted the first time at the age of fifteen and had served with Pershing on the Mexican border, in a later battle was blasted into the air by an artillery shell and left for dead by his buddies. Two weeks in a field hospital, and he was back in action. If Mears enjoyed a sound sleep on the trip to Elaine, it was no accident. He couldn't hear a thing out of his left ear.[44]

Truly, the men on the train were a rolling killing machine. The commanding officer of the group was Col. Issac C. Jencks, a West Point graduate, a veteran of the World War I, and a former Indian fighter. The colonel was supremely confident that his troops would have no problem in dealing with the Negroes. By the time the troop train pulled out of Little Rock, only four white men had been killed by the supposed horde of rampaging blacks. It is not known whether the colonel wondered privately if perhaps the rumors of a black revolt had been overstated and if his main problem was going to be his own troops.

While Brough's troop train was winding its way to Elaine, Ulysses Bratton, whose son was reported to have been taken prisoner, was spending a long night in Little Rock. Bratton had a very different view from the governor of what constituted justice in the Arkansas Delta.

Ulysses Simpson Bratton (called Ulis by his close friends) would play a pivotal role in the aftermath of the Elaine affair, but his first worry would be to try to get his son out of the Helena jail where he was ultimately taken on October 1. To his great anger and lasting bitterness, it would be a full month before his son would be released.

The key to understanding Ulysses Bratton is understanding his people and their values, for Ulysses was an Arkansan like no other white man of his time. His grandfather, Ben Bratton Sr., described himself at the age of almost ninety as being from Tennessee and of old-line Whig stock.[45] He had come to the wilds of northern Arkansas in the 1830s and lived to the age of ninety-eight. It took a train-track accident to kill him, an accident that severed both his legs. An uncle of Ulysses, James Bratton, told a story about how his father had kept a pet bear that took great delight in throwing him down as a child and sucking his ears. The Brattons settled near Marshall in Wiley's Cove in rugged Searcy County, an area unsuited to growing and sustaining cotton. When the Civil War broke out, three uncles of Ulysses Bratton were conscripted into the Confederate Army. They ran off, and by 1863 had joined the Union Army. Too young for service when his brothers were conscripted, Benjamin Bratton Sr., the father of Ulysses, eventually joined too, and all survived. When they returned to Searcy County, their houses had been burned and their fences torn down.[46]

Ulysses Bratton, born in 1868, would become a fierce Republican stalwart and a devout Methodist. Doubtless shaping his views was his stint as an assistant U.S. attorney in Little Rock during the Taft and Roosevelt administrations, a stint during which he sued planters in the Delta for violation of federal peonage laws—or debt slavery, as it was known. With little cash after the war, planters needed a system by which they could continue to operate. Throughout the South, the sharecropper system met this need. A tenant would be furnished supplies and carried on credit until the cotton crop came in during the fall. The tenant would then give a percentage (from a half to a third, depending on whether he had his own tools and equipment or had to be furnished them by the landlord) of his crop to the planter as rent in lieu of cash. Invariably, the tenant was said to owe money after these arrangements were carried out because of the supplies he had obtained during the year. Often unable to read or figure and understandably reluctant to challenge the word of his landlord, especially if the tenant was black, he had little recourse of his own. Until federal peonage laws outlawed this practice, the tenant would not be allowed to leave until his debt to the planter had been paid.

Ulysses Bratton was of the view that tenants were routinely cheated by their planter landlords in the Arkansas Delta and that debt slavery existed on a wide scale even after its formal abolition. Forced to resign as assistant U. S. attorney by President Theodore Roosevelt due to a charge of conflict of interest, Bratton continued to practice law and Republican politics.[47] Though he managed to secure the job of postmaster of Little Rock, by the second decade of the 1900s he found himself increasingly out of step with the mainstream of the Republican Party in Arkansas. Bratton had always sided with the faction of the party that had encouraged blacks to participate. After repeated defeats by the Democrats, many Arkansas Republicans saw black participation as a dead weight and acted accordingly to do their best to discourage their membership.[48]

By 1919, in practice in Little Rock with his son Guy and with a branch office and associate by the name of G. R. Casey in Helena, Bratton had gained a reputation among blacks as a white attorney who would act as a vigorous advocate for them in court. In the fall of 1919 his firm was contacted about representing a group of black sharecroppers from Phillips County who wanted to get better settlements with their planters. It turned out to be an unlucky coincidence that he sent his son Ocier to Phillips County on October 1 to gather information about their case and collect a retainer.

Ulysses Bratton's earlier experience in federal court with a sympathetic Republican judge in the Delta may have given him confidence that he could handle whatever was thrown at him in that region of the state. If so, he would find out in the next thirty days just how wrong he was. Eastern Arkansas, he would find out, had its own way of doing things.

CHAPTER 2

The Law of the Delta

The only thing the white people demand here is white control and while I am
Northern born, I realize the absolute necessity for that.
                                    —*E. M. "Mort" Allen*

September 1, 1919
Phillips County

Mort Allen had his fingers in so many pies in Phillips County that it
was a wonder he ever got any sleep. Phillips County was a seamless web
of business opportunities. Allen had come in 1906 from the North by
way of Fort Smith, on the western border of Arkansas. He was in part-
nership with the industrialist Harry Kelley, whose plan it was to develop
four thousand acres in the area. Kelley had the money; Allen would attend
to the details. Along with being the base of a logging and cotton operation, by 1911 the townsite of Elaine had been cleared, the streets graded
and lots platted, but there was a long way to go. At one point Allen lived
in the train depot, the only building in Elaine. In Arkansas, he had met
and married Harriet Key (affectionately called "Big Sister" by everyone),
a young woman whose family owned a plantation in Wabash, just a few
miles from Elaine. By 1913 Allen, now with a young daughter, Marsha,
to raise, had moved to Helena and opened an insurance agency along with
his other business interests. He had done so well that he was president of
the National Association of Insurance Agents.[1]

Then in 1915 Gerard Lambert made his mind-boggling purchase of
twenty-one thousand acres. With the immense logging operation he set
up to clear the land, it appeared that Elaine had to boom. Besides the
Lambrook enterprise, owned by Lambert, there were Chicago Mill and
Lumber, the Theodore Fathauer Company, and Lundell Land and
Lumber. A schoolhouse was built, the land on which it sat courtesy of
Allen and Kelley. In 1919 four white students graduated from the eighth
grade.

Kelley and Allen had conceived the town as bone-dry (as indeed the entire state had become on January 16 as it struggled with prohibition), its deeds containing prohibitions against the sale of liquor. In fact, this covenant was not honored, and the town's founders would have been naive to try to enforce it. The logging operation was manned by hard-drinking Irishmen as well as by blacks. After hacking through the canebrakes and swamps of southern Phillips County, a man needed a drink or two at the end of the day to kill his thirst. Without the constraint of family, single mill hands and lumber workers were some of the hardest drinkers around. As it happened, one of America's most famous African American writers, Richard Wright, spent time in Elaine as a boy until his uncle, an owner of a prosperous black drinking establishment, was murdered by white men in 1916 for refusing to sell them his business. In *Black Boy* Wright describes their move for a time to West Helena before they left Arkansas for good: "Why had we not fought back, I asked my mother, and the fear that was in her made her slap me into silence."[2]

Besides owning the townsite in Elaine, Mort Allen was now treasurer of the Lambrook operation, which had contracts with 650 sharecroppers. Whatever the old South had been in the minds of whites, with its images of faithful darkies and banjos being strummed, it was no more for some. Gerard Lambert, also from north of the Mason-Dixon Line, justified the events in Elaine in his autobiography with the following observation: "Ours was a primitive and pioneer country where racial hatred was close to the surface. Here we had a tinderbox to be set out by the slightest spark. For this was the numerical imbalance. The colored men outnumbered the whites by at least ten to one. White men, with their families on their minds, were constantly alert for the first signs of what they considered danger to their women and families. And the Negroes knew this. If they got out of line, they realized that there would be no compromise with sudden death."[3]

Whites made the determination of what was out of line, but some things in the Delta didn't have to be said aloud.

Yet thanks to the national Republican Party, there had been a time when blacks appeared to be somewhat in control of their own destiny in Phillips County. That time had been, of course, after the Civil War. "Under Reconstruction this county was placed entirely under Negro rule. . . . This condition of affairs continued for ten years [until 1878]," Greenfield Quarles, one of the white lawyers from Helena who was appointed to represent the black defendants, told an Arkansas historian in 1920.[4] This wasn't exactly the case. The fusion principle—meaning that blacks and conservative white Democrats entered into a power-sharing arrangement on the county level—operated in some of the Delta counties, including Phillips. The following quotation from the 1997 *Phillips County Historical Review* suggests that racial politics in the Delta were complicated during Reconstruction and its aftermath: "A prominent black Phillips County politician, James T. White, supported this alliance [between blacks and conservative whites], and swore vengeance on 'carpetbaggers and rings' in 1874. He later said, in 1878, that the Southern white man was the black man's best friend."[5] Phillips County did indeed have a black sheriff, H. B. Robinson, who served from 1874 to 1878. Blacks also served at the county level as coroner and assessor. Several blacks from Phillips County served in the Arkansas legislature, including the state senate.[6] A former slave from Phillips County interviewed in the 1930s by the WPA project reminisced: "We had colored officers here. Austin Barrier was sheriff. Half of the officers was colored at one time. John Jones was police."[7]

As late as 1891, eleven black men, including J. N. Donahoo and John H. Carr from Phillips County, sat in the Arkansas legislature. As late as 1895, a black was still on the Helena police force. In its firing of Officer Jones, who had been a policeman for twenty years, for using force against a white man, the city was said to have had no choice. The *Helena World* commented: "There was strong pressure, however, brought to bear to relieve the police force of all negroes, and Chief Clancy yielded to it inasmuch he considers it his duty to serve the people acceptably."[8]

With the federal branches of government patently withdrawing support for antidiscriminatory treatment of black Americans, it was just a matter of time before most blacks in the South would be disfranchised and segregated. By passing the Separate Coach Act of 1891, an act requiring segregation on railway cars, the Arkansas legislature began that process in Arkansas. This was followed by a number of segregationist measures, including a poll tax, the white primary, and other Jim Crow laws. Yet, segregation by "custom" (the polite term in the South for coerced behavior that required no enacted law) in Arkansas was just as effective as passage of legislation. For blacks who lived in the growing urban areas of Arkansas, these measures were bitter pills to swallow. However, on the plantations in the Delta where the work of bringing in the cotton was done, it rarely could have made much difference that blacks represented the Delta in the Arkansas legislature or held municipal and county offices. As the article in the *Phillips County Historical Review* implies, Phillips County was never "entirely under Negro rule."

The reality was that blacks in Arkansas, to a greater or lesser degree, had always been subject to acts of intimidation, harassment, and violence by whites.[9] Violence against blacks in Arkansas immediately after the Civil War could generally be placed in a political context. As allies of white Republicans during Reconstruction, blacks had to deal with the Ku Klux Klan and with other native Arkansans who were determined to "redeem" Arkansas as a Democratic state. When the "Redeemers" triumphed in 1874, Augustus H. Garland, governor between 1874 and 1877, grandly pronounced in his inaugural address: "Let people of all parties, races and colors come and be welcomed to our State and encouraged to bring her up to a position of true greatness."[10]

And blacks, recruited by labor agents who painted a picture of a tropical paradise, did come to Arkansas by the thousands from Mississippi and other Deep South states, many of them coming to the Delta. Violence against them never vanished, but for a time it lacked the intensity it would have after the drive beginning in the 1890s to eliminate blacks as a political force and create a formal and informal system of apartheid. One particular episode of violence in southern Arkansas in 1883 eerily foreshadowed what occurred in Phillips County thirty-six years later. On August 2, 1883, the *Arkansas Gazette* reported that blacks were "on the warpath" in the northwestern portion of Hempstead County, in the southern part of the state. Blacks had killed a white man named Thomas Wyatt and were believed to be planning an insurrection. "[The] affair was the premature explosion of a deep-seated plot," according to R. G. Shaver, a former Confederate general and later sheriff and a prominent lawyer and citizen of Howard County at the time of the violence.[11] Though never proven, a white account of the affair stated that "at secret meetings they made out a list of several white men whom they proposed to kill, with Wyatt's name at the head."[12] Posses numbering 250 men hurried to the scene. The governor sent the commander of the state militia to investigate. Soon, twenty-seven blacks were in custody on murder charges in Howard County; three more charged with murder and forty-four charged with rioting were confined in the Hempstead County jail at Washington. Four African Americans lay dead, three of whom had been killed by accident. "The killing of Eli Gamble, Lonzo Flowers [*sic*] and a boy sixteen years old, was altogether a fatal mistake on the part of the attacking squad under the command of Capt. John Bell, of Nashville," a *Gazette* report perfunctorily commented on August 5.[13] No whites were charged.

Blacks had been aroused by the possible rape of a black woman, a niece of one of the principals in the affair; according to them, they had determined to make a citizen's arrest of Wyatt (which was legal at the time) when whites failed to take action.[14] For years the cases were fiercely litigated, resulting in reversals and new trials ordered by the supreme court of Arkansas. One black man, Charles Wright, was eventually hung, the others released immediately or after prison terms.[15]

A number of the blacks who poured into Arkansas in the 1880s lured by the hope of better conditions soon began to look elsewhere. Kenneth C. Barnes describes the long reign of political terror, whose principal victims were blacks, against Republicans in a north Arkansas county after the Civil War. Hundreds gave up on Conway County, which had once been seen as an oasis for African Americans, and moved on to Oklahoma, some going to Liberia as part of the back-to-Africa movement. Barnes poignantly quotes one of the new immigrants as writing home that one of the things he liked about Liberia was that "there are no white men to give orders; and you go in your house, there is no one to stand out, and call you to the door and shoot you when you come out."[16]

As long as cotton needed to be picked by hand, the Arkansas Delta, in particular, would be a lightning rod for racial strife. In the fall of 1891, an organization called the Colored Alliance called for a strike by cotton pickers. The call was ignored except in Lee County, adjacent to Phillips County. Though the details are obscure, a young black man by the name of Ben Patterson got together a group of around twenty-five men and rode onto a Lee County plantation encouraging others to join the strike. A fight broke out, and two pickers were killed along with a plantation manager. Posses soon caught up with the strikers and killed fifteen, apparently all of them black. Six blacks went to prison.[17]

Phillips County came in for its share of violence against blacks, even when this violence caused class conflict between poor white sharecroppers and plantation owners. White sharecroppers often competed unsuccessfully with black sharecroppers, who were preferred by planters because blacks would make contracts for considerably less than whites. The whites would then don the white caps of the past and drive off the blacks, much to the consternation of the planters and the white establishment. "If they [whitecappers] are caught while at their unlawful work they should be shot down like dogs, for the man who would burn his neighbor's barn and substance is worse than an assassin," fumed the *Helena Weekly World* in 1898.[18] Prosecutions were apparently rare, and convictions were rarer still.

Violence, disfranchisement, and apartheid required an explanation. It was an obvious one. Blacks had always been deemed utterly inferior to whites, but with the imposition of the Jim Crow era, the contempt inherent in white attitudes hardened with each rationalization of white actions. Blacks in Phillips County were inferior in every way, morally, intellectually, even spiritually. An 1898 obituary of S. D. Gibson, the minister of the Second Baptist Church, stated: "He was regarded as one of the best colored preachers, or rather he had a better knowledge of the art of entertaining his congregation than many of his kind."[19] The June 12, 1895, *Helena Weekly World* contained this characterization of two black preachers: "Jim Harvey and Sim Gibson are just a couple of common negro broilers, neither of them know anything about christianity, nor are they governed by any consideration except a desire to work the gullible fools in the congregation for all the money they can get."[20] In writing about the attitudes of white residents of Phillips County, Susan Huntsman notes that Phillips County whites sneered openly at most displays of black religion "as a joke, a cheap and flawed imitation of white worship."[21]

Citing stories about black crime from the period, Huntsman demonstrates that blacks were often represented as having a "scheming nature." When their plans failed, it was due to their stupidity. Paradoxically, "although blacks were often depicted as ruled by their emotions and lack of self-control, they also rarely committed a crime without it being premeditated or in cold-blood."[22]

When a black was praised, it was for those qualities that made him easy to control: "'Napolen is an industrious and enterprising farmer, and is reliable and trustworthy in every respect.'"[23] Had Napolen joined a sharecropper union in October 1898, the date of this item in the *Helena Weekly World*, it is not likely that he would have received such a positive mention in an article about farmers. As Huntsman notes, "More importantly a good black was faithful, reliable, trustworthy, steady, quiet, and peaceful."[24]

Thus, in order to justify white domination, the views of Phillips County whites about blacks were *necessarily* contradictory. Blacks were stupid but could scheme. They lacked self-control, but when they murdered whites, their actions were premeditated and planned. They were treacherous and lazy but loyal and industrious if they worked hard. They were docile but capable of acts of sudden ferociousness.

After thirteen years in Phillips County, Mort Allen shared the prevailing racial views of his adopted region. Months after the fighting at Hoop Spur he would write a letter to the governor of Kansas about the leader of the union, Robert Hill. Supporting Hill's extradition back to Arkansas, Allen argued: "Hill had the ability of rousing the spark of savagery lying dormant in every negro's heart."[25] At the same time, he felt that blacks were easily led. The mulatto Robert Hill "had simply played upon the ignorance and superstition of a race of children—most of whom neither read nor write," Allen would say in a statement to the *Helena World* on October 7.[26] These stereotypes of the former slave made white domination nonnegotiable. In Allen's letter to the Kansas governor, he wrote, "The only thing white people demand here is white control and while I am Northern born, I understand the absolute necessity for that. "[27]

Other stereotypes abounded as well. The plantation system, for example, was fair and equitable. As Allen would write William Avery of Hampton, Virginia, on November 20, 1919: "It is absurd to say that negro farmers as a class were being exploited by white planters. Too many proofs to the contrary are in evidence all over the South. There may have been individual cases of this sort but not enough to condemn the white planters as a whole."[28]

Only occasionally would there be a crack in the armor. From slavery onward, religion had been used as a handmaiden of the status quo in the Delta. In the early part of the twentieth century God and economic progress were particularly seen as working the same side of the street. Thus, ministers were careful not to interfere in plantation economics.

One Reverend Burke Culpepper, however, apparently took his calling more seriously than most. The *Helena World* gave this account of one evening's activities in 1916: "The evangelist took up another line of spiritual wickedness in high places in this community, in the unfair treatment of labor especially of colored farm labor, on the part of those whose positions as financial and social leaders should make them above such practices. The evangelist evidently knows that some large fortunes in Helena have been founded on unfair and unrighteous treatment of negro farmers, and held all men guilty of such action up for the severest condemnation. . . . At the conclusion of the speaking, another large number of persons, most of them men, and many of them men of real worth in the community, went forward and professed conversion."[29]

This remarkable acknowledgment of ill treatment of black labor by whites in Phillips County was so unique that it deserves comment. This brief moment of self-examination was almost over before it began. Blacks were commonly believed to have too little self-control to save their money, instead making foolish purchases. Why go to the trouble of keeping detailed accounts when blacks didn't keep up with their money themselves? Yet for one emotionally charged moment, someone within this tightly knit system pointed his finger, and hands were raised in recognition.

Was this simply an emotional moment at a revival, or was cheating of tenants routine in the Arkansas Delta? Ulysses Bratton, the white Republican lawyer from Little Rock who sent his son to meet with members of the union, would make a serious charge of peonage to the U.S. Department of Justice in November 1919 that will be explored in chapter 7. However, an interview with a white resident of Helena decades after the Elaine affair also provides a clue. In October 1919 Alvin Solomon was one of a handful of young Jewish men from Helena who had come back from the war. After the clash at Hoop Spur on the night of September 30, he became part of the Phillips County posse, composed of ex-servicemen, that went to Elaine. Solomon defended the actions of the posse; however, on the subject of planter-sharecropper relations, he remembered: "Most of these tenant farmers didn't get a break. They [the planters] kept the books on them, and they were always in debt. They'd give them what they wanted to give them. There were exceptions to that, but the exception was just against the rule."[30]

Despite its drawbacks for tenants, the system worked well enough for many landowners. In fact, under white control progress seemed inevitable. If Elaine with its population of just four hundred was the future, Helena, the sixth largest city in Arkansas, was the present. Mort Allen had a real estate office in the Solomon Building on Cherry Street. As a real estate man, Allen knew better than anybody that growth was not only good; it was the only game in town. Thanks in no small part to his leadership, business in Helena was going through the roof. The Business Men 's League that he had helped start was working tirelessly to help the city grow, and the results were little short of spectacular. Recently, the league had put together a brochure entitled, "Why Helena is Your Natural Market." It boasted that Helena offered four banks, one trust company, and two oil mills and then listed all the progress of the past year. Besides investments in new roads and streets, two hundred thousand dollars would be spent on river terminals. One million dollars had been spent on new building construction. Two hundred homes had gone up.[31] The Business Men's League had also been working for months on a new train for Helena and had just gotten the news of a new daily Missouri-Pacific route from Memphis to Natchez that would stop in Helena. That would make six daily arrivals in the city. The stores were filled with goods and advertised fashions "created by the foremost millinery artists." Auto dealers offered Jordans, Hupmobiles, Reos, Studebakers, Hudsons.

The Business Men's League had its share of planters, hundreds of whom had come together in Phillips County in February 1919 and tried to gain more control over their markets by agreeing to reduce their acreage in order to raise prices. Some had also repeated a tactic from the year before: in order to hold onto their labor they delayed settlements for months, claiming that they were waiting for cotton prices to reach their highest level.[32]

Mort Allen had not been so busy heading up the Business Men's League that he neglected his own bottom line. Besides his other financial interests, Helena's newest one-hundred-thousand-dollar department store, Ellis, Gemmill and Love, was to have its grand opening on October 3. A member of the board of directors, Allen was to have represented the Business Men's League at the festivities along with T. W. Keesee, his relative by marriage, welcoming the new store to the area. Allen's wife, Harriet, was on the women's welcoming committee and was to have made food for the event. There was going to be something for everybody. The Boy Scouts were to escort children to a special showing of a Charlie Chaplin movie at the Jewel Theatre.[33] Mort Allen was not a man who left things to chance.

In business he took everything into account before making a decision, but one factor was a given: docile black labor was the fuel that ran the county's engine of progress. If it didn't burn smoothly, sooner or later every enterprise in the county would ultimately begin to sputter. Rule number one: the white power structure had to be in control to make sure nothing disturbed the labor supply. Whether you were a planter, a real estate agent, or a politician, you understood that basic fact. The war had caused all kinds of problems. Detroit and Chicago were beckoning with the promise of jobs, and blacks had left the South in droves. Yet thousands of blacks were needed in Phillips County to bring in the white gold. If conditions became too harsh and violent in the Delta, blacks would continue to head north and stay, and all those thousands of acres of lovely, rich soil wouldn't be worth a yard of manure. Rule number two: see rule number one.

Dealing with labor wasn't easy, and problems had been brewing for years. In 1916, investigators from the United States government had come to Arkansas and noted: "As a result both of the evils inherent in the tenant system and of the occasional oppression by landlords, a state of acute unrest is developing among the tenants and there are clear indications of the beginning of organized resistance which may result in civil disturbances of a serious character."[34]

"Organized resistance" meant labor unions, and Phillips County was not immune to efforts in that direction. In 1917, two white labor organizers tried to recruit black railway workers to join a union. Not in Phillips County. Roy Dramer and Red Wiggins were whisked off to jail and charged with "threatening and intimidating" black workers. The Helena municipal judge had no trouble in reaching the conclusion that Dramer and Wiggins were deserving of five-hundred-dollar fines and twelve-month jail terms. The judge pointed out that "in the present crisis of the country it was a most unpropitious time for creating dissension in the ranks of labor."[35] Nobody was going to mess with Phillips County's black labor. It was treated very well, thank you. Just three weeks earlier the Business Men's League had used its clout to reverse the successful efforts of the United States Department of Labor to recruit Phillips County blacks to work on the construction of Camp Pike near Little Rock. The blacks were fired and "encouraged" to go back to Phillips County. "Army Posts will Use No More Negro Labor," was the August 10 headline in the *Helena World*.[36]

Yet the news of strikes and violence elsewhere continued to saturate the media. By May Day 1919 the news and editorials reported by the *Helena World* seemed to indicate an unending stream of worker unrest. But during the summer of 1919 Allen and others in the white power structure did not believe that the signs of labor unhappiness in the communities of southern Phillips County were significant enough to warrant taking decisive action to stop meetings from taking place.

Allen clearly did not believe that blacks were capable by themselves of taking collective action that would threaten the existing labor relationship. Had there been white agitators present on the scene before October 1, he would have been in the forefront, making certain that action was taken immediately. Some whites, however, apparently had taken the signs more seriously. Many years later it would be claimed that Sebastian Straub, who furnished supplies to sharecroppers all over Phillips County, and others, including Joseph Meyers, who owned the Bee Bayou plantation, had been suspicious and had hired black detectives from

Chicago to see what the blacks were up to with their secret meetings around Elaine. Charles Straub, the son of Sebastian Straub, told interviewers in 1960 that he was present at the interview at which the detective told his father:

> that the plan of the union was to kill a number of planters in the Elaine vicinity on or about October 6. The Negro union members were assured by the Negro organizer that he would see to it that the Government would give to each union member 40 acres of land and a mule after the planters were killed (this was in the detective's report). I saw and read the last report of the detective engaged to do this work, and remember very well that I saw it about the middle of September, 1919. After this report it was arranged that should any report of trouble come from Elaine the telephone operator would notify a number of designated citizens of Helena and ask them to report to the Acting Sheriff.[37]

In a written statement made in preparation for the same *Arkansas Historical Quarterly* article, written by Helena residents J. W. Butts and Dorothy James, Lynn P. Smith said he was living in 1919 on the Bee Bayou plantation: "As well as I remember, there was a committee formed here, and Jos. Meyers was one of the committee, and they employed negro detectives, at different times to investigate. . . . The reports showed that there were a number of planters to be killed, and the names of the negroes who were to kill them. These planters were notified, but they did not believe it, and therefore the men quit hiring the detectives. The detectives were hired nearly a year before September of 1919, but not all the time. I don't think they had any detectives here for about a month before the trouble started."[38]

One has to seriously doubt the allegation that detectives said that blacks had drawn up a list of planters to be killed, if for no other reason than the fact that the Committee of Seven, whose members became the official investigators of the riot and included Sebastian Straub, never claimed that planters had been told in advance that they were on a list marked for death but hadn't believed it. Nor was any of this information ever brought out in the extensive trial proceedings that followed the massacres. Certainly, the revelation that black detectives had uncovered a plot to kill planters would have enhanced the version of the story told by the Committee of Seven, the version that claimed that blacks were planning an insurrection. That this particular claim surfaced for the first time more than forty-one years later has to make one suspicious, especially when the Committee of Seven made such an extended effort at the time to convince the public that blacks had planned an insurrection. This information would have been compelling evidence that an insurrection had been planned. Again, why wouldn't Sebastian Straub have revealed it?

The "written report" of the unnamed detective has never been found or made public. Another reason for doubting the story is that if black detectives had discovered a plot to kill planters, Robert Hill and any union members thought to be planning wholesale murder would have been arrested immediately. It isn't conceivable that evidence of an insurrection plot would have been simply ignored.

In September 1919 Allen either didn't know who Robert Hill was or wasn't concerned about him. He did know the blacks in Helena who related well to the white power structure. As preachers, teachers, lawyers, and small businessmen, they had carved out a niche for themselves. They had made their way by cooperating with whites, not confronting them. Their leader was one of the most well-known African Americans in the United States. Dr. Elias Camp Morris was the president of the National Baptist Convention and pastor of the Centennial Baptist Church in Helena. In 1908 Booker T. Washington had been his guest for a meeting in Helena, an event that had attracted fifteen hundred spectators and over one hundred white guests. Like Scipio Jones in Little Rock, Camp Morris was the consummate black insider who worked with the "best whites." In 1917 he had "humbly" recommended a raise in wages to meet rising prices, pointing out that blacks would continue to leave for the North if this didn't occur.[39]

Morris was no ordinary "broiler" of the type sneered at by the *Helena World.* His white blood obvious in his thin lips, Morris had the countenance of a dreamer but was intensely practical. Vigorous well into his sixties, he had come to Arkansas as a young man and had built the Centennial Baptist Church up from a handful of adherents into a church whose membership numbered in the hundreds. Morris was everything the white community wanted a black person to be—infinitely patient, industrious, and respectful. He counseled racial uplift and hard work. In a speech to black churchmen in Pine Bluff in 1902, he recounted what he had seen blacks endure in the state. First there had been slavery, then freedom. They had gained the ballot, but now it was being taken away. Lynching of blacks was on the increase. Painting the present as optimistically as he could, he called for patience and said it was racial prejudice that "gives employment to every Negro preacher, every Negro teacher, doctor, lawyer, that built all the Negro churches and school [sic], started every Negro store, hotel and restaurant, every bank, every insurance company, and in fact every enterprise owned and operated by the race."[40] Only when blacks had built themselves up to a degree that whites couldn't ignore them would politics be useful to them, Morris said (though he was himself active in the Republican Party). He advised diligence, the acquisition of property, and righteous living. Seventeen years later, neither he nor other "black leaders" would be prepared for the emergence of a labor union whose members protected their meetings with guns. A week before the outbreak of violence at Hoop Spur, black leaders of the newly formed Helena colored YMCA wrote a letter to the *Helena World* to complain of the rumors linking the colored YMCA to the union. They wanted the readers of the *World* to know that they were rejecting the blandishments of these men who had urged them to more militant action. The hope of the race lay in education, recreation for the young, and cooperation with Helena's "best white people."[41] Given Morris's attitudes, it must have come as a shock to the white community when he later refused to rubber-stamp its "investigation" of the racial violence in Elaine.

By 1919, however, a different kind of black sharecropper had begun to emerge in Phillips County, though these sharecroppers represented a small percentage of the total population. Often they were men who had been to war on behalf of the United States. Now they were home and expected to be treated differently and were not going to wait until the white man decided to change. "We helped you fight the Germans, and are ready to help you fight the next fellows that get after you, but we want to be treated fairly," a fugitive Robert Hill (who apparently did not go off to the war) would explain in a December 1919 letter to the *Arkansas Gazette* that was reprinted in the *Helena World.*[42] It has been estimated that more than a thousand black men from Phillips County entered the military during the war years. Testimony in the trials would indicate that some of the Elaine Twelve had military experience.[43]

And it wasn't just the war. Escalating cotton prices during the war years had encouraged rising expectations. In increasing numbers—though again as a minute percentage of the total—blacks were able to purchase their own farms, thus giving some an independence they had never dreamed of. Too, they were given hope for a better day by black newspapers like the *Chicago Defender* that made their way into Arkansas and Phillips County. The *Defender* not only contained inspirational stories about black achievement, but it also denounced Jim Crow and violence against blacks. One measure of its influence was that Governor Brough would try to ban it and the NAACP's *Crisis* from coming into the state after the violence in Phillips County. Blacks in the Delta knew that workers were going on strike in other parts of the country. A fifth of the nation's workforce had walked out. Why shouldn't they?

Part preacher and part salesman, as any union leader must be, the mulatto Robert Hill seemed an unlikely union leader for Phillips County blacks, but he possessed the right combination of innocence and shrewdness to appeal to black sharecroppers who were sick and tired of walking away from the cotton scales at settlement time with little if anything in their pockets. Hill, a farmer who was married with two children, would be demonized by Mort Allen and the white power structure in Phillips County, but he and the union he represented had little in common with Allen's portrayal.

The original founding of the Progressive Farmers and Household Union of America is obscure, but by the time Robert Hill brought it to Phillips County, its aims were hardly revolutionary: farmers must come together and act jointly. One of the union's primary songs contained the following words:

> Your calling was the first on earth—
> Organize, oh organize!
> And ever since has proved its worth—
> Organize, oh organize!
> Then come ye farmers, good and true;
> The die is cast—it's up to you—
> Organize, oh organize![43]

Instead of pledging themselves to a foreign brand of radicalism, applicants were required to agree that that they would "defend this government and her constitution at all times." Sometimes, Hill raided the Bible for material. One of his proclamations read in part: "O, you laborers of the earth, hear the word. The time is at hand that all men, all nations, and tongues must receive a just reward! The union wants to know why it is that the laborers cannot control their just earnings which they work for."[44]

At the same time Hill was not above trying to puff his credentials or attempting to increase the coffers of his organization (or perhaps his own pocket) through some dubious ploys. Though general membership cost one dollar and fifty cents for men, he advertised a special rate. If you paid more than five dollars, you had a right to attend the congresses of the union and speak on the floor. Ten dollars would give you a share in a union headquarters building to be built in Winchester, Arkansas. Fifty dollars or more would get your name engraved. He identified himself to union members as a "U.S. detective," a silly, self-important claim that would get him charged with a federal crime, that of impersonating a federal officer. A correspondence course from Saint Louis that taught its students how to be "detectives" had produced a badge that read "U.S." Perhaps Hill believed his claim himself. In November 1919, he would write to the NAACP: "I am a detective on the case for the farmers in Phillips Co., and hope that you all will get up for my help."[45] Whatever Hill's abilities or personal motives, he and the officers of the local "lodges" were striking a nerve among ordinary sharecroppers in the black settlements in the area around Elaine.

In any event, within twenty-four hours of the shoot-out at Hoop Spur, Mort Allen had surely realized how big a mistake he and his friends had made in not shutting down the union before it had built up a head of steam. He would not make the same mistake twice.

CHAPTER 3

The Boys from Camp Pike

All you have to do is remain at work just as if nothing had happened.
—From a circular distributed to Phillips County blacks,
October 7, 1919

October 1–2, 1919
Elaine

Historians writing about Elaine have uniformly accepted the United States military's account of its role in the Elaine affair in part because the military is thought to have saved hundreds of lives by disarming the white mobs that came to the Elaine area on October 1 before the troop train arrived shortly after eight in the morning on October 2. Additionally, historians have had another reason for glossing over the military's performance in Phillips County: Arkansas governor Charles Hillman Brough and other members of the white power structure in the state acted oblivious to the fact that soldiers from Camp Pike, sometimes acting together with white civilians and sometimes acting alone, engaged in acts of murder, torture, and devastation of black-owned property in Elaine during the seven days they were in the area. On October 10, 1919, after most of the troops had returned to Camp Pike (some troops remained in Helena guarding the Phillips County courthouse to prevent lynchings of the hundreds of blacks detained there), Brough wrote Secretary of War Newton Baker: "These five hundred troops, composed of representatives of the Third Division, the 'Rock of the Marne' and the Fourth Infantry, under command of Col. I. C. Jenks and Major Callen, rendered invaluable service and their presence unquestionably checked a wholesale massacre of whites and blacks alike."[1]

Brough's letter goes on to describe the "racial disturbances in Phillips County" as having been "nipped in the bud."[2] Brough's letter, which was placed in the official military reports, would become part of the successful effort to cover up the behavior of some of the troops. Brough's use of the word "check" is telling. He does not say "prevent." This is the closest

Brough would come to admitting publicly that white mobs had roamed the Elaine area at will, murdering blacks.

History has been kind to Governor Brough and to the United States military. Brough's role in the Elaine affair has always been taken at face value. Since it has been assumed that his prompt action saved lives of black Arkansans, his willingness to ask for troops and, indeed, his eagerness to accompany them to Elaine have ended the matter for historians. Yet Brough's actions in conjunction with the military have to be reexamined in light of evidence of the slaughter of blacks by the white mobs and the troops.

To appreciate the evidence to be presented of massacres by troops and by white mobs coming into the area, one must first keep in mind that only one soldier from Camp Pike, Luther C. Earles (Earle in some accounts), lost his life in what fighting did occur between soldiers and blacks. In total, only five whites, including Earles, lost their lives. Four of them were either Phillips County law-enforcement personnel or members of the Phillips County posse that was hunting down blacks on October 1. Secondly, one must keep in mind that there was no black insurrection at Elaine. It will be shown that the story of a planned insurrection was concocted on October 2 by the white power structure in Phillips County in order to legitimate the actions of white mobs the previous day.

If one accepts the evidence that massacres by the military and white mobs took place, then the actions of the principals afterward take on an entirely different meaning and character. Thus, it is essential to interrupt our narrative in order to evaluate the evidence that massacres of innocent blacks by the military and white mobs occurred in the Elaine area.

In 1925, a slender paperback appeared in Little Rock with the quaint title, *What a Preacher Saw Through a Keyhole in Arkansas.*[3] It was the second published work by the author, Louis Sharpe Dunaway, whose first book was about Jeff Davis, the demagogic three-term governor and United States senator from Arkansas. Born in 1870, Dunaway made a career of traveling the state and selling subscriptions to newspapers, primarily the *Arkansas Gazette.* He also worked as a reporter. His obituary in 1959 in the *Arkansas Gazette,* perhaps because of his visits to every county in Arkansas, stated that he was "once described as the best known newspaperman in Arkansas." The obituary writer said of him that "his travels and keen interest in politics made him known in every newspaper office and courthouse in the state."[4]

Composed mostly of his subject's speeches, Dunaway's first book, on Jeff Davis, did not purport to be a deeply researched work. Though Dunaway's observations are more than fair to him, Davis, who hated the *Gazette* because of its editorial stance against him, referred to Dunaway from the campaign stump as "that *Gazette* Yankee."[5]

However, Dunaway, a Faulkner County native who attended well-regarded Hendrix College in Conway, thirty miles northwest of Little Rock, from 1892 to 1895, was no Yankee out to bash the South. But for one chapter, *What a Preacher Saw* is a "feel-good" book. In its foreword, Dunaway says that he wrote it "with a view of replying to the slanderous lines penned by one Mr. Jackson, and circulated by that ill-advised and uninformed gentleman who delights in his authorship of *On a Slow Train Through Arkansas*."[6] The book Dunaway refers to, by Thomas Jackson, made Arkansas hillbillies a favorite subject. Dunaway set out to defend the state. In chapter after chapter he extols the native beauty of Arkansas and gives facts and figures purporting to show the state's progress. One chapter, for example, is entitled, "Diamond Cave, Probably Largest Cavern in the World, in Newton County, Arkansas." *What a Preacher Saw* is an inoffensive, bland book with folksy humor designed to make the reader feel better about his home state, seemingly nothing more than an exercise in boosterism: "Many are the visitors who go through there every month in the year and are guided through the marvellous passage-ways, which have been pronounced equally as huge and wonderful as the noted Mammoth Cave in Kentucky."[7]

Dunaway's promotion of Arkansas and her people fills every page until suddenly one reaches the chapter, "The Blackest Page in State History." This chapter is an account of the events in Phillips County in 1919, an account in which Dunaway over and over again accuses the troops from Camp Pike and "low-lived" whites of engaging in an outright slaughter of the blacks they encountered in the Elaine area. He baldly states, "It has been charged and not denied that 856 negroes were killed during the first days immediately following the first trouble in Elaine."[8] Pages later, he insists again that "a fair count showed 856 dead negro bodies with a wounded list probably five times greater."[9]

Until Dunaway's accusations not a single person from Arkansas had alleged in print that the men from Camp Pike had acted in any way but as heroes. Nothing in Dunaway's background or previous journalistic efforts prepares his readers for the following outburst: "The thing that 'stumps' us, however, is by what authority did a coterie of Federal soldiers, aided and abetted by a collection of low-lived creatures who call them-selves WHITE MEN, march down among the ramshackle homes of good old innocent, hard-working Darkeys, and then unlimber their guns on those poor servants of the rebellion, finally snuffing out their lives before passing onto the next house, where the same cruel scene was enacted, thus leaving a path strewn with aching hearts and besprinkled with the blood of innocent humanity." The soldiers "committed one murder after another with all the calm deliberation in the world, either too heartless to realize the enormity of their crimes or too drunk on moonshine to give a continental darn."[10]

The documentation provided by the author for such claims is sparse. Dunaway cites an unidentified schoolteacher from Miller County who was teaching in Phillips County at the time as the "authority for the state-ment that 28 negroes in one bunch were killed and their bodies thrown into a pit and burned."[11] None of these individuals was connected with any of the fighting at Hoop Spur or afterward. The same source told Dunaway that sixteen other blacks were hung from a bridge four miles outside of Helena by the soldiers. He also cites a Professor J. C. Fretwell, who had lived in Phillips County, as an informant. Fretwell had allowed two or three soldiers to stay at his home during the trouble. He said that "they counted upon their fingers the numbers of negroes who had been killed during the day by their party and by the machine gun and made no attempt to conceal the facts."[12]

The above is the sum total of documentation for Dunaway's auda-cious claims. Dunaway's target was primarily the U.S. military. A loyal Arkansan, he went out of his way to exonerate the local power structure in Phillips County. Their actions in killing blacks were justified: "It was nothing more than expected, when a chivalrous white citizenship took up arms and immediately avenged the killing of seven or eight of their own color. While this summary action is not conducive to good govern-ment, yet it is not assailed for the reason we know of some of the leading characters in this tragedy, and we know them to be big and brave and true to the traditions of the 'Old South.'"[13] Indeed, Dunaway ranked the slaughter of the blacks as not the "the deepest regret" of the Elaine affair. That designation went to the loss of the lives of the white citizens of Phillips County.

It would be easier to dismiss Dunaway's claims if the rest of the chap-ter didn't provide a serious, unusually competent, and detailed summary of the complex legal proceedings that followed the massacres. This chapter is not a hit-and-run operation by an embittered cynic with a grudge against the United States military, and it is certainly not the work of a man sympathetic to blacks: Dunaway clearly shared the sentiments of Arkansas whites of his time. Rather, his diatribe seems prompted by simple outrage that innocent people were murdered. Despite the lack of documentation, the reader senses that something terrible occurred in Elaine that was hushed up. But Dunaway absolves the governor: "We know that Gov. Brough did not sanction the soldiers' death-dance; we know that he was not aware of the butchery that was taking place in the guise of 'peace making.'"[14]

So far as can be determined, Brough never commented publicly on this chapter of Dunaway's book, nor did Dunaway state how he knew that Brough was ignorant of the troops' actions. Yet Brough was aware of Dunaway's book because the author presented him with an autographed copy. Unfortunately for his credibility, Dunaway gives no hint of how he determined the number of African American dead, other than what is stated above.

Just as history cannot take Dunaway's word for the number of blacks killed in Phillips County, neither can it take his word that Brough did not sanction the military's actions or that he was ignorant of them. As in the impeachment proceedings against President Nixon, among the questions that we shall explore is the question of what Brough knew and when he knew it. Equally as important will be the question of whether Brough bears any responsibility for the actions of the military.

Though Dunaway ignores the question of how Brough could have been unaware of the killings (the governor returned to Little Rock the next day, on October 3), he doesn't spare his profession, resorting to rare sarcasm: "It is a strange 'coincidence' that newspapermen, quick to get the news and usually accurate in their figures, were 'unable to get the known Negro dead,' or furnish a true description of the soldiers' march of death through the cotton fields of Phillips County. And it is a 'strange come-off' that these same 'news hounds' found time to write only 'half the story' of all the Elaine troubles."[15]

Dunaway appears to have self-published both books. *What a Preacher Saw* apparently sunk like a stone. The book is barely mentioned in his obituary, the chapter on Elaine not at all.

At least two of the historians writing about the events in Elaine were apparently not aware of Dunaway's chapter on Elaine. It is not cited in either Arthur Waskow's 1966 *From Race Riot to Sit-In: 1919 and the 1960s* or Richard C. Cortner's 1988 *A Mob Intent on Death: The NAACP and the Arkansas Riot Cases.*[16] However, the book is cited in B. Boren McCool's *Union, Reaction, and Riot: The Biography of a Rural Race Riot,* published in 1970.[17] Three times McCool cites Dunaway's chapter on Elaine in his summary of the court cases, but he does not even mention in a footnote Dunaway's account of the soldiers' behavior. More recently, in an *Arkansas Historical Quarterly* article, Jeannie M. Whayne, mentioning in a footnote Dunaway's claim that 856 blacks were killed, refers to the book as "eccentric"; in a comment on an earlier draft of this work, Whayne calls Dunaway's effort "a ridiculous little book." [18] Yet Dunaway's chapter on Elaine cannot be dismissed so easily, for Dunaway painstakingly tracks for his readers the subsequent legal proceedings in federal and state courts with a tenacity and accuracy that meets the highest standards of investigative journalism; this is the work of a reporter who made certain he was getting right the details of a complex series of events.

Acknowledging that Dunaway, as a reporter, was a victim of his own class and racial prejudices, which led him to excuse the Delta planter class and Brough in the events in Phillips County, does not easily translate into believing that he deliberately or negligently misrepresented the U.S. troops involved in the massacres. Had his motive simply been to protect the local power structure in Phillips County, he could have laid the massacres entirely at the feet of the "low-lived whites" who participated in the slaughter of blacks.

Dunaway would not be the only person to claim that the military was involved in the massacres. In 1955 writer James Street, also once a reporter for the *Arkansas Gazette,* included a brief summary of the Elaine affair in his book, *James Street's South.* In commenting on the military occupation of Elaine, Street states:

> [The] soldiers mounted machine guns on the main street and watched the Negroes of southeastern Arkansas shuffle down the streets, apparently without malice in their hearts.
>
> Finally, however, some thoughtless Negro fired a shot at the soldiers. A volley from the machine gun was the answer and the war was on. Without comment and without haste the soldiers went about the tedious duty of ending the riot. They marched through the swamps shooting Negroes without question. Those who were not shot were herded into cattle cars for safety. For two days, the slaughter continued, but the riot was broken.[19]

Street, whose other books include *Tap Roots,* apparently gathered his material from another reporter and did no research of his own. Thus, his account of the Elaine story is a vastly inferior account to that given by Dunaway. His four-page summary filled with major factual errors (Street didn't even get right the number of blacks to be executed), Street's work is useless as a history of the events. Yet for the second time the word "slaughter" had found its way into print to describe the soldiers' actions. It wouldn't be the last time.

Significantly, the prosecuting attorney in the Elaine cases, John E. Miller, would in 1976 provide secondhand corroboration, fifty-seven years after the events, that the United States military had played a part in the massacre of blacks. Then eighty-seven years old and the senior federal judge in the state, Miller sat for an oral interview conducted by Dr. Walter Lee Brown, a professor of history at the University of Arkansas in Fayetteville, along with two employees of the university library. The interview covered Miller's life, but a good part of it focused on the events in Phillips County. His taped interview, which has been transcribed, is at times rambling and unclear, in the manner of oral histories, and after so many years Miller naturally misremembered some of the details. By then Miller, a native of Missouri, had enjoyed the fruits of Arkansas politics for much of his adult life. For the past thirty-five years he had been a United States district court judge for the Western District of Arkansas. Before that he had served in the United States Senate as an anti-Roosevelt independent (having been a congressman), though he would not remember it that way: "I was about half and half. I supported a lot of New Deal legislation until I thought we had gone far enough."[20] To get him out of the Senate, Franklin Roosevelt offered him the juiciest political plum an attorney could obtain, and eager to get out of Washington, Miller took it.

During his interview, Miller apparently could not help eventually referring to blacks as "niggers." Asked about what had occurred in Elaine, he answered: "Brough sent the national guard [*sic*] in there. The Negroes had been told that the army would come in there and protect them and they were looking for it. And a train with boxcars with state militia largely on the boxcars went out of Helena and down towxxds [*sic*] and just before it got to Elaine, the niggers thought the train had U.S. troops, they rode up on both sides with their guns, two or three hundred of them on both sides, and by g—that alerted the national guard and the national guard fired on them and they must have killed 100 niggers right there."[21]

At this point in the interview Miller, who said he had not been present but had been told "a great deal" about the incident, began to digress, recalling that he had been in court in Marianna when the fighting started.

Brown: One of the things that we are trying to find out today is what really happened in that county out there, southxxx [*sic*] and southwest. You said you were told that the troops shot these blacks down that rode up on each side of the railroad tracks. Did the Negroes shoot back?

Miller: Yes, they did.

Brown: The blacks shot back?

Miller: Yes you see that is what caused, really, the firing, that real slaughter down there. There was some shot fired . . . but they were fired in celebration of the army being there. That is what happened. There wasn't a soldier hit or anything.[22]

That real slaughter. Miller's statement that the blacks fired their guns in the air in celebration of the arrival of the United States troops seems to be an explanation designed to make it appear that the slaughter of blacks was the result of a tragic misunderstanding. But it seems highly unlikely that men who were being hunted down would spontaneously act in such a manner upon seeing perhaps hundreds of heavily armed soldiers. The impetus for such an account probably came from Miller's memory that only one soldier had been killed and that whites had said that Robert Hill told union members that the United States government would come to their aid. This scenario was just as much of a concoction as Miller's story. While Hill wrote the national NAACP that he was a "U.S. detective," there is no credible evidence that he led union members to expect aid from the U.S. military.

The *Memphis Press* reported on October 4 that a few miles outside of Helena corpses of blacks lay beside the road: "Enraged citizens fired at the dead bodies of the negroes, as they rode out of Helena toward Elaine. When the troops rounded up the negroes, hardly any had guns or ammunition. . . . The soldiers used their machine guns on one group of negroes. . . . Two negroes were killed outright and the rest threw up their arms and surrendered." The reporter gave the figure of African American dead as twenty.

Further, anecdotal evidence suggests that nonresisting blacks were gunned down by the military and that the total of blacks killed by soldiers was far higher than admitted by Colonel Jenks, his intelligence officers, or the local press. Roger C. Mears Jr., the son of the same Roger Mears who was a hero at the Second Battle of the Marne, stated in a 1999 interview that his father, in telling him about the events at Elaine, had said that troops were ordered to fire into a building where blacks were said to be. Roger C. Mears Jr., who proudly provided the details of his father's undeniable heroism in World War I, said that his father had told him that he had not wanted to do this. When he was pressed for more details, none were forthcoming.[23] The implication, however, is obvious: the blacks inside the building were not resisting or were unarmed.

In a tape transcribed in 1995 by Thea Bratton Crossier, the great granddaughter of Ulysses Bratton, Ulysses Bratton Jr. told a local historian by the name of James Johnston the following: "The guard was called out and they killed scores of colored boys out in the woods. I had lunch in Little Rock about that time and I sat next to one of the guardsmen and he said they were shooting them down like rabbits. He didn't know who I was of course. But it meant a lot to me because I knew who was involved."[24]

Since he was speaking some seventy years after the event, Ulysses Bratton Jr.'s memory of these events had its lapses, just as Judge Miller's did. It was not the Arkansas National Guard that went to Elaine, but regular Army soldiers from Camp Pike. In another part of the interview, Ulysses Bratton Jr. incorrectly said that Ocier, his brother, was held for several months instead of one month. What gives Bratton's account of the military's actions credibility, however, is that neither Ulysses Bratton Sr. nor any members of his family ever displayed any signs of bitterness against the U S. military. In fact, Guy Bratton had served as an intelligence officer in France and had joined a local American Legion Post upon his return. The family's understandable hostility was reserved for the people of Arkansas for driving them out of the state.

Edward Molitor, whose great uncle was named by Amos Jarmon as one of the men who shot the four Johnston brothers, who were from a prominent black family in Helena, recalled in a July 1, 2000, interview that his Aunt Mary, born in 1907, once told him that "the troops fired on the blacks killing from between fifty and fifteen hundred."[25] This estimate, of course, is meaningless, except that it implies that stories about the military's actions circulated among the locals in the area.

In his autobiography, *All Out of Step,* published in 1956, Gerard Lambert, the Northern owner of the twenty-one-thousand-acre Lambrook plantation outside of the town of Elaine, includes a brief, error-ridden account of the events, yet he records two incidents that also support the view that Louis Sharpe Dunaway's account is not fiction. By the time Lambert arrived at the scene, the soldiers were already in Elaine. He recalls the soldiers shooting an individual who tried to run from a building and then taking his body up to the second floor: "Two men calmly picked up the body and carried it to a spot beneath the windows of the room where the others were confined. As they dropped it on the ground they looked up at the staring faces of the Negroes in the window and told them this should be a lesson to them. For the first time I felt sick. Later, when I left the building, the man's body was still there, covered with flies."[26]

The second incident recounted involved "the colored leader at Lambrook" who had been taken into custody by the military. Lambert states that he was told:

> Troopers brought him to our company store and tied him with stout cord to one of the wooden columns on the other porch. He had been extremely insolent, and the troopers, enraged by the loss of two of their men that day in the woods, had pressed him with questions. He continued his arrogance, and one white man, hoping to make him speak up, poured a can of kerosene over him. As he was clearly unwilling to talk, a man suddenly tossed a lighted match at him. The colored man went up like a torch and, in a moment of supreme agony, burst his bounds. Before he could get but a few feet he was riddled with bullets. The superintendent told me with some pleasure that they had to use our fire hose to put him out.[27]

The above account adds another dimension to the soldiers' behavior—that of torture committed during interrogation in complicity with local whites. We shall see that interrogation became a function of the military's role and that it was often performed in concert with white civilians in the area. The evidence will also show that nonmilitary personnel engaged in acts of torture at the Phillips County jail to make blacks testify against each other during the trials.

The full record of the military's actions will never be known. What seems likely is that individual units of the military contingent in Elaine acted differently toward the blacks, probably depending upon the attitude of the individual in command. Unquestionably, a number of blacks were allowed to surrender to the troops without incident. The trial of one of the Elaine Twelve illustrates the care that was taken by some of the troops. Barely one month after the massacre, Albert Giles, who was nearly killed in an exchange of gunfire on October 1 that resulted in the death of James Tappan, a member of the Phillips County posse, testified to the following:

Q: You had no medical attention before the soldiers came?
A: No sir.
Q: The soldiers dressed your wounds?
A: Yes sir.
Q: Where did you go then?
A: They dressed it there at the house and taken me away from there, they put a board under my arm and wrapped it up and carried me away, and they carried me over there and brought me to the hospital.[28]

The evidence that there were massacres of innocent blacks by white mobs and soldiers from Camp Pike (though not necessarily at the same time) should be understood in the context of later efforts by both the U.S. military and the white power structure to make it appear that white planters and their families were in danger and that only blacks who were fighting were killed. Simultaneously, it has to be understood that once the word spread that there had been a shoot-out at the Hoop Spur church and that blacks were continuing to resist on October 1, whites in the Elaine area were most definitely afraid that they would be attacked and totally panicked. Again, none of the whites killed or wounded were planters or their families. As will be shown, both the military and the white power structure in Phillips County (including Governor Brough) would make much of the argument that a massacre by blacks was averted by the quick response of the military. In fact, had blacks wanted to kill white planters and their families, because of their numerical superiority and proximity they had ample opportunity to do so on October 1, before the posses and the military arrived.

From the beginning, the national NAACP claimed that innocent blacks had been killed by white mobs. In articles written for national magazines such as the *Nation* and the *Survey,* published in December 1919 and January 1920, Walter White publicly drew attention to an issue that no one in Arkansas was willing to talk about—the behavior of the posses and the troops. The difficulty was in determining the true proportions of the massacres and would never be resolved by the NAACP, a dilemma admitted by Walter White. "A large number of colored people who were killed were put to death by troops who used machine guns to mow down colored people. Citizens' posses, however, murdered a great many more," he wrote in a letter dated January 31, 1920.[29]

Though the NAACP gave different estimates over the years, its highest figure of the number of blacks thought to have been killed was put forth in a press release on January 14, 1925, the date the last of the men were released from the penitentiary: "Mr. White reported that Negroes were being hunted and 250 shot down like wild beasts, in the Arkansas cane brakes, because they had organized to employ a lawyer in an endeavor to obtain settlements and statements of accounts from the landlords under the share-cropping system." In an article published in 1919, White had written, "White men in Helena told me that more than one hundred Negroes were killed."[30]

It would be 1921 before any of the whites who had been in the fighting would publicly support these claims. Two extraordinary affidavits of former security employees of the Missouri-Pacific Railroad who were then living in Memphis would crack the wall of silence about the massacre by white mobs. By 1921, efforts were underway to litigate the Elaine cases in federal court. Defense counsel attached to their petition for a writ of habeas corpus two sworn statements from T. K. Jones and H. F. Smiddy, who were members of the posse from Phillips County on October 1.[31] Since the cases involving these particular affidavits never went to trial and thus were never tested in court, questions will always remain about the veracity and accuracy of the assertions in them; however, the fact that the prosecution went to such lengths to discredit H. F. Smiddy in particular and then settled the cases without additional trial suggests the fear their prospective testimony engendered in the white power structure of Phillips County. Taken together, the affidavits are astonishing, for Jones and Smiddy admit to participating in acts of torture to compel confessions and identify their accomplices by name. Almost incidentally, the affidavits give a picture of what occurred before federal troops arrived on October 2. Smiddy and Jones, Smiddy's supervisor, were both participants from the beginning in the initial effort to investigate the death of Will Adkins in the early morning hours on October 1, and both remained in the area for the rest of the day. Smiddy had been called as a witness in the William Wardlow trial to establish what time the body of Will Adkins had been found on October 1. (He is misidentified in the Wardlow trial transcript as "H. L. Smith").[32]

Little is known about T. K. Jones beyond what is contained in his affidavit, but H. F. Smiddy would become a part of the Elaine saga because of the persecution he would suffer. With a wife and four children to support, Smiddy was not out of work at the time he signed his sworn statement, but he soon would be. Smiddy stated that he quit working for the railroad in late November or early December 1919 and went to work for the chief of police in Helena as a plainclothes policeman. Two or three months later he quit that job and worked as a deputy sheriff for Phillips County, staying there one year until Sheriff Frank Kitchens died and a new sheriff was elected. His future correspondence with the NAACP and Jones and McHaney reveals him to have been a weak and pitiable lower-class white, but one who had a conscience. And though he would need money and protection, he stubbornly maintained that his motivation was pure. "It was not the money I did what I did for the Colored People in the South, I knew the streight [sic] of the thing and I wanted to see them come out of it, and I did this for them and I don't think I ought to suffer for it," he wrote Walter White on February 15.[33]

In his ten-page affidavit Smiddy states in part: "Between nine and ten o'clock on the morning of October 1 a great many people from Helena and other portions of Phillips County, and from other surrounding counties, began coming in, quite a large number of them, several hundred of them, and began to hunt negroes and shotting [sic] them as they came to them."[34] Smiddy implicates himself as well as others. He admits to wounding one of the individuals who later pleaded guilty: "I shot Milliken [sic] Giles myself. He was in the edge of the thicket trying to hide. When I shot him he was not trying to shoot anybody and didn't have a gun."[35]

Earlier in the affidavit he admits to having been present when other blacks were shot: "As we marched down the thicket in the southwest I saw about five or six negroes come out unarmed, holding up their hands and some of them running and trying to get away. They were shot down and killed by members of the posse. I didn't see a single negroe [sic] during all the man hunt that was armed, and I didn't see a single negro fire a shot."[36] In another portion of the affidavit he mentions the activities of a band from Mississippi who arrived that afternoon: "They shot and killed men, women, and children without regard to whether they were guilty or innocent of any connection with the killing of anybody, or whether members of the union or not. Negroes were killed time and time again out in the fields picking cotton, harming nobody."[37]

Until July 15, 1921, for approximately six years, T. K. Jones worked for Missouri-Pacific and was "in charge of the Memphis Division," which included the Memphis to Marianna run and Helena to Clarendon and Brinkley. Jones, Smiddy's supervisor, states that he was not in one of the groups that went out to hunt blacks but was assigned during the morning to guard a road near the Hoop Spur commissary with the Helena chief of police, Sam Austin, and then later to guard a house that was rumored to be about to be attacked by blacks. His affidavit lends support to the view that though whites may have expected blacks to come after them, that didn't occur: "The local freight train on the Missouri-Pacific Railroad made several trips up and down the road during the day with the caboose loaded with men, and if the negroes had desired to kill anybody they could have killed them."[38]

Jones also states that he helped torture blacks and confirms Smiddy's affidavit as to the names of others who joined in: "Those that did the whipping of the negroes in the Phillips County jail other than myself and Mr. Smiddy were Mr. Dick Dazell, Louis Anselman, Charlie Gist, and some others whose name [sic] I do not now recall."[39]

Their affidavits reinforce each other. Though Smiddy and Jones do not name individuals who participated in the mass killing of blacks, they had an intimate knowledge of the Elaine affair from before the shoot-out at Hoop Spur through the trials in November.

An unsolved mystery is how Edgar McHaney, one of the attorneys for the defendants, persuaded Smiddy and Jones to provide affidavits. Traitors to their race, they had both testified in the trials of the convicted men. As we shall see in chapter 11, Smiddy especially became a marked man. He was charged with numerous offenses and later depended on the defendants' counsel for financial support.[40]

In assessing the content of the affidavits, one has always to keep in mind that these were appellate documents, their sole purpose to cast doubt on previous incriminating testimony. Scipio Jones and Edgar McHaney were not trying to write a history; they were trying to save their clients' necks. Thus, neither affidavit mentions the activities of the military. Why not? The answer seems obvious. The legal fight was between the state of Arkansas and the black defendants. Why take on the fabulously popular "doughboys" if you didn't have to?

The part of the affidavits concerning the "bunch from Mississippi" would be corroborated years later, in 1927, in a master's thesis written on the events in Elaine by an Arkansan named Bessie Ferguson. Ferguson graduated in 1925 from Hendrix College in Conway, Arkansas, which Louis Sharpe Dunaway had attended many years earlier. Her advisor for her thesis was Thomas Staples, a highly respected Hendrix College professor who had written a book on Reconstruction in Arkansas and who followed the Dunning interpretation of Reconstruction, which viewed the aftermath of the Civil War as a rape of the South. From Moro in neighboring Lee County (whose county seat is Marianna), Ferguson, whose alumni card from Hendrix shows that she lived at some point in Helena (perhaps during her research), shared the racial views of the typical white resident. Though her biases are apparent, her work contains some interviews of individuals from Elaine, both black and white. The stories Ferguson got were so contradictory that she simply divided her paper into separate sections. Unfortunately, she did not usually identify by name the persons with whom she spoke. In her conclusion, she states in part:

> The killing of Adkins started four days of fighting between the white people and negroes and a much longer period of unsettled conditions. Five white men were killed and at least five times as many negroes is a conservative estimate. The negroes were killed because they resisted the authorities. The results would have been the same if white people had resisted officers of the law and government troops.
>
> The negroes greatly exaggerate the indiscriminate killings which took place. A party of twelve men from Mississippi equipped with eleven guns and an axe created havoc wherever they went. One instance of their brutality being the murdering of a harmless crazy negro woman, Frances Hall. Such slaughter was not sanctioned by the authorities. Barberism [sic] such as cutting off the ears or toes of dead negroes for souvenirs and the dragging of their bodies through the streets of Elaine are told by witnesses.[41]

In this last sentence the reader is given a glimpse of the horror that occurred in Elaine, but Ferguson does not provide the names of persons killed, other than the individual listed above, or mention the witnesses' names. It would have been useful had she reported how many deaths blacks said they had suffered, but her work seems determined to minimize them. Given the social pressure Ferguson must have been under, perhaps it is commendable that she gives as much of the story as she does.

However, it is not realistic to believe that Arkansas residents acted with greater self-restraint than their neighbors from just across the Mississippi River. Frank "Happy" Kitchens, the sheriff of Phillips County, was notorious for his brutality involving blacks. A correspondent of Brough by the name of Harry Anderson (who addressed the governor as "Hillman"), wrote him on October 7: "Knowing Frank Kitchens and his crowd as well as I do, I am quite sure your action was the direct cause of saving a great number of lives—both black and white down there. Nothing would have suited Frank better than to have been given free hand to hunt 'Mr. nigger' in his lair."[42] As has been noted, Frank Kitchen's crowd and others sharing his sentiments had ample opportunity to murder blacks on October 1 before the military arrived. Ironically, Kitchens himself apparently never made it out to the hunt. Apparently ill for some time, he appointed Sebastian Straub as acting sheriff during the morning of October 1, though he resumed his duties later that day.

Judge John Miller's interview corroborates the role played by Mississippians but also implicates Arkansans in the massacre of blacks:

Brown: I've talked to blacks that are young now, second generation, but they told me that their parents were hidden by friendly whites to keep them from being found. Whites would hide blacks to keep them from being found by the mob.
Miller: I don't doubt that a bit.
Brown: Looking for blacks to kill them.
Miller: Now that came about when that damn Mississippi contingent came over there. They started the marauding. We wouldn't have any of that until—now I understand they had plenty of help over there in Arkansas. All they needed was some agitator and leader.[43]

Miller thought he had nothing to hide. As we shall see, he had obviously forgotten a letter he wrote to Governor Thomas McRae in 1921, in which he had concealed information about the role of the white mobs and the military.

Finally, evidence of a massacre comes from the lips of the black sharecroppers who were sentenced to death for their part in the fighting. Ida B. Wells-Barnett, an intrepid African American woman who became a fierce antilynching advocate and passionate defender of equal rights for blacks, became interested in the plight of the convicted men. Then living in Chicago and a member of the Equal Rights League, she wrote a letter about the men that was carried by the *Chicago Defender* on December 13, 1919. It was read by one of the men (almost certainly Ed Ware, although Wells-Barnett keeps his identity a secret), who wrote her a letter thanking her for her efforts to free them. It can be assumed that Ware's letter was most likely smuggled out of the prison by Scipio Jones. Though she does not give the date of her visit, Wells-Barnett took the train to Little Rock and met with some of the wives of the men. The men had already been convicted and probably were awaiting the results of an appeal to the Arkansas Supreme Court. Pretending to be a family member, Wells-Barnett was allowed entrance to the prison and took statements from them. The results of her interviews can be found in a pamphlet entitled *The Elaine Riot*.[44] Since Wells-Barnett was convinced that the fighting at the Hoop Spur church was a result of the blacks' determination to form a union, the pamphlet itself makes no pretense of examining the evidence from the planters' side.

Because of the manner in which the trials were conducted in November, information from African Americans about the conduct of whites was not brought out. The "statement" of Ed Ware begins with events of September 26, 1919. According to Ware, on that date, "my merchants, Jackson & Longnecker, came to buy some cotton I had just ginned and offered me 24 cents and then 33 cents for it. I refused to take it, and they said they were going to take the cotton at that price. I rejected their offer and said I'd take my cotton to Helena to sell." After he was threatened by them, Ware says, he went into Helena on September 29 and "gave my business over to an attorney so I would not have to deal with them." He also found out that "Woolen and Davidson were paying 44 1/2 cents for short cotton."[45]

As to the events of the night of September 30, Ed Ware's statement makes no mention of his role during the shoot-out: "Some automobiles were heard to stop north of the church and in just a few minutes they began shooting in the church and did kill some people in the church."[46] His statement becomes quite specific concerning the events of the next morning. Ware states that he and others had just received news:

> They were coming to kill me and all of the other Negroes that belonged to the union and then I began to look for myself. I went out in the field about 200 yards from my house, sitting there talking to two other men about the threats that I had just received. I happened to look up and I saw a Negro by the name of Kid Collins running down the road in front of my house and followed by a crowd of white men. The Negro and all of the white men were armed with guns and they had almost surrounded my house when the old man, Charley Robinson, and Isaac Bird and myself began to run. The old man was crippled and could not run and they shot him down and took him up from there and carried him and put him in my wife's bed and let him stay there four days. They took the coun-

try broadcast and began to shoot down everything they saw like a Negro.[47]

Ed Coleman, who was seventy-nine years old and had been at home the night of September 30, states:

[I] was living two and one-half miles from that trouble. By the Negroes running, I was awakened from my sleep and they told me about the white people shooting into the church on them. Then I was afraid to death near. When the morning had come, I saw about 200 white men in cars shooting down the Negroes. . . . And at 11:30 that day we saw near 300 white armed men coming and we all ran back of the field and when we got back of the field there was a big crowd of white men shooting and killing Jim Miller's family. We turned and went to the railroad. The white men tried to cut us off. When we got to the railroad, some of them were shooting at us. It was only two shots made from we colored men. There was not any life taken whatever. We was still running and made it to the woods, where we were hid all night and all the next day. Then I came home to get my wife. She was about dead herself. When I got there, the white men had went and shot and killed some of the women and children. The next day I found her, then I taken her . . . in the bushes and hid for all night and all the next day and part of the next night.[48]

There is also evidence that the military and civilians pursued a scorched-earth policy during the massacre. In his interview with John Miller, University of Arkansas historian Walter Brown states: "George Tendril [sic], who teaches in North Carolina, said when he was going through some papers he found that the blacks in that county [Phillips] two or three years later, applied to the Slater fund for money to rebuild school buildings because they said all the black schools and churches had been burned in a large area."[49]

The men sentenced to death and their wives told Ida B. Wells-Barnett that whites stole their cotton and personal belongings. "I lost all of my household goods and 121 acres of cotton and corn, two mules, one horse, one Jersey cow, and one farm wagon and all farming tools and harness and eight head of hogs, 135 chickens and one Ford car," reads Ed Ware's statement.[50] In a chapter entitled, "What White Folks Got From Riot," Wells-Barnett writes that Ed Ware's house was ransacked: "They shot into the mirrors of the house and took fiendish delight in destroying things. . . . Longnecker and Jackson gave the Ware's [*sic*] three rooms of furniture to poor whites whom they afterwards moved on the place."[51]

Lula Ware was put in jail for four weeks and then released. She and seventeen others were "told to go back home and go to work as they had always done, and never join nothing more unless they got their lawyer's or landlord's consent." Mrs. Ware went back to get what she had left and found nothing. She saw her safe in a Mrs. Forsyth's house, and a Mr. George had her chairs.[52]

Frank Moore's wife received similar treatment:

> His wife got away and was gone till she saw in the papers four weeks later that all was quiet and people could go back and gather their crops. When she went back to her house, everything was gone. She went to the landlord's wife and told his wife she had come to gather her crops and pay what she owed. She also asked Mrs. Archdale what had become of her furniture and clothes and where her husband was. Mrs. Archdale told her she would get nothing even though Mrs. Moore saw some of her furniture and clothes in Mrs. Archdale's house. She also was told her husband was in jail in Helena and they were going to have him put in the electric chair. Mrs. Moore asked why. "Did he kill anybody?" "No," she said, "but he had just come from the army and he was too bigoted."[53]

Wells-Barnett concludes her chapter with an itemized list of the crops that thirty-four of the convicted men had lost, estimating that the "white lynchers of Phillips County made a cool million last year off the cotton crop of the twelve men who are sentenced to death, the seventy-five who are in the Arkansas penitentiary and the one hundred whom they lynched outright on that awful October 1, 1919!"[54] Even the convicted men had no idea of the scope of the tragedy.

In recent years stories handed down by whites have placed the total number of African American casualties much higher than the Army and the white power structure were willing to admit. Otis Howe III, a white resident of Little Rock whose family still lives in the Elaine area, related in a 1999 interview that he was told by a white man that over a hundred bodies of blacks were loaded on a flat car and taken down by Snow Lake (the southernmost point of Phillips County) and dumped into the wilderness.[55] His father, Otis Howe II, denied at the conference in Helena that locals had acted out of any motive but self-defense but said that if whites had killed blacks indiscriminately, this had been done by the bunch from Mississippi.

Oliver McClintock, an uncle of the author, reported in a 1999 interview that he was passing through Elaine in 1946 on a train and was told by an old white man that during the trouble "niggers were stretched out as far as you can see."[56]

A black man living in the area who refuses to allow his name to be disclosed reports that there is a mass grave in Elaine and that family members (not his) living in the area can pinpoint the spot. He refused to give permission to disclose the name of the family, asking how the author would protect him and this family if the information were made public.

One indication of the number of African Americans killed is burial insurance claims. George Washington Davis, grand secretary of the Pythian Lodge (a black fraternal order and insurance company), wrote the NAACP in November 1920 that the company had paid benefits for 103 individuals. Having lost three sons during the Elaine affair, Davis, who was from Pine City, alleged that he "knew personally" of seventy-three others. He also said that an equal number of whites died but provided no documentation of this.[57]

This last allegation is false. The white Phillips County residents who died were considered heroes, their deaths reported in banner headlines by the *Helena World*. As we shall see, Governor Brough gave an interview on October 3 in which he eulogized by name each white who had been killed. Newspapers in surrounding counties that provided posse members mention no deaths of whites in the fighting. Given the fact that each white from Phillips County who died was given a martyr's funeral, it is unlikely that the number of whites exceeded five. Individuals who wish to believe that blacks engaged in massive resistance during the Elaine affair have a difficult time explaining why the number given by whites of their deaths was so low when each white death was thought to add credibility to the claim that blacks were engaged in an insurrection. The best evidence that blacks did kill more than five whites comes from a video interview with a black man from Phillips County who said that he had seen white bodies stacked in a wagon.[58] Again, however, the extensive coverage by white newspapers of white deaths does not support this claim. Regrettably, black newspapers in the area from this time have not been found.

If perhaps hundreds of innocent blacks were murdered in Phillips County, how could their deaths be concealed for even a month? Why didn't blacks tell Bessie Ferguson about the actions of the United States military? Why didn't Arkansas blacks who knew about the military's actions raise a voice in protest? A combination of factors was involved, and we will suggest answers as the narrative resumes. Some of the answers will seem cowardly, unless one keeps in mind what a dangerous environment Arkansas blacks had to endure and how they coped with it.

Louis Sharpe Dunaway gave one of the leading African Americans in Arkansas an opportunity to give his observations in his book about the events in Elaine. The offer was accepted. Joseph A. Booker was president of Arkansas Baptist College in Little Rock and figures in the narrative. It appears that he had a perfect opportunity to confirm anything Dunaway had said. Instead, he wrote: "I have always felt the negro was greatly in debt to the Southern white people for what he is, and for what his children may yet be." Booker claimed that "no one at the same distance from the scene could have been more agitated over the Elaine riot" than himself. But the questions he wanted to address were "not the comparative number on each side destroyed; the main questions with me and with thousands of other negroes in the state were, 'How can this thing be stopped?' 'What can we do to prevent a repetition of it in other parts of the state?'"[59]

To say publicly that blacks had been slaughtered at Elaine would have caused Booker distress that he had spent a lifetime trying to avoid. Booker was interested in survival. In his view—and in the view of the black middle class and surely, after Elaine, in the view of Arkansas Delta blacks)—survival was best achieved by not saying anything to rile the white man in Arkansas.

In light of the above, the reasons why Louis Sharpe Dunaway and Bessie Ferguson didn't name their sources seem obvious. Both were educated people; both knew that without documentation they cheapened the value of their work to the point where it wouldn't be taken as seriously. However, they and their sources *knew* what would happen if their names were revealed. Neither Ferguson nor Dunaway could guarantee their sources that they would not experience retribution, any more than the author can make such a promise today.

Finally, for further proof that massacres by whites occurred the reader must consider the informal conspiracy of silence that was to develop around the activities of the white mobs and soldiers who came to the Elaine area. Sharpe Dunaway's sarcastic comment that it was strange that his fellow reporters had difficulty coming up with the number of black casualties has particular relevance here. The failure to "notice" the activi-

ties of the mobs and soldiers after they arrived became the hallmark of
the response in the Delta, whether of the governor of Arkansas; of the
commander of the soldiers at Camp Pike; or of newspaper editors in
Arkansas, Tennessee, and Mississippi.

From the standpoint of news reporting the story of armed whites
coming to the area was very big indeed. Every editor in the area knew
immediately the possible results of such a development and could not
ignore its significance. The *Arkansas Gazette* correspondent in Helena on
October 1 informed his editor in Little Rock in a story for the next day
that "additional posses were expected to arrive during the night and the
forces will be swelled to 1,000 men, exclusive of the troops en route from
Camp Pike."[60] The October 2 Memphis *Commercial Appeal* quoted a
train conductor who worked for the Iron Mountain Railway: "Coffin also
reported that motor car loads of men, heavily armed, from the Mississippi
side had been passing through Helena at frequent intervals during the day
en route to Elaine about 20 miles west."[61] Already censoring itself, the
afternoon *Helena World* did not even mention the posses coming in from
outside Phillips County on October 1, despite the fact that the mayor of
Helena had telegraphed the governor that six hundred were expected by
six o'clock that afternoon.

Other papers in the area reported the departure of men from their
communities. The *Daily Graphic,* one of two daily papers in the town of
Pine Bluff, forty miles southeast of Little Rock, reported on the swift
response of the military and added that there was "even prompter action
of hundreds of white men of this community in rallying to the defense
of Elaine citizens Wednesday night."[62] The *Brinkley Argus* mentioned on
October 2 that men from Holly Grove, approximately twenty-five miles
from Elaine, had joined others there.[63]

In any story involving what from the beginning appeared to be a violent racial clash, one would normally expect detailed coverage of the activities of these men. And there was a great deal of newspaper ink devoted
to the fighting involving the posse from Helena, in which two whites were
killed. However, there was virtually a news blackout throughout the Delta
concerning the activities of the hundreds of others who flooded the area.
For example, neither the *Pine Bluff Graphic* nor the *Brinkley Argus* mentioned in their coverage the activities of the men from their locales.

Any mention of these men from outside the area after they had
arrived would follow a pattern. In the first accounts some details would
be given. The *Arkansas Gazette*'s front-page story on October 2 read:

"Posse men reaching Helena from Elaine late tonight said that bodies of at least fifteen negroes were lying in the streets and outskirts of the town and that more probably would be found in the woods."[64] However, the story does not give the circumstances regarding how there came to be at least fifteen blacks lying in the streets of Elaine on October 1.

The afternoon *Memphis News Scimitar* also gave its readers a hint of what had occurred on October 1. In its coverage on October 2, the paper stated: "The number of Negroes dead and wounded from yesterday's fighting has not been ascertained, but according to one member of the posse from Helena, who came in from the scene of the fighting late yesterday, 'there are plenty of them.'"[65] The *Commercial Appeal* account on October 2 mentioned an interview with Clarence Osmont of Memphis, who had been engaged to take his bloodhounds to the Elaine area. Osmont stated that "he had seen two white men killed, two whites wounded, and several Negroes killed. One Negro killed, he said, was struck by 26 bullets."[66]

The *Arkansas Democrat* reported on October 2 that two black men in the community of Mellwood, just two miles south of Elaine, were shot down in the street by residents and officers. The justification given by the paper was that the two men, whose names aren't given, were "heavily armed" and were "making remarks about the whites and race trouble at Elaine."[67] Though the brief page-one account virtually admitted the men had been murdered, there would be no follow-up nor need for further explanation. With the exception of a prominent black dentist from Helena (D. A. E. Johnston) no efforts by the media would be made to give the names of blacks who had been killed by the white mobs or soldiers.

What the posses from outside Phillips County did during that day and evening the newspapers do not tell us either. "The emergency posses assembled there [Elaine] were estimated to have a total strength of about six hundred men. They camped for the night with chain guards posted about the town and the camp," the *Arkansas Gazette* said. "Edward Bevins of Helena, sworn in as a special deputy sheriff, was in command of the camp at Elaine tonight. Sheriff Kitchens was unable to direct the attack against the uprising yesterday [October 1] on account of serious illness."[68]

A close reading of the newspapers in the area shows that all of the reporting focused almost exclusively on the activities of the posse from Helena and the description of the deaths of James Tappan, Clinton Lee, and O. R. Lilly. The papers studiously avoid mentioning what the other six hundred to one thousand men did. Many of the stories were simply rewrites and verbatim accounts from the *Helena World* and the *Arkansas Gazette*. Once the newspapers realized the carnage that had occurred in and around Elaine to the black population, with little loss of life to the white population, they censored their reporting. The newspapers in Tunica and Greenville, Mississippi, relied on Associated Press reports and did not mention their residents going over from the east side of the river; however an editorial in the *Tunica Times* on October 4 counseled in unusually savage terms that there was no need for restraint. Entitled "The Cause and Effect," the article called the situation in east Arkansas "regrettable" and laid the blame on "a paid lot of marauders who are working nightly through the South, sent hither by a league of New York and Chicago, whose supreme efforts are to incite the negro to rebellion." The notion that the trouble was homegrown was patently nonsense: "The Negroes of the South are a far superior lot to these disturbers of the North. They have lived in this land of peace and plenty for lo, these many years, and they know better their condition than all the world. No human mind can destroy their usefulness; and the mongrel who strews his filth and slime among them, for naught save personal gain, is not deserving of a court trial."[69]

Did this last sentence indicate indirect approval of the work of the individuals from Mississippi, who were said to have come over with blood in their eyes? Perhaps. Perhaps it was a reference to Robert Hill. But the inference seems clear: this writer saw lynching as a way to deal with the problem of blacks who would tamper with existing labor conditions. If these "instituters" came to Tunica, "they will have a reception which they can keep in their diary, and carry home to their masters of their origination."[70]

The *Arkansas Gazette* did not follow up on its story of the dead in Elaine, though it had announced that it was sending a reporter to accompany Governor Brough and the troops. After their arrival papers would primarily report only the statistics confirmed by the military and the white power structure in Phillips County.

The sole reference to the posses in the *Helena World* on October 2 was the following: "Parties of armed men who came to Helena from Clarendon, Marianna, Marvell, and other points near Helena on the Arkansas side, and other parties from Lula, Tunica, Friars Point and Clarksdale, Mississippi aided in patrolling the streets of Helena last night, and assisted in preserving order in the troubled zone. Some of these visitors left for their homes this morning."[71] The *Commercial Appeal* in its front-page headlines on October 2 stated: "HUNDREDS OF DEPUTIES ARE SENT TO ELAINE" but neglected to follow up on such a newsworthy event. The litmus test was whether whites had been killed.

Daniel Goleman describes how humanity copes with painful information: "In order to avoid looking, some element of the mind must have known first what the picture contained, so that it knew what to avoid. The mind somehow grasps what is going on and rushes a protective filter into place, thus steering awareness away from what threatens."[72]

To "avoid looking," the papers focused not on the activities of the men who came to Elaine but on the valiant members of the Phillips County posses. "Included in the force at Elaine is a detachment from the American Legion Post at Helena. Members of the post volunteered for service for the slayers of Adkins and the men have been acting as a unit in the posse under the leadership of Herbert Thompson," said the *Gazette* on October 2.[73]

What about the names of any other of the more than five hundred men who had come into the area? Who was commanding them? What had they done all day? Had they fired on anyone? Been fired upon? The papers are silent. We will never know in any detail how the white mobs went about murdering blacks on October 1. It was a subject more taboo than incest. Avoiding unpleasant news about white behavior toward blacks had become a part of the Southern psyche since the days of slavery. Goleman explains this phenomenon: "From the need to soften the impact of threatening information, lacunae arise. They operate on attention, through a variety of tactics, all of which filter the flow of information. These strategies for dealing with the world come to define the shape of responses as well as perception. Their outlines become the frame of character."[74]

Yet one would think that newspapers would be immune from the kind of self-deception that went on in reporting this story, because their stock in trade is bad news. But this was not so in the South—not on the race issue, particularly at that time in history. Newspapers reported the bad things blacks did, not the bad things whites did to blacks. This lack of honesty became part of the character of most Southerners, including owners of newspapers. Goleman says, "Favored tactics of defense become a sort of armor-plating on experience, a gathering around of preferred bulwarks in the battle against unsettling items of information."[75]

In the South in times of racial conflict the "favored tactic of defense" of white Southerners was to claim that it was the blacks who were always the aggressors. In Elaine that tactic was adopted consistently. The *Arkansas Gazette* declared on October 2 that "early reports said that between 1,000 and 1500 negroes had assembled in the vicinity of Elaine and were armed with high-powered rifles."[76]

Elaine, however, was never attacked by blacks, though it would be reported at first that it was: "In a message Chief Deputy J. R. Dalsell [*sic*] in charge of the posse at Elaine telephoned that his force was greatly outnumbered and that fire had become general." The *Gazette* added, "Later, it was reported that the negroes had been driven from Elaine, but that fighting was still in progress a mile to the north, where the band was supposed to have received reinforcements. Fighting in this vicinity continued late in the afternoon."[77]

In fact, none of the United States military reports mentions that Elaine was ever attacked by blacks. Additionally, Ocier Bratton, who was kept a prisoner in Elaine during much of the day on October 1 before he was transported to Helena in the afternoon, detailed his experience in a letter to his father on November 5, 1919. He mentions no attack on Elaine, though there were fears of one. "I was then conducted to a brick store in Elaine," wrote Ocier Bratton, "which I soon learned had been chosen as the safest place for the citizens to make their defense from. The store was soon full of people, including women and children. I with two Negroes from Ratio were chained together in the back of the store. Shortly the report came that the Negroes were coming in on us and I was given a sack of flour and told by a deputy sheriff (and he was a real friend and worried to death for my life) to sit on it if the Negroes began shooting, as they might shoot me through a window."[78] However, there was no attack, and Bratton was later transported to Helena.

The *Arkansas Democrat*, the Little Rock–based rival to the *Arkansas Gazette*, at one point had two correspondents in Phillips County—one with Brough and one in Helena. The *Democrat* assured its readers that "absolutely no violence has been done to the law-abiding negroes" but reported nothing about the activities of the white mobs.[79]

As we resume the narrative in the next chapter we shall see that the newspapers were not the only representatives of the white power structure to avoid mentioning the activities of the posses. The commanding officer of the troops that went into Elaine and the governor of Arkansas would do the same, as well as the white power structure of Phillips County. It is difficult to overstate the significance of the presence of the white mobs that came into the area. Whatever reports Brough was receiving from Helena, he would have known from his knowledge of history and his own personal experience how totally unlikely it was that blacks were engaged in an armed insurrection. By the time he received the third telegram informing him of the presence of a mob of up to one thousand whites, he would have known that the far greater danger involved a massacre of blacks. The next chapter's focus will be Governor Brough and Colonel Jenks, the commanding officer of the Camp Pike troops. Did either man make any effort to minimize the use of force against African Americans? Did Brough and Jenks, working with the white power structure in Phillips County, cover up a massacre by the white mobs? Did Brough cover up knowledge of a massacre by the United States military? Did Jenks cover up a massacre by his own troops? Surprisingly, these questions have never been addressed by historians.

CHAPTER 4

A Committee of Seven

I have just had a very thrilling experience in Phillips County, in connection with the race riot there.
—Letter from Charles Hillman Brough, October 3, 1919

October 2, 1919
Phillips County

To the great relief of the white populace, the troop train rolled into the Elaine depot shortly after 8:00 A.M. on the morning of October 2: "Upon detraining we were met by a committee of civilians who explained that the negroes of the surrounding country had assembled and were killing the whites whenever they ventured out to their farms. The white population had armed themselves as best they could and were assembled at Elaine, the Negroes holding the woods around the twon [*sic*] and prevented them from getting out."[1] This almost completely inaccurate statement (neither the *Helena World* nor the *Arkansas Gazette* ever reported an actual attack by blacks against white planters or their families on September 30 or October 1, before the military arrived) is from a military intelligence report by Capt. Edward Passailaigue, dated October 7, 1919. The captain does not go on to acknowledge that in fact the information contained in his report was later shown to be false.

If troops under Colonel Jenks's command participated in the slaughter of innocent blacks, the official military reports of the time Jenks spent in Phillips County take on particular significance. Were the reports accurate? Or were they designed to cover up a slaughter by Camp Pike soldiers? The most obvious way to cover up a slaughter would be to understate the number of victims. However, knowing that figures might be challenged, one might prepare the report in such a way as to make it seem that whatever force was used was appropriate to the situation at hand. Doing so might mean inventing emergencies that didn't exist and including documents from others congratulating you on a job well done.

We shall see that Jenks attached to the reports newspaper accounts from the *Arkansas Gazette,* which hailed the troops as heroes.

From the moment of their arrival the primary mission of the troops was crystal clear: to engage blacks, compel their surrender, and bring them into custody. Thus what had begun originally as a racial incident resulting in the death of a white deputy sheriff would become an assault against anyone with a black skin. The morning *Arkansas Gazette* reported on October 3: "Major Callen, second in command of the soldiers at Elaine, said he expected to give all negroes an opportunity to surrender and receive protection from the troops. Those who fail to give themselves up and show an inclination to fight it out, will be shot on sight, it was said."[2]

Before the morning of October 2 was over, the Army had sustained its one death. Those blacks who remained in hiding out of fear for their lives became marked for extinction. One of the difficulties in challenging the military's version of the events in Elaine is documenting when the slaughter by the troops commenced and when it ended. Neither Dunaway's chapter nor the brief account of James Street is any help in answering the question of when the slaughter of blacks by the military began and ended. Did it occur before the white posses began to leave the Elaine area on October 3? It seems logical that excessive force would have occurred when some blacks were still resisting.

In determining whether the reports and the documents attached to them that Jenks and his officers sent were intended to hide the troops' activities, it must be kept in mind that Jenks would have known that there were hundreds of armed whites who had come into the area from outside the immediate vicinity. Further, he, like Brough, would have known in advance that these men were intent on hunting blacks and may have already killed hundreds on October 1. Though he may have received initial reports that white farmers and their families were being killed, he would have quickly learned that these stories were false. He would have learned that neither Elaine nor any other town in the vicinity had been attacked by blacks. In short he would not have had any verifiable information that blacks were engaged in an insurrection.

In his report to his commanding officer at Camp Pike, Colonel Jenks wrote that he immediately began to secure the area by ordering the placement of a machine gun on the top of the Elaine Mercantile Building. He then directed that a company from the Third Division, armed with two machine guns, proceed to Helena to guard the jail and prevent lynchings. He told his officers that he wanted four companies front and center for the march to Hoop Spur three miles north, where there were reports of fighting, and directed a Major Baxter to remain in Elaine with the detachment from the Fifth Army and to begin the process of disarming the civilian population, both black and white.[3]

No reports from Jenks or his intelligence officers were made as to how the disarming of civilians in Elaine was carried out. It seems unlikely that posses from outside Elaine would have turned in their weapons, since they would have argued that they needed them for self-protection on their way out of the area. It would seem probable that at this point, as reported by the *Helena World,* some or most of these individuals would have begun to leave the area.

Neither Jenks nor his intelligence officers commented in their reports on the information that hundreds of whites had come in from outside the area. Jenks merely stated: "Upon arrival, we found the town in great state of excitement. Hundreds of white men all carrying fire-arms, were on the streets, near the station and in groups, all over town."[4] This failure to acknowledge either the entry of white mobs into the area or what they were doing speaks for itself. The only plausible explanation for the omission is that the military was seeking to cover up its own activities.

Not satisfied merely to ride with the troops to Elaine, Governor Brough set out on the three-mile march to Hoop Spur. One must wonder if Jenks had conferred in advance with Major General Sturgis, the commanding officer of Camp Pike, about the governor's participation. Jenks did not mention in his report that Brough was present, though an intelligence officer did and, of course, so did the newspapers. Brough was acting out his own childhood fantasy. There was no military need for his presence. It was as if Woodrow Wilson had accompanied the troops into action in World War I. Brough carried no weapon and went off to the battle in his suit accompanied by a military chaplain from Boston. "I have just had a very thrilling experience in Phillips County, in connection with the race riot there," he wrote a friend in Mississippi a day later, on October 3, after he returned to Little Rock.[5]

One of their first encounters was with an old black woman, her body shattered by a shotgun blast. Though Jenks ordered a medic to treat her, her condition was terminal.[6] Who had killed her and why he didn't speculate. As they neared the settlement of Hoop Spur, Jenks reported, they encountered canebrakes that stretched two hundred yards deep and extended for two miles. Suddenly, four black men bolted across the road in front of them, like quail flushed from a thicket. One of them reportedly turned and fired. No one was hit. It would be variously reported in the newspapers that Brough had been fired upon, three bullets whizzing over his head.[7]

Along the way the troops ran up on a cabin two miles from Elaine where about sixty "helpless" white children, women, and old men were being guarded by ten white males. Captain Passailaigue opined that "had troops not arrived, the fate of that party would have been much more disastrous."[8] Without a doubt the individuals were extremely frightened, but they were not in the danger described by Passailaigue, since there were never any reports of whites being attacked on their property.

Though in his report Jenks states that there was fighting three miles outside of town, his account is curiously devoid of details concerning the actual battle waged by his troops. He reports that Cpl. Luther C. Earles was killed and that another man, Sgt. Pearl Gay—who later returned to duty—was slightly wounded but makes no mention of fire returned by his troops: "We searched thoroughly and carefully the whole terrain in this vicinity and cleared it completely."[9]

Captain Passailaigue gives more details of the encounter but again fails to mention that the troops even fired their weapons, much less the number of casualties inflicted by them:

> With the assistance of civilian guides a thorough reconissance [sic] of the country was made. Before reaching the woods where the negroes were last reported, Major Callen, deployed the Battalion as skirmished and started forward. One company was held in reserve and followed two hundred yards in rear of front line in squad columns. Colonel Jenks took his position just in rear of the center of the formation.
> . . . In this manner the woods and fields were thoroughly combed.
> . . . About fifty armed negroes were captured and placed in the School House at Elaine under guard.[10]

The report made by Colonel Jenks and his aides is in sharp contrast to one initial account of events on October 2. The *Memphis Press* reported that a major battle by the soldiers was underway: "Many negroes are reported killed by the soldiers. Two soldiers are seriously wounded. The negroes are surrounded in the woods near Elaine by nearly 500 soldiers and have refused to surrender. A battle to the finish is expected. The negroes are well drilled and armed. The soldiers have trained machine guns on them. Constant fighting is now in progress."[11]

None of the other papers noted a major battle shaping up in their reporting on October 2. For example, the *Memphis Press*'s rival, the *Commercial Appeal,* which had its own correspondent in Phillips County, though mentioning that Brough had been fired upon, summarized the day's events as follows: "Within a few hours after the troops arrived, the promiscuous shooting ceased and but a few negroes resisted arrest."[12]

One has to wonder how many blacks were killed on October 2 by the military and why Jenks failed to report that even one shot was fired by his troops. Armed with seven machine guns, the troops had plenty of firepower. One can only surmise that reporting the actual number of blacks killed and wounded would have raised a red flag in light of the Army's casualties.

Jenks's report continues in this vein. He mentions sending "a detachment of one half of one company of the 57th Infantry (25 men) [*sic*] to Millwood [*sic*], where I had seen ten or more citizens (white) arrive with rifles and shot guns. . . ." Yet he gives no report of what occurred when they arrived. He states: "Outposts of from twelve to twenty-five men were sent to two plantations. . . . Outposts were also posted to protect the town of Elaine and a permanent guard placed at Hop [*sic*] Spur."[13] Again, he does not describe what, if anything, happened at these places.

Instead, he gives a summary: "Several hundred Negroes were taken into custody, examined and if found to be reliable turned loose. . . ." Jenks fully accepted the planters' contention that blacks had planned an insurrection: "Members of the union here plotted to kill twenty-one of the leading landowners—send mounted messingers [*sic*] called 'Paul Reveres' over the country to notify all members that this had been done after which all male whites were to be killed. The date fixed for this was October 6th."[14]

In Jenks's entire report he only mentions that *two* blacks were killed by soldiers. After stating that four blacks (the Johnston brothers) were killed by civilians, he reports: "The same night two more were killed, one wounded and one captured by our outpost guarding women and children. This was due to their continuing to advance on the building sheltering the refugees, after being ordered to halt."[15] He concludes by attaching newspaper clippings and by stating: "The behavior of the troops was excellent throughout."[16] He especially commends Major Callen as well as other officers.

In contrast to his commanding officer, Captain Passailaigue is a bit more forthcoming about the number of blacks who were killed by the troops: "To the best of my knowledge about 20 negroes were killed by soldiers for refusing to halt when so ordered or for resisting arrest. In all cases, all of these negroes were armed."[17] Another intelligence officer, Maj. Eugene Barton, states that in all fourteen blacks were killed, "with about twenty two wounded."[18]

Each of the reports is vague about what occurred. Given other accounts, it is impossible to believe that the troops did not fire a shot in their first and only reported battle with blacks. The failure of Jenks or his officers to give a plausible account of the events of October 2 taints the entire military perspective. On balance, the evidence suggests that the military used excessive force and may have killed perhaps hundreds of blacks, as alleged by Louis Sharpe Dunaway.

Indeed, one has to reassess how much resistance blacks actually put up between October 1 and October 3. Other than the shoot-out at Hoop Spur, in which one white was killed, fighting by blacks appears to have been rather minimal when the actual evidence is examined. On the morning of October 2, there was fighting at Hoop Spur in which two members of the Phillips County posses were killed, but as the trial transcripts in chapter 7 will show, there may have been only a few shots at most fired by blacks.

As stated earlier, though there were rumors of imminent attack, the newspapers did not report a single shot fired by blacks on farmers or their families before the troops came. There was a report in the papers that a train going into Helena that contained women and children had come under fire: "One train bearing refugees concealed in a steel gondola was fired upon by Negroes who had climbed trees beside the railroad tracks where it runs through dense canebrakes. None of the refugees was hurt."[19] However, even this report is made suspect by Ocier Bratton, who on October 2 was brought into Helena by train. He wrote his father, "The run to Helena was uneventful. In passing Hoopspur [sic] the men stayed from in front of the windows, however."[20]

On paper the military had acted impeccably. Jenks's military objectives upon his return to Elaine included preventing lynchings and protecting "the colored people from any kind of violence and enabl[ing] them to return to work under the protection of U.S. troops."[21] Further objectives included taking blacks into custody and interrogating them about their activities. In the next few days hundreds would be detained in temporary stockades until the owners of plantations where they worked had vouched for them.

The military position would coincide with the governor's view of his accomplishments. Together they had prevented a wholesale slaughter of whites in the area. "Upon examination, negroes confessed that they had planned to kill all the whites they saw in the outlying districts and then march on and 'Clean Up' the town of Elaine," wrote Passailague.[22]

This summary of what blacks were alleged to have confessed to is not credible. Again, not a single white "in the outlying district" was reported to have been fired upon. Also, as stated earlier, given their vast numerical superiority, had any blacks wished to kill whites, they would have done so in the hours before the posses began arriving from Phillips County and elsewhere. Passailague's summary is also unsupported by the names of those individuals who supposedly confessed. Given the techniques of torture (e.g., pouring gasoline on blacks) that the Army employed, any "confessions" would have produced the desired information.

In evaluating Governor Brough's performance in the first twenty-four hours, we are properly warned against reading history backwards. For a Southerner, Brough had "advanced" views about blacks. Certainly, he was one of the best educated and brightest in the nation at a time when almost every white person was utterly convinced of the inferiority of blacks. Given the time and circumstances, can Brough be legitimately criticized for his actions? In retrospect, it appears that he was justified in requesting troops, especially in light of the news of mobs coming into the area. However, there is no evidence that Governor Brough ever cautioned Jenks or any military officer that they might not be encountering an insurrection and must not use excessive force. Should he have been expected to forcefully convey this opinion to Jenks? Leaving aside his education and background, he would have known just from reading the newspapers that any time there was violence between whites and blacks, blacks suffered far greater consequences. Had Brough not been so determined to play at being soldier, might he not have been more concerned about the peril blacks were in from the beginning, both from the military and from the white mobs?

If Brough gets credit for asking for troops, he has to take some responsibility for their actions. But Brough was a patriot, and patriots don't enhance their reputations by casting a critical eye on the military. A governor who was a bit less starry-eyed about the military would have perceived that the battle-tested troops with their twelve machine guns were possibly a bigger threat to the black population of Phillips County than the white mobs. The most benign view of Brough's actions is that he was so caught up in the drama of participating in his first military campaign that he failed to insist upon any accountability. The longer he was at Elaine, the more suspicious he would have become. In marching with the troops he would have seen the body of one black woman who lay dying. He would have asked questions about the activities of the five hundred to a thousand civilians who had flooded into Elaine to go on a "nigger hunt." Brough may have been an idealist, but he wasn't naive about the capacity of Southerners to rouse themselves into a white heat of fury at the thought of blacks arming themselves and having the temerity to fight. He would have been told about the group from Mississippi even if Arkansans were minimizing their own actions.

What did Brough know, and when did he know it? It was much too soon on the afternoon of October 2 for him to have known in full and for certain what had and hadn't occurred in Elaine. He may well have thought an insurrection was being attempted, but with only one soldier dead after several hours in the field and with not a single injury to planters or their families, he could not have believed it was amounting to much. True, he would have seen the fear and panic in the faces of the women and children crowding into Elaine and heard them voice their belief in an impending attack on Elaine, which never came. He said he went to Elaine to get a true picture of the events, but there is no indication that he ever tried to get the black version of what was occurring. By accompanying the troops to Elaine and going into the field with them, he forfeited any sense of objectivity that would have allowed him to assess the situation and try to insure that the military and the white mobs who remained acted with as much restraint as possible.

Too, a darker scenario exists: Brough understood as early as October 2 that some kind of massacre of innocent people had occurred the day before and was aware of the military's massacre (assuming it occurred October 2) but chose to act as if neither had happened. After all, blacks had fired over his head. Blacks had to be taught a lesson, just as blacks had been taught a lesson in his hometown of Clinton. That lesson was one of white supremacy. There is nothing in Brough's behavior or comments to suggest that he felt blacks didn't need to relearn the same lesson in Arkansas. Did he at some point tell Jenks to do what he had to do and then go into Helena so that he wouldn't be around to witness it? We don't know. Unlike the Watergate cover-up, there are no tapes to tell us what Brough knew and when he knew it. To believe that he was *never* aware that indiscriminate killings took place suggests that he was a man of childlike naivete about race relations—which, as has been suggested, Brough

Gov. Charles Hillman Brough, a native of Mississippi, was serving his second term as governor of Arkansas when the fighting began in Phillips County. *Courtesy of Butler Center for Arkansas Studies, Central Arkansas Library System.*

The Elaine 12, photographed at "the Walls," the Arkansas State Penitentiary outside the city limits of Little Rock, which housed prisoners on death row. *Courtesy of Butler Center for Arkansas Studies, Central Arkansas Library System.*

Soldiers from Camp Pike escorting prisoners at Elaine. *Courtesy of Butler Center for Arkansas Studies, Central Arkansas Library System.*

Governor Brough speaking to crowd in Elaine on October 2, 1919. *Courtesy of Butler Center for Arkansas Studies, Central Arkansas Library System.*

Governor Brough with Col. Issac C. Jenks, commander of the Camp Pike troops, on October 2, 1919, in the Elaine area. *Courtesy of Butler Center for Arkansas Studies, Central Arkansas Library System.*

D. A. E. Johnston, a dentist and one of Helena's black elite, was killed with his three brothers by whites on October 1, 1919. *Courtesy of Butler Center for Arkansas Studies, Central Arkansas Library System.*

was not. His "advanced views" on race stopped at the moment that blacks in any number took up arms.

The most likely scenario is as was reported by the *Memphis Press* on October 2—that the machine guns were active in that first encounter and that Brough was present. In his mind it would have been the Clinton "riot" all over again. Excessive force was necessary to imprint upon the psyche of blacks that they would not be permitted to even think that they could resist whites. The federal government had not intervened after blacks were slaughtered in Clinton and in fact would be a willing instrument in the slaughter of blacks in Arkansas. In Brough's view, the fury of the white response to black resistance, whatever its size, was inevitable and correct. Whatever it took to maintain white supremacy was non-negotiable. As we shall see, when the NAACP and the black press dared to point out that blacks had been slaughtered in Arkansas, Brough would take extraordinary (though unsuccessful) measures to keep this news from reaching the ears of Arkansans.

Only eight years after, still in the heart of the Jim Crow era, an Arkansan governor would use National Guard troops to quell white mob violence against blacks during the last lynching that occurred in Little Rock.[23] Though the circumstances were different (blacks did not offer any resistance), the decision of Governor John Martineau (who figures prominently in this narrative) shows that it was possible for a Southern governor to use force on behalf of blacks to protect them and not against them.

October 2, 1919, Evening
Helena

As Mort Allen and six others (E. C. Horner, a planter, lawyer, and businessman who was developing the town of West Helena; T. W. Keesee, Allen's brother-in-law—they had married sisters—and also a planter; Sebastian Straub, the furnish merchant who had supposedly hired the detectives to infiltrate the union; H. D. Moore, the county judge, who under Arkansas law was the chief administrative officer of Phillips County; J. C. Knight, the mayor of Helena; and Frank Kitchens, the county sheriff) prepared to meet Governor Brough in Helena on the afternoon of October 2 at the Phillips County courthouse on Cherry Street, they knew they had to regain control of the situation in the county immediately.[24]

By that evening they would have begun to hear that white mobs had killed innocent blacks and engaged in atrocities on October 1. The stories coming out of Elaine spread quickly. In the October 3 *Helena World,* there was a hint of what had actually occurred buried in a self-congratulatory editorial. The paper boasted: "The whole world expected us to lose our heads and go wild. Even the troops which came to assist in quelling the disturbances expected to find the mob spirit prevailing." Despite the lack of "mob violence," however, the writer conceded that there were "disturbing rumors which persist into getting into circulation."[25] The "disturbing rumors" were, of course, of the very acts of white mob violence that the paper was claiming had not occurred.

Rumors. Just rumors. It is in this editorial that one can almost see the writer's psychological effort to avoid the conclusion that the second-worst nightmare of whites in the Delta had taken place. The worst nightmare naturally was that blacks would exact retribution for the decades of slavery, rape, exploitation, and contempt they had experienced at the hands of whites. The second-worst nightmare was what was happening in Phillips County—that whites would engage in an orgy of violence against blacks that would far exceed anything before or after it. The editorial in its acknowledgment of the "disturbing rumors"—and in its immediate dismissal of them—characterizes the process by which whites throughout Arkansas and indeed the nation could make themselves actually believe that no massacre had occurred.

There were several reasons to "not notice" that a massacre of blacks had occurred. First, to acknowledge a massacre would be to confront the fear that blacks might at some future time retaliate against whites. Though no actual attacks in the outlying areas had occurred, the reaction of whites was one of hysteria. If news got out that blacks had been slaughtered, whites would never be able to close their eyes at night again. Second, advertising the news of a slaughter might result in blacks leaving the Elaine area right at harvest time. Therefore, there couldn't have been a massacre. A few blacks had been in revolt, and whites had simply defended themselves, killing as few blacks as possible. It made no difference that blacks would know there had been a massacre.

If the idea that whites convinced themselves there had been no massacre seems farfetched, it should be pointed out that at no time in the state's previous history had its white citizens behaved any differently. The reaction of white Arkansans to almost every act of violence—whether the rape of black women during slavery or the murder of black men during the nineteenth and twentieth centuries—was the same: it either hadn't occurred (despite a significant mulatto population) or it was justified. Daniel Goleman writes:

Our favored defenses become habitual mental maneuvers. What has worked well in key moments, keeping anxiety under control with rewarding results, is likely to be tried again.

Successful defense becomes habit, habit molds style. These familiar tactics become second nature; when psychic pain confronts us, we fall back into their soothing arms. What may have been at first a serendipitous discovery in the battle against anxiety comes to define our mode of perception and response to the world.[26]

The racial perception and response of white Southerners was as entrenched by 1919 as the act of breathing. Thus, white males didn't rape black women; black males raped white women. Whites didn't murder blacks; they defended themselves against blacks. Whites didn't cheat blacks; blacks were natural thieves. And so on. Ever since the end of Reconstruction, very little had stood in the way of Arkansas whites' desire to construct a reality that suited their need to reduce their own anxieties about what the past and present were really like.

The failure to acknowledge that whites had engaged in a slaughter of blacks on October 1 had profound consequences. Because of the failure to acknowledge what had occurred, the door was opened for similar behavior by the United States military. Had Governor Brough or any member of the white power structure in Phillips County been willing to confront the "disturbing rumors," the dynamics of the military presence would have been significantly different. Blacks would have been seen as the victims they were instead of as the aggressors. However, instead of trying to make his own independent evaluation in Elaine (and for this failure he bears a heavy responsibility), Colonel Jenks took his cues from white civilians. Had anyone in the civilian white power structure been willing to point out that a massacre had already occurred, further slaughter would have been avoided. Jenks would have realized that his troops' own behavior would be judged similarly and would have taken steps to avoid the "shoot on sight" orders given by Major Callen.

After the arrival of the military, the needs of the white power structure in Phillips County would have been apparent. In Mort Allen's view, what surely was at stake in his meeting with Brough was control. Here was the governor, a notorious Negro sympathizer, and they were going to have to deal with him. Given that Brough was not in their hip pocket, Allen and his group could have easily feared the worst. What if the governor insisted on taking charge of the investigation into what had occurred? What if he demanded that Negroes, maybe even Negroes from outside the county, be part of any investigative effort? The governor would no doubt have questions about what the activities of the mobs had been. He was known to be an outspoken critic of lynchings. Well, the way to handle that problem was to point out that no lynchings had occurred. And that was true: no blacks had been dragged from jails and put to death. The posses and the military had put down an insurrection. Would Brough buy this? They couldn't have been certain exactly how he would react. He was an egghead professor; they were planters and businessmen. But how could he not agree that there had been an insurrection? All he had to do was look at the faces of the women and children crowding into Elaine. They were scared to death. And blacks had shot at him as recently as that morning. But the problem was that other than the rumors and the fear, there was little evidence that blacks had attempted an insurrection. Allen and his group would tell Brough that they would get to the bottom of the matter, but the most important thing was to regain control without any interference from Brough or anyone.

By the afternoon of October 2, Allen and his group had obtained information that blacks had actually formed a union that had engaged the services of the Bratton law firm. From that point on, it would have been absolutely clear to Allen that a massive effort would have to be undertaken by himself and the others to identify the ringleaders of the union, to interrogate them, and to convict them as soon as possible, before the situation got any worse. The responsibility for the "racial disturbances" was squarely on the back of the union. Any acts of violence against blacks could be explained.[27] Though it would quickly become clear that no insurrection was taking place (since no white planters or their families had been attacked), it would be a small step for Allen and his group to claim that an insurrection had been planned but disrupted prematurely. Thus whites had acted to prevent their own slaughter. Blacks had been planning an insurrection. But first Allen and his group had to find out if Brough needed convincing.

Meanwhile, before his meeting, Brough was milking his military experience for all it was worth. The *Arkansas Gazette* reported, "Governor Brough marched at the head of the troops from the passenger train to the business district of Helena tonight."[28] Thrilling indeed. How many professors could say they had ever done the same? Brough's fantasy was complete.

There is no record of the conversation that took place between the seven men and Governor Brough. Probably they would have begun by sorting through the information that each person had. Since late Tuesday night (September 30), when Will Adkins was killed at Hoop Spur, there had been one confused tragedy after another. The headlines in the afternoon *Helena World* had reported on October 1 that "Bootleggers Ambush Three Peace Officers" and that Clinton Lee had been killed when his gun had accidentally gone off. These stories were wrong. There had been no bootleggers, and Clinton Lee had been killed by a black. The seven men would have told Brough that they were already far down the path of finding out what had happened. They had begun interrogating blacks since Tuesday morning. Instead of bootleggers killing Adkins and wounding Pratt, the fault lay with a labor union of black sharecroppers who had been planning an insurrection. If Adkins hadn't stopped to change a flat tire (he and Pratt had been accompanied by a black trusty named Kid Collins and had been on the way to Elaine to arrest a bootlegger named Clem) and prematurely touched off the shooting at Hoop Spur, there was no telling how many whites might have been killed. Black guards outside the Hoop Spur church had begun to shoot first, killing Adkins outright and wounding Charlie Pratt, a deputy sheriff. After Collins had managed to get word to Helena after the shooting, a group had gone out to Elaine but had been fired upon in the early morning hours. Frank Kitchens had been too sick that day to take charge and had appointed Sebastian Straub as acting sheriff. When it was light, Straub had sent a posse from the Richard L. Kitchens American Legion Post out to Hoop Spur to engage the blacks, who numbered up to fifteen hundred. It was in the area around Hoop Spur that two of the Legion boys had been killed. Clinton Lee had been picked off while sitting in an automobile; James Tappan's jaw had been shot off by blacks firing from a canebrake, and he had died later in the hospital at Helena. Then O. R. Lilly, a city alderman and real estate man, had been killed by a Helena black named D. A. E. Johnston (or Johnson in some accounts), who appeared to have been one of the ringleaders of the union. Johnston, along with his three brothers, had been shot instantly. Johnston's business on Walnut Street had been searched. Twelve high-powered rifles had been found, along with union literature. Blacks were already confessing that those who were part of the union had planned an insurrection that was to begin on October 6. Blacks were planning to kill planters on that day and seize their land.[29]

Brough would have wanted to know about Ocier Bratton. In Elaine, he would have been told that Bratton had been taken to Helena the afternoon before. Brough was worried that Bratton would be lynched but was assured that now that troops were guarding the jail, that wouldn't happen. The town of Helena itself had remained quiet. Allen and the others had gone to E. C. Morris and other preachers, both black and white, who had done their jobs well. The *Helena World* had nothing but praise, declaring hopefully on October 2: "Dr. Morris holds the confidence of the white citizens of Helena and wields a powerful influence among members of his own race."[30] Helena had been shut down completely, and with the troops patrolling the town, it would be safe.

Allen would finally have gotten to the point with Brough. He wanted the governor to publicly recognize his group, the "Committee of Seven," as the de facto law enforcement agency in Phillips County. They would be responsible for conducting the investigation. They would determine the causes of the riot. They would report what had happened.

Allen may have held his breath, but he needn't have bothered. Apparently, Brough rolled over without a fight. Brough had no authority to anoint a private group whose desire it was to take over local law enforcement functions, but it couldn't have hurt anything for him to make a statement that a committee of the town's leading citizens had stepped in to insure public order. The next day the *Helena World* blared the news: the Committee of Seven was in control and was acting "in full cooperation with the governor."[31]

Given the times and circumstances, should Brough have been expected to have acted impartially and to have demanded an independent investigation or at least to have refrained from endorsing the committee? Not in the South of 1919, where white control was a given. As we shall see, just two months later, he would appoint blacks to a statewide biracial committee in Little Rock that had no formal authority to investigate Elaine, though in private Elaine would be discussed, apparently at length. But Helena was not Pulaski County.

So what did Brough get in Helena? A pledge that there would be no lynchings in Phillips County. The Committee of Seven would have been delighted. Absolutely, Governor. No lynchings. We've never had one in Phillips County, and we won't have one now. The implicit agreement to ignore the fact that in Phillips County for the last day and a half there had been one lynching after another symbolized the mindset of almost the entire white population in the state. There had been no lynchings. It had been an insurrection. Well, not an insurrection that was actually carried out, but one that was prematurely set off and promptly squelched.

What Brough did not do at Helena in his meeting with the

Committee of Seven was as important as what he did do. He did not make an issue of the activities of the hundreds of men who had poured into Elaine, of the behavior of residents of Phillips County, or of the conduct of the military. The next day he would praise Phillips County residents, though he would also be conspicuously silent about the posses who had come into Elaine.

There is some evidence to suggest that the slaughter by the troops may have started in earnest on October 3. The *Arkansas Gazette* reported the following: "Helena, Ark. Oct. 3. A message sent by the railroad station agent at Elaine late today said that a report received there indicated that several negroes had been surrounded near the village of Modoc, east of Elaine, and a detachment of soldiers had started for the scene to arrest them. He reported considerable shooting in the canebrakes about Elaine, where soldiers were engaged in a search for hiding places of the negroes."[32] As usual there was no follow-up by the paper the next day.

On October 6, the *Arkansas Gazette* reporter on the scene, William Wilson, told the paper's readers that the troops had been "anxious to get into battle with the blacks—not because they wanted to kill them but because they realized the negroes . . . should be stopped before women and children and more white men should be murdered."[33]

By sending this article and others on to his commanding officer, General Sturgis, Colonel Jenks was protecting himself from future criticism. Jenks knew that the reality was that blacks had put up little resistance and had not killed a single woman or child or white male who was not involved in efforts to bring them in. Assuming that the military participated in a massacre of its own, Jenks and others in charge would have had ample reason not to criticize the five hundred or more men who had come into Phillips County for *their* behavior. Had Jenks done so, he would have faced the charge that his troops had engaged in indiscriminate killing as well. Thus, the more discreet course of action was to insist that blacks had been killed only in the line of duty and to ignore the actions of the posses.

An in-depth investigation at the time could have come close to the full story. D. Y. Thomas, a history professor at the University of Arkansas, corresponded with a number of individuals (e.g., Mort Allen and Ulysses Bratton) in 1920 and ultimately concluded ten years later in his book, *Arkansas and Its People,* that the insurrection theory "was later shown to be incorrect."[34] He failed, however, to research and analyze the dimensions of the events. History, often impeded in any case, was a perpetual victim of the racism of the era. Out of fear, out of shame, many of those who knew what had happened wouldn't and couldn't tell the truth. And as we shall see, some of those in the white community of Phillips County with whom Thomas corresponded simply lied about what had happened.

CHAPTER 5

More Than One Version

Let them [blacks] beware of the voice of strange teachers and new prophets. . . .
—From an editorial in the Memphis Commercial Appeal,
October 24, 1919

October 3, 1919
Phillips County

The front page of the October 3 issue of the *Helena World* advised its readers in inch-high headlines: "ELAINE INSURRECTION IS OVER: COM-MITTEE OF 7 IN CHARGE." The first decision made by the now "official" Committee of Seven was to not release the names of its members to the public for the time being, perhaps out of fear of retribution by blacks. A statement released in the names of Sheriff Kitchens; Mayor Knight; Mort Allen, president of the Business Men's League; and Joseph Solomon, president of the Board of Trade read:

> Quiet having been restored at Hoop Spur, it is expected that nor-mal conditions will be resumed today. Most of the Negroes in the Elaine territory have already returned to work. Naturally many rumors and reports of the fighting have been terribly exaggerated.
>
> The negroes at Hoop Spur have been under the influence of a few rascally white men and designing leaders of their own race who have been exploiting them for personal gain. The people of Phillips County have never stood for mob violence and will permit none to occur under any circumstances. There has been no trouble whatever in Helena.[1]

The only accurate item in this news release was that there had been no trouble in Helena. Mob violence had already occurred in Phillips County. Most probably the death toll of blacks was in the hundreds. The black population of the county was now living in terror. Certainly, they were not going back to work. Hundreds of blacks were being detained in both Elaine and in the Phillips County jail in Helena.

The Committee of Seven was faced with four tasks: first, it had to break the union once and for all; second, it had to get blacks back in the fields to complete the harvest; third, the committee had to prevent more rampages by whites, which would only worsen the problem of getting blacks back to work as well as fuel blacks' desire for revenge (or so whites would fear); fourth, it had to put in place the fiction that there had been an aborted insurrection that had been put down with a minimum amount of loss to the black community. Three of these goals would be accomplished, but getting blacks to go back into the cotton fields as if no massacre had occurred would be the hardest goal to achieve. The committee tried. It distributed a circular that read:

> TO THE NEGROES OF PHILLIPS COUNTY
> Helena, Ark., Oct. 7, 1919
> The trouble at Hoop Spur and Elaine has been settled. Soldiers now here to preserve order will return to Little Rock within a short time. No innocent Negro has been arrested, and those of you who are at home and at work have no occasion to worry. All you have to do is remain at work just as if nothing had happened. Phillips County has always been a peaceful, law-abiding community, and normal conditions must be restored right away. Stop talking! Stay at home— Go to work—don't worry![2]

The tone of the circular belies the panic of the white power structure. Publicly, all was normal. Years later, Allen would admit, "The forward progress of the town [Elaine] was retarded for several years. My own financial losses were dastardly, but I managed to avoid bankruptcy."[3]

Allen was not alone. A Mississippi newspaper, the *Greenwood Commonwealth,* told the truth about the disaster that was occurring:

> With a splendid cotton crop in the field and no prospect of getting it gathered, that is the problem confronting the planters of near Helena, Arkansas. . . . Mr. Carruth [a resident of Elaine speaking two weeks after the massacre] told Mr. Bonner that outsiders had no idea of the serious conditions confronting the people there as a result of the race riot. He said many of the negroes were in jail while the riot was being investigated and scores of others had left the county. He stated labor was scarce and that few negroes could be secured to gather the cotton crop. White people will have to be brought in from the outside if they are able to save the crop, he

declared. He told of one planter who had 300 acres of fine cotton and not a negro on his plantation.[4]

The number of blacks who ultimately left Phillips County as a result of the massacres is not known. It may have been in the hundreds, perhaps more. A 1925 agricultural census revealed a drop of 592 black farm tenants in Phillips County since the previous count, in 1920. White tenants increased their ranks during the same time period by seventeen.[5] However, since blacks from all over the Arkansas Delta and the rural South were heading north during this period, no conclusions can be drawn from this data.

Meanwhile, nothing could be admitted, and the insurrection theory had to be established. White control meant that the white version of what had occurred was the official version. And every story told by whites that involved a white death had to link the victim to the insurrection even when it strained the credulity of everyone, black or white, who heard it. On the front page of the October 3 issue of the *Helena World* was the "true" story of how O. R. Lilly had been killed by the four Johnston brothers. No deaths during the massacre of African Americans would cause more anger in the black community in Helena and nationally. Son of private school teachers and a graduate of the Chicago School of Dentistry who had married the daughter of a wealthy black businessman, A. H. Miller, David Augustine Elihue Johnston, in addition to his successful dental practice, was a member of the National Negro Business League, begun by Booker T. Washington. His older brother, Louis H. Johnston, was a physician in Oklahoma City. Two of the brothers were in the automobile business, one of whom had been wounded at Château-Thierry.

An abbreviated version of Lilly's death had run the day before.[7] But for every "official" story of the death of a white resident of Phillips County in the Elaine affair, there is at least an alternative version. In the case of O. R. Lilly, there are three other accounts and even more interpretations. However, Amos Jarmon, Phillips County treasurer, gave the official version. Four black brothers had been apprehended outside of Wabash near Elaine on October 1. Jarmon told the paper: "We had no handcuffs, so we chained the Johnsons' [*sic*] feet together and placed them in the rear of Mr. Lilly's Oldsmobile."[8] In the front seat were James "Jim" Carruthers, Lilly's black chauffeur; Jarmon; W. H. Molitor; and Lilly. According to Jarmon, they stopped the car to see if they could assist some individuals from Helena and Elaine whose automobile appeared to be broken down. Jarmon asked if they needed help, and at this moment, D. A. E. Johnston grabbed Lilly's gun and shot him. Then Jarmon and Molitor fired and killed Johnston. The men in the other automobile got out then and opened fire on the other three Johnston brothers, killing them instantly.

The "black" version, however, is contained in an undated report about the massacre sent to the *Crisis,* the militant NAACP magazine edited by W. E. B. Du Bois and distributed all over the country. In this version, the Johnston brothers were betrayed by white men posing as friends who encountered them while they were hunting and told them about the riot, saying that it would be dangerous to be found on the road. They had just boarded a train when they were arrested by a group of white men:

> The officers had with them a man named Lilly, a friend of another white man whom Dentist Johnson [*sic*] had thrashed the week before. The white man had tried to whip Johnson [*sic*] and Johnson [*sic*] beat him up. The Johnson [*sic*] brothers were men who did not truckle and cater to white men. They never looked for trouble, but if a white man tried to bully one of them, they always took their own part. They were known as brave men who knew no fear.
>
> The men were taken off the train and placed into a car. When they had gone a few miles down the road from which they had just come, they encountered a mob led by the "white friends" who had warned them to take the train. As the mob approached, Lilly and the officers began to get out of the auto. The Johnsons [*sic*] saw they had been led into a trap by their supposed "white friends." They were handcuffed, but they tried to put up a fight. Just as Lilly was climbing out of the car, preparing to turn over the helpless men to the mob, Dr. D. J. [*sic*] Johnson [*sic*], although shackled, managed to grab Lilly's pistol from his hand and shot him. The officers and the mob then shot the men literally to pieces.[9]

The person who wrote this account is not identified, but it was probably Walter White of the NAACP, who might have heard this version of the events while he was in Arkansas investigating the massacres. In a slight variation on the "black" version, Ida B. Wells-Barnett wrote that "as he [Lilly] started to drive the auto away, members of the mob blazed away at it, and killed the Johnston brothers, also the white driver, and filled the auto full of holes."[10] This account is in error at least to the extent that the driver of the automobile was Lilly's black driver, James "Jim" Carruthers, who survived. In this version too, though, the Johnstons appear as passive victims.

A third version of the killing of the Johnston brothers is reported by historian B. Boren McCool. McCool refers to "certain evidence which indicates that a prominent plantation owner whose name never appeared in the reports of the incident was also in the car. Local rumors alleged that a personal enmity existed between the man and Lilly; and that enroute to Helena, the man shot Lilly three times and then turned on the Johnstons, who were killed by him and the other three deputies."[11] In a footnote to this paragraph McCool states: "D. A. Keeshan, undertaker at Helena, in a private conversation with J. W. Butts stated that Lilly was not killed with his own gun but with the gun of a local white man."[12]

While writing his book, McCool was given temporary possession of the original research material for the Butts and James piece that would eventually appear in the *Arkansas Historical Quarterly*, including transcriptions of interviews and notes. What McCool does not disclose in his book was that J. W. Butts had obtained from D. A. Keeshan the name of the man who may have killed Lilly. In a handwritten note appended to the end of an unnumbered document and signed with his initials, "JWB," Butts wrote, "D. A. Keeshan, undertaker, says bullets from Jos. Meyer's gun killed *Lilly-*."[13] Joseph Meyers is the individual who along with Sebastian Straub supposedly hired detectives from Chicago to investigate the union. He owned a plantation in the Elaine area.

The significance of McCool's disclosure that Lilly, the owner of the car in which the Johnstons were riding, may have been killed by a white man who then turned his gun on the four brothers is not clear, but it may be that Meyers turned his gun on the three brothers after he shot Lilly in order to keep them from talking and to give himself an alibi. To complicate matters further, O. R. Lilly's son, James Lilly, has written that "Keeshan-Lambert Funeral Home Owner-Manager said 46 bodies were brought in B &W. . . . They murdered your dad."[14] Were the Johnstons simply innocent bystanders who were made scapegoats for the murder of Lilly by Meyers or a group of men? James Lilly says that he talked to the manager-owner about his claim but was given no further information.

James Lilly also claims that a number of years after the Elaine affair his Uncle Charles (his father's brother) received a letter from Jim Carruthers, the black chauffeur, who had moved to Chicago. The letter allegedly said that Carruthers was told that he would be allowed to live if he moved from Helena and never returned—an offer he took up. In the letter, now lost, Carruthers allegedly wrote that Lilly had been killed by a posse.[15]

In any event, it was never proved that the Johnston brothers had any connection with the union. Nor would this have been likely. Given the family's willingness to defend themselves, the Johnston brothers may have been sympathetic to the fact that blacks were defending themselves with weapons, but that hardly made them members of a union or leaders of an insurrection.

The deaths of the other three residents of Phillips County—Will Adkins, James Tappan, and Clinton Lee—were equally problematic but more important to the white community since these deaths became the basis for the prosecution of the Elaine Twelve and dozens of other blacks. The trials for the deaths of these three men would start in a month.

October 3, 1919
Little Rock

Back in Little Rock by two o'clock on the afternoon on October 3, a tired-looking Governor Brough held a press conference in his office and showed off a bullet used during the fighting. Two days earlier he had said he was going to Elaine to "obtain correct information." He now reported, "The situation at Elaine has been well handled and is absolutely under control. There is no danger of any lynching. The saying is current among the white citizens that Phillips County has never had a lynching and would not have one now even in this crisis. The white citizens of the county deserve unstinting praise for their actions in preventing mob violence."[16]

Given the fact that "the white citizens of the county" had participated in the killings of the past forty-eight hours and had part of their county overrun by white mobs that they did nothing about, this was an astonishing comment, though apparently no member of the press challenged it. Apparently some whites had hidden blacks during the massacre, yet in his statement Brough baldly ignored the presence of the white mobs that had streamed into the county on October 1. Who were these citizens that deserved "unstinting praise," and what had they done? The press never asked. Brough may have been referring to the fact that Ocier Bratton had not been lynched at Elaine. Brough's performance must have had a surreal quality to it. Everyone who was present at the press conference knew about the white mobs, but it was as if they had never existed at all.

Without any investigation Brough called Lilly's death an "assassination" by D. A. E. Johnston, stating that twenty-one high-powered rifles had been found on Johnston's property along with a great deal of ammunition. The implication was that the four Johnston brothers (including the physician brother visiting from Oklahoma) were part of the insurrection, which Brough knew had not been proved. It seems most unlikely that a medical doctor would give up his practice in another state to join an armed revolt of black sharecroppers.

By this point Brough had obviously committed himself to a position of totally denying that blacks had been massacred. He praised the valor of the whites who had been shot: "I deeply deplore the death of Corporal Earle with whom I had just talked. With the deaths of Tappan, Lee, Adkins, and the expected death of Proctor [this soldier did not die], Phillips County will have lost some of its most promising and most patriotic citizens."[17] The governor mentioned none of the names of the blacks who had been killed. They were the enemy. Like the soldiers in France, the whites had merely done their duty. The meeting with the Committee of Seven had confirmed the cause of the trouble in Elaine. The possibility that blacks were merely defending themselves was not an issue Brough addressed. Resistance from blacks was synonymous with revolt.

Yet one of the most important molders of public opinion in the state initially had doubted that blacks had planned an insurrection. The *Arkansas Gazette,* which billed itself as the oldest paper west of the Mississippi, was already eighty-three years old when the Heiskell family from Memphis bought a controlling interest in it in 1902. The man who was to run it and make it into a journalistic powerhouse was J. N. "Ned" Heiskell, a witty, bookish newspaperman whose humor could turn to sarcasm in the blink of an eye. A graduate of the University of Tennessee, Heiskell had worked for papers in Knoxville, Chicago, and Memphis. Aloof and agnostic, Heiskell labored on Sundays because he said he could get some work done then. Like Brough, after dinner he visited his library. If Brough was "to the manner born," he had nothing on Heiskell, whose father had served in the Nineteenth Tennessee Infantry and was a circuit court judge in Memphis. Heiskell had the Old South in his veins. At the beginning of his career, he had justified the lynching of blacks on the theory that some plantations were so remote that there was nothing else that would deter their savage behavior. Later, he came out against lynching as uncivilized. The *Gazette* had also favored a movement to end black voting by a repeal of the Fifteenth Amendment.[18]

The *Gazette* was dubious of the claim there had been an insurrection: "Can it be believed that D. A. E. Johnson [*sic*], for example, could have let himself believe that the negroes could put down the whites by armed

MORE THAN ONE VERSION

insurrection and take over the land for themselves? A negro of Johnson's [sic] intelligence must have known that for negroes to hold control of a certain region through the force of arms was a thing inconceivable and that an insurrection could only have one result."[19]

The paper called for an investigation, though expressing confidence that the whites in charge would get to the bottom of the matter. If blacks had been misled by some evil whites, this would be found out in due course. Shortly, the paper would accept the Committee of Seven's report of an insurrection in its entirety and never again waiver in its commitment to the belief that the deaths of the Elaine Twelve should be carried out. The *Gazette*'s rival, the *Arkansas Democrat*, as the story unfolded over the years during the course of the litigation, would not be so sure.

On October 7, Mort Allen announced the results of the investigation of the Committee of Seven in a long statement to the press. Run on the front page of the *Helena World* and in many other newspapers, it began: "The present trouble with the negroes in Phillips County is not a race riot. It is a deliberately planned insurrection of the negroes against the whites directed by an organization known as the 'Progressive Farmers and Household Union of America,' established for the purpose of banding negroes together for the killing of white people. This 'union' was started by Robert L. Hill, a negro 26 years old of Winchester, Arkansas, who saw in it an opportunity of making easy money."[20]

Allen's explanation of what the blacks thought they would gain by killing whites was little short of absurd, but there was such contempt for the intelligence of most blacks that no story would seem too ludicrous to be believed:

> He told the darkies that he was an agent of the government and because the senators and representatives at Washington were white men and in sympathy with the white men of the South it was impossible for the negroes to get the rights that had been promised them for service in the Army and so the Government had called into existence this organization which would be supported by the Government in defense of the negroes against the white people. He told them that it was necessary for all members of the Union to arm themselves in preparation for the day when they should be called upon to attack their white oppressors.[21]

Then, in a total contradiction, Allen charged that Hill had formed the union as a "get-rich" scheme, an allegation more plausible in light of all the dues and other dubious fees Hill charged to members. But this logically negated Allen's contention that Hill was masterminding a violent revolution, since it would have involved risking the geese that were laying his golden eggs. If one is profitably bilking others, one does not send them out to be killed. Allen's statement contended that Hill:

> urged all lodges to decide upon a plan of campaign when the day came to strike and designate the part to be played by every man. He told them that the Government was erecting at Winchester three huge storehouses where arms, ammunition and trained soldiers would be ready for instant use. On Wednesday morning after the first fight at Hoop Spur, the negroes crossed the track and lay in the weeds all day waiting for Hill's army to materialize. They were within easy range of automobiles going to and from Hoop Spur all day and could have easily fired into them, but they wished to wait for Hill's Army in order to clean up in one fell swoop.[22]

Here was the old stereotype reborn: a Negro smart enough to scheme but at the same time a savage idiot with a harebrained idea that had no chance of succeeding, unless success meant getting all his men killed or prosecuted for murder. According to Allen, "He [Hill] was very adroit in making use of certain circulars issued by the Government and in distorting the purpose of the Arkansas Warehouse and Ginners Law to convince the negroes that the United States Government was endeavoring to correct evils which he alleged existed among the farmers."[23]

No logic was too convoluted for Allen. Somehow, the United States government was a part of Hill's plan even though it had acted against blacks' financial interest: "He further told the negroes that the plan of Secretary Lane to provide homesteads for the soldiers had been carried out where the white soldiers were concerned, but the negroes had been refused participation in it."[24]

What were the blacks to get? Allen's answer to that question was that blacks believed they would be allowed to take over large plots of land "after all the white people had been driven off."[25]

And how did the Committee of Seven know all of this? "I have cross-examined and talked to at least 100 prisoners at Elaine," Allen's statement read. "They belong to different lodges in that section. The stories they tell are almost identical as to the promises and representations made by Hill."[26]

Like most successful lies, Allen's account contained snippets of innocent facts that he characterized as sinister. He wrote, "The slogan of the organization is 'We Battle for Our Rights.' The password of all the lodges was 'We have just begun.'"[27]

By the time Allen was through, he probably believed his story himself. "A remarkable thing about the development," he wrote, "is that some of the ringleaders were found to be the oldest and most reliable of the negroes whom we have known for the past fifteen years. He [Hill] had made them believe that he had been entrusted with a sacred mission which had to be carried out regardless of the consequences."[28] The idea that blacks thought they were being cheated by the system and needed a labor union was dismissed by Allen in a single sentence: "As far as the oppression is concerned many of the negroes involved own mules, horses, cattle and automobiles and clear money every year on their crops after expenses are paid."[29]

It is not known whether the Committee of Seven and other planters engaged in acts of torture themselves or used underlings (as in the Phillips County jail) to make blacks confess to whatever whites wanted to put in their mouths. It is naive to believe that torture was limited to the Phillips County jail. As noted earlier, Gerard Lambert, in his autobiography, remembered being told of the methods used on his plantation to make blacks talk.

Again, it is noteworthy that Allen didn't mention that black detectives from Chicago had been hired to infiltrate the union and had uncovered the insurrection plot but hadn't been believed, as would be alleged forty years later in the *Arkansas Historical Quarterly* article by Butts and James. Allen's statement to the press on October 7 would have been the logical time to mention this.

Within a month scores of blacks would be charged with murder, and not a single detail contained in Allen's statement would be offered into evidence by John E. Miller, the prosecuting attorney for Phillips County, and his assistants. In any place but the South this remarkable absence of proof of a plot at the trials of the very men accused of murder would have completely undermined the Committee of Seven's story. But in the South, in fact, the absence of such proof was ignored by everyone.

The bottom line was the key to the Southern white position. An editorial on October 8 in the *Arkansas Gazette* placed the blame on the North. It was a scheme, as usual, cooked up by vile politicians and manufacturers to entice black labor from the South. This was not a particularly original theme. What makes the editorial jump out at the reader, however, is its attitude toward white violence against blacks: "Unless something is done there will be other outbreaks in the South. Each outbreak will mean more decided action against the negroes until finally an outbreak will mean annihilation of the negroes in the affected district."[30]

The meaning of this was clear as a bell. It took as given the notion that white Southerners would not tolerate "trouble" from blacks. The *Gazette* had no particular interest in inquiring how close to annihilation blacks had come in Phillips County. An earlier editorial had already exonerated whites. "There was no bursting of all restraints and no uncontrollable disorder which reigned in Washington and Omaha and Chicago," the *Gazette* had claimed on October 7. The thrust of the present editorial was that someone must put an end to the notion that blacks could do something about their economic situation: "The correction lies largely with negro leaders, and the sooner they begin work the better. Any change in the condition of the negro will come by evolution and not by revolution. To those who have lived in the South this truth must be apparent."[31]

Every black who read this editorial could only interpret it as a warning. It wouldn't be the only one blacks received. Newspapers in the Delta were equally explicit. An editorial in the *Commercial Appeal*, from across the river in Memphis, which was reprinted on the front page of the *Courier Index* of Lee County on October 24, 1919, did not pull any punches either. Entitled, "To the Negroes: Beware of New Prophets and Strange Teachers," and "addressed directly to the negroes in the South," the editorial began by professing to be written for their welfare but was clearly intended to put blacks on notice. The editorial noted that the past year had been a time of unrest. Blacks had gone north, but many had returned. Simply because blacks had certain rights to move about, that didn't mean it was always a good idea to exercise these rights. While it was true that some of them had been exploited by their landlords, so had white tenants. Millions of Americans had suddenly gotten the idea that they were entitled to higher wages for less work, and these ideas had filtered down to blacks as well. Some had gone to the war in France and had come backing thinking that conditions that applied there should also apply in the United States. Obviously referring to relations between men and women and the lack of European prohibitions against blacks and whites marrying, the editorial bluntly stated that such "conditions" were off limits to blacks.

The editorial then became even more blunt. After reciting the events that had occurred in Phillips County, the editorialist warned, "In killed and wounded, the Negro will always get the worst of the fight. . . . This is a time for negroes to be patient. This is also a time for them to be cautious. Let them beware of the voices of strange teachers and new prophets."[32]

In Little Rock black leaders such as Scipio Jones and others would take heed.

CHAPTER 6

Little Rock and New York: An Uneasy Alliance

You put down the riot, you stopped the mob, you restored order. . . .
—Letter from Scipio Jones and other black leaders to Charles
Hillman Brough, October 19, 1919

October 10–11, 1919
Little Rock

There could not have been two blacks more dissimilar in their out-
look on how to deal with the racism of their time than Scipio Africanus
Jones and Walter White, the twenty-six-year-old assistant field secretary
for the NAACP, which had sent him to investigate the Elaine massacres.
Because of their very different viewpoints neither could have possibly
trusted the other. Their initial visit, which took place in Little Rock during the second week of October 1919, could not have inspired mutual
confidence.

Like his friend and fellow Republican in Helena, Dr. E. C. Morris,
Scipio Jones had spent a lifetime building trust and credibility with
Arkansas whites. As the unquestioned leading black attorney in the state
at the age of fifty-six, he had already appeared before the Arkansas
Supreme Court in twenty-four cases, including a number on behalf of
the Mosaic Templars insurance company.[1] Most attorneys, white or black,
have much less appellate experience in their entire careers. Jones had won
most of these cases. Yet he was careful not to step on any white toes. It
was said of him in 1939 by J. H. Carmichael, a white lawyer and former
dean of the Arkansas Law School, that "in his appearances in court, he
always conducted himself in such a way as not to offend the sensibilities
of the white jurors, the white judges, and the white attorneys, appearing
in the cases."[2]

Jones and other members of the black elite believed they had per-
fected the best way to deal with racial trouble. They found the most sympathetic white men with power and cultivated them assiduously. They

felt they had no choice. Only whites could stop whites from going off as they had in Elaine. All it would take was a single incident, and all they had worked for would go up in flames. Jones had little tolerance for those Northern blacks who wanted blacks in the South to stand up and demand their rights. He accepted segregation. What else was a black person in the South to do? It was the law of the land. More importantly, it was the law and custom of the South. When a local chapter of the NAACP formed in Little Rock, Jones had declined to join. It was easy for Northern blacks to tell Southern blacks what to do. They weren't risking their lives.

Though he had never given up on politics, Jones was a Booker T. Washington man in many respects. African Americans desperately needed to build themselves up. He was third vice president of the National Negro Business League, but this organization had never seemed to catch hold and grow. Still, it had been an honor to meet and talk to Washington on the three occasions when he had come to Arkansas. The dedication of the Mosaic Templars Building had been proof of what blacks could achieve.[3]

As difficult as it was becoming to remain a Republican, Jones had learned the hard way that he had no place else to go politically. When he was almost forty, he had foolishly run for the Little Rock school board. Out of over two thousand votes cast in his ward in 1902, he had received only 181.[4] Since then he had confined his political efforts to the Republican Party, but even that was becoming more problematic. He had been a good Republican all his life. In 1909 he had been recommended for a patronage job in Washington, D.C., as a recorder of deeds, but it hadn't come through.[5] Now Republican whites in Pulaski County were gearing up for another one of their efforts to purge blacks from the party. At one time the Republican Party had been the party of freedom. Those days were becoming harder to remember.

Jones was also a businessman, though he had never developed the knack for making the kind of money that his mentor, John E. Bush, cofounder of the Mosaic Templars of America, an insurance company and fraternal organization, had displayed. At the time of the trouble in Elaine, Jones was starting up a venture with a number of partners that he hoped would become the largest icehouse in the country owned by blacks. Years earlier, he had begun with others a real estate business, but it had not been successful.[6] Yet the potential was there. Scipio Jones knew well what blacks in Little Rock had to lose if Arkansas whites took out their resentment on them. A single night of mayhem could wipe out a generation of effort and progress.

The mostly black neighborhood where he lived, at 1911 Pulaski

LITTLE ROCK AND NEW YORK

Street, lay just south of the newly constructed state capitol and was the center of black cultural life in Little Rock and home to black profession-als like himself. Philander Smith College sat across the street from Arkansas Baptist College. If Thirteenth Street was college row in the black community, then Ninth Street, beginning at Broadway and running west to Izard, was the heart of black commercial life. In 1919, Ninth Street was thriving. The offices of black physicians, dentists, and life-insurance executives sat next to the business establishments of black barbers, restau-ranteurs, and photographers. But the jewel of the black community was the Mosaic Templars Building at Ninth and Broadway. The Mosaic Templars of America, with its headquarters in Little Rock, was a black fraternal organization that provided insurance to its members. Phenomenally successful as a business and a showplace of the black com-munity, the Templars at its peak in 1928 would be operating in twenty-six states and have members in Central America and the West Indies.[7] In 1919, in addition to the insurance company offices, the Templars build-ing leased space to three black physicians, two dentists, and a lawyer, as well as a druggist. As the attorney for the Templars, Scipio Jones would move his office into the Templars building in 1920.[8]

Though a stalwart Republican, Jones counted himself a friend of one ex-governor of Arkansas, George Donaghey, but it was Brough who received most of his attention.[9] For his efforts to sell Liberty Loan Bonds, Brough had arranged for Jones to be appointed by Woodrow Wilson to the national colored advisory board to the Liberty Bond effort.

As far as Jones was concerned, the national NAACP rarely stopped to think about the practical effects of its activities on local blacks. Blacks could never be sure how widespread white violence against them would be. For a while, it had seemed that lynchings of colored men had begun to decline in Arkansas, but when Jones began to count them up, he was able to recall four since December 1918.[10] There had been no lynchings in Little Rock since 1892, but the possibility was always present.

No black man in Arkansas watched whites more closely for clues to what they might do. Politics and economics ultimately ruled every deci-sion white folks made. As far as what would happen to the men who were in jail in Elaine, Jones knew the final word always rested with the gover-nor. It was a foregone conclusion that some black men in Phillips County would be sentenced to die in the electric chair if they could avoid being lynched. It would be Brough who would have the power to commute their sentences. It never did any good to alienate the one person who

could help your people. That was the problem with the NAACP: it sometimes acted as if it forgot the individuals involved so that it could stand
on principle.

Meanwhile, while the NAACP ranted and raved from its safe offices
in New York about how Negroes in the South should act, Jones would
continue to show up in court immaculately dressed, even something of a
dandy with his walking stick that was purely for show. Yes, he had a
Cadillac and a chauffeur to drive it.[11] And yes indeed, his wife, Lillie, had
a maid even though there were no children in his house now that his
daughter, Hazel, was married and living in Chicago. Rich white folks had
all of those things. Why shouldn't blacks? If he still deeply missed his first
wife, Carrie, who had died so young, that was his private business.[12] All
in all, he knew he had been lucky. His white father, Sandford Reamey,
had helped pay for his education at Philander Smith and across the river
at Shorter College in North Little Rock.[13] He had seen to it as well that
Scipio Jones, alone of his family, had learned to read.[14] Scipio Jones had
worked hard too, first as a field hand and then a teacher. And he had
worked all the while he was reading law in white men's offices in Little
Rock. White men had helped him all his life.

Despite his success as a lawyer, it hadn't been easy. Whites were always
watching for him to try to go too high. Twice he had been publicly humiliated in the papers. Once he had bought a mule that had been crippled.
A story on the front page of the *Arkansas Gazette* had ridiculed him.[15] He
knew what he could say, how far he could go. As a black attorney, he could
plead a black criminal defendant's case. He wasn't too proud to beg a white
jury for mercy, saying that his client was just a colored boy who didn't
mean any harm.[16] He had a reputation for being able to cross-examine
black witnesses better than anyone else around. Cases involving claims of
blacks against the Mosaic Templars insurance company presented no
problem. Trial judges—all of them white, of course—listened to his arguments and either accepted or rejected them according to their understanding of the law. After all, the disputes involved just Negroes, so the
judges usually had no reason to be biased. Jones had even been elected as
a special judge by the other lawyers for a case involving two blacks in Little
Rock municipal court. Even that had caused something of a furor when
a lawyer who had just recently moved from Mississippi objected.[17] What
Scipio knew he was forbidden to do as an attorney was to challenge the
system of white supremacy directly and be successful at it. In 1901 he had
been able to preserve an objection in a criminal trial that his client had

95

been denied his constitutional right because of the absence of blacks from the jury. He had won that case in the Arkansas Supreme Court against George Murphy, then attorney general.[18] But for a black attorney to challenge the entire economic system of the Delta, as Ulysses Bratton had done, would have been ridiculous. When all was said and done, if a black man was going to accomplish anything in the state of Arkansas, he had to know his place.

Though Jones counted whites among his friends, his work and talent brought him into close company with the most well-known African Americans in Little Rock. They formed an informal but tight club. Besides himself, the most influential members of his race at this time in Arkansas were mainly educators and preachers now that John E. Bush and Mifflin W. Gibbs—a lawyer and a businessman—were dead. Chester Bush had succeeded his father at the Mosaic Templars, but nobody would take the place of John Bush, whose drive and energy had made the organization so successful.

Walter White, the man sitting across from Jones, did not look in any shape, form, or fashion like a black representative of the national office of the NAACP. As if to mock the idea of racial classification, Walter White's hair was blonde, his eyes blue, and his lips thin. Yet, he *identified* himself as a Negro. His knowledge that despite his color he was forever a black man came as an epiphany during his youth in the middle of the Atlanta riots in September 1906. He had been helping his father, a postal worker, in downtown Atlanta when the murders had started. They had watched in shock as a white mob ran down and killed a crippled black man. Running to Houston Street in the black community to protect his five sisters and his mother, he could not have known that this single night of violence would forever transform his life. Yet it soon would, because as the mob came down the street toward their house, his father handed him a pistol and told him to fire when the first man crossed their lawn. He knew then that *nothing* could protect him, not his light skin nor how hard he worked, not how much he could achieve nor the good will of some whites. In White's autobiography he wrote: "In the flickering light the mob swayed, paused, and began to flow toward us. In that instant there opened up within me a great awareness; I knew then who I was. I was a Negro, a human being with an invisible pigmentation which marked me a person to be hunted, hanged, abused, discriminated against, kept in poverty and ignorance, in order that those whose skin was white would have readily at hand a proof of their superiority, a proof patent and inclusive, accessible to the moron and the idiot as well as to the wise man and genius."[19]

Ironically, his white skin enabled him to do for the NAACP what no one else in its employ at the time could: infiltrate the enemy. Thus, when he went to work for the NAACP in 1918, White would pose as a white man to get information. Soon after he started he volunteered to go to rural Tennessee to determine the facts of the death of a black man murdered and tortured by a mob. White pretended to be looking for a farm to buy and gained the confidence of the locals, who naturally gossiped about the details of the murder. When he returned to New York, his account was documented with firsthand sources and widely published, to the delight of the NAACP, which depended on contributions from rich white benefactors as well as its local chapters.

In 1919 the chairman of the board of directors of the NAACP was a fifty-four-year-old socialist and Unitarian white woman from Brooklyn named Mary White Ovington.[20] The only woman to sign the NAACP incorporation papers in 1909, Ovington had helped to draft the famous "Call" and its invitation list, which had resulted in bringing together for a meeting such liberal luminaries as William Dean Howells; W. E. B. Du Bois (now on staff as editor of the *Crisis*); Jane Addams; Lincoln Steffens; John Dewey; and Ida B. Wells-Barnett, the antilynching crusader.[21] Now, ten years later, the NAACP had 220 branches all over the country and more than fifty-six thousand members. With a private income, Ovington, who wrote extensively, had the time and inclination to work closely with the NAACP staff, which included the office workers, the field secretaries, James Weldon Johnson (her favorite), Walter White, and William Pickens—all of whom were black. The man who bore the title of executive secretary, John Schillady, was white, but he would never recover emotionally from a severe beating he received in Texas on NAACP business. He resigned in 1920.

In the field, White's modus operandi would continue to include deception of whites regarding his identity, a tactic necessary to gain information, but Scipio Jones was undoubtedly angered and upset (he would within a week take pains to distance himself from White's actions) when he learned that White had interviewed the governor during the trip to Little Rock by pretending to be a white newspaperman from the *Chicago Daily News*. In his autobiography, White brags about his meeting with Brough, made possible by fake press credentials provided by the managing editor of the Chicago paper, Charles H. Dennis: "I purposely led him

[Brough] to believe that I had little knowledge of the Negro question and was open-minded to whatever facts he, as chief executive of the state, cared to give me."[22] Brough, taken in completely, was delighted to correct the "foul lies" that were being circulated by the *Chicago Defender* and the NAACP about the riot and to set the record straight with the story he had been telling continuously since returning from Phillips County a week earlier. Characteristically, Brough gave White a picture of himself, complete with his famous signature, an ornate inscription that trumpeted to the world the self-regard of the writer. More importantly, he wrote a letter of introduction for White, who told him he was going to Helena to get the real story of the Elaine riot.[23]

The news that White was taking the train to Helena did not please Scipio Jones. He warned the younger man not to talk with any blacks in Phillips County. It would only get them into trouble. Whites would be watching and listening. Before he left for Helena, White did make a contact in Little Rock that would prove to be invaluable: Ulysses Bratton provided him journalistic material on the system of informal peonage that prevailed in the Arkansas Delta. White and Bratton were probably introduced by Scipio Jones (Bratton and Jones, both attorneys, were allies in the Republican Party); it would be a fateful meeting. Four years later, Bratton would help argue to the U.S. Supreme Court the case of *Moore v. Dempsey*, which would eventually result in gaining the freedom of six of the Elaine Twelve.

Walter White did make the trip to Helena, though he had spent only a few hours there before he was warned that his identity was about to be discovered. In the chapter of his autobiography entitled, "I Decline to be Lynched," he describes his getaway: "I sped down the railroad tracks, keeping out of sight as much as possible. Just as the train pulled in, I climbed aboard from the side opposite the station platform. The conductor looked at me quizzically when I offered payment in cash. I explained to him that I had important business in Memphis that evening and had not had time to buy a ticket." The conductor told him he was leaving "just when the fun is going to start. . . . There's a damned yellow nigger down here passing for white and the boys are going to get to him."[24]

Despite the drama of his leave-taking, in terms of useful information, he got almost nothing in Helena except a lifelong anecdote. He did talk to the sheriff, Frank Kitchens, but he interviewed no one in the jail. It didn't matter. Stories would have begun to get out as soon as black refugees made their way out of Phillips County and could talk freely.

A war of words was about to start. And Walter White would have plenty to write about. On October 11, the NAACP held a press conference in New York, announcing White's findings. In this and subsequent articles in the future, the NAACP would give a counterversion of the riot in Elaine: blacks had formed a union in response to the continuing conditions of peonage and then had been shot down by the authorities when they had stood up for themselves. White wrote in the *Chicago Daily News* on October 19 that the contention that there had been a planned insurrection was "only a figment of the imagination of Arkansas whites and not based on fact."[25]

The NAACP's blasts at the state of Arkansas put considerable pressure on the black middle class of the state. Scipio Jones did his best to make sure his friend the governor would not hold Walter White's deception against himself and the black community. On October 19 a letter signed by Jones and other prominent Little Rock blacks appeared in the *Arkansas Gazette*. In part it read: "We are writing you this letter to assure you that we appreciate very keenly your prompt action in handling the very serious situation at Elaine. . . . You put down the riot, you stopped the mob, you restored order, thus saving many lives in both races and much destruction of property. We are on the ground, we know what you have done, and wish to again assure you that the best colored people of the state of Arkansas endorse your stand and stand shoulder to shoulder in all things that tend to bring peace and good will between the races and for the uplift of Arkansas."[26]

This letter was signed by James Monroe Cox, the venerable president of Philander Smith College in Little Rock. Cox had been at Philander Smith since 1886 and had been president of the school for the last twenty-three years. Like Scipio Jones, he had been born into slavery, as had Joseph A. Booker, president of Arkansas Baptist College. The other signers included Rev. J. P. Robinson, pastor of the largest Baptist church in Little Rock, and Bishop J. M. Conner of the African Methodist Episcopal church. Another signee was John Hibbler, a lawyer and business partner of Scipio Jones. All of these men were pillars of the black elite in Little Rock.

They of course were not alone in their desire to assure the white power structure that they posed no threat to the existing order. Blacks all over the state, fearing they would be next to feel the wrath of white mobs, were acting accordingly. Middle-class blacks in Arkansas (and by implication middle-class blacks elsewhere in the South) have been criticized for their lack of solidarity with the masses during the Jim Crow era. For example, Fon Louise Gordon, an African American historian who received her doctorate at the University of Arkansas, points out that Joseph A. Booker, during the 1891 debate at a meeting of blacks over legislation that resulted in the Separate Coach Act, did not oppose the legislation as such but urged a modification that would allow a distinction based on class. She notes that "the primary interest" of speakers at a second meeting "was protecting their own privileged position. The speakers expressed no concern for the obvious political and economic ramifications of the proposed caste legislation. Instead of presenting a black community unified in its condemnation of the law, black leaders willingly accepted modifications which would have relieved the middle class of the shame of segregation but still relegated the poorer classes to inferior facilities."[27] Gordon further points out that the black elite in Arkansas benefited from segregation. Indeed, as has been mentioned, Dr. E. C. Morris, making lemonade out of a lemon, forthrightly challenged his Baptist flock to view segregation as an economic opportunity. It was a question of pride. Poor blacks, uneducated and unemployed, shamed the black elite.

How much of Gordon's criticism applies to Scipio Jones personally is a valid question but an easy one to answer. There is no record of what he thought about issues such as the Separate Coach Act. Unquestionably, he identified with black elite values in social matters. But if he is judged by what he did as an attorney throughout his life, including in the Elaine cases, it is obvious that he never turned his back on the great mass of poor blacks who lived in Arkansas. He once collaborated with Jeff Davis (of all people) to make it easier for prisoners at the county farm to pay off their fines and be released sooner. Early on, he took the cases of poor blacks who could not have paid his fee, and his persistence throughout the Elaine cases would become the stuff of legend.[28]

Jones claimed to know nothing of Hill's sharecropper union, which, at first blush, strains credulity, but may possibly have been essentially correct. In a buried item in an article that apparently went unnoticed by the white power structure (and historians) in the October 6, 1919, issue of the *Arkansas Gazette*, the name of Thomas Price, Scipio Jones's law partner, surfaces in connection with the union. On page three, toward the end of an article about the organization of the union, the reporter mentions that the Committee of Seven turned up a union "membership card" that was signed by Robert Hill but also by a "T. I. Price, general attorney, Little Rock, Ark."[34] Nothing is known about Thomas Price's involvement with the sharecropper union beyond this obscure reference, and thus Scipio Jones's possible participation as counsel to the union would be a matter of pure conjecture, since neither man mentions this in their correspondence with the NAACP or apparently with anyone else. At a minimum, Jones would have likely known of so singular a group of clients who had retained his younger partner. However, this was not information that either would have wanted circulated, since it could have only caused problems (including arrest) for them.

In any case, Jones's papers have not survived. It is not known if he kept a diary. Always discreet, perhaps he did not care to record his deepest feelings about whites or about his own motivations in his dealings with them. By the time Jones signed the letter of support for the governor, he would have heard the stories that there had been a massacre of blacks in Phillips County. Instead of publicly confronting Brough with these accounts, he chose to endorse his actions. In light of his subsequent actions in taking the cases of the men in Phillips County, Jones's motive had to be that whatever the governor knew or didn't allow himself to know, Brough, with his power to pardon, would ultimately be the last hope in Arkansas. Viewed from the offices of the NAACP in New York during the first three weeks of October, Jones's action in signing the letter supporting Brough would have been highly suspect. Brough was the enemy. Walter White had humiliated him. And in turn Brough had declared war on the NAACP, seeking to ban its publication the *Crisis* (along with the *Chicago Defender*) from being distributed in Arkansas.

If Scipio Jones felt the self-hatred and shame that inevitably accompanies the journey through a life as caste- and class-ridden as his own, that would have been entirely normal. Had he lived to see the Civil Rights Movement in the 1960s, his manner of relating to whites would have been called obsequious. Yet he would demonstrate courage and persistence that few advocates in any era have exceeded. And in the process, he would come to appreciate the humanity of the twelve sharecroppers on death row, the Elaine Twelve.

October 1–November 2, 1919
Little Rock

If Scipio Jones had come to terms with his life long before the Arkansas race massacres, the events in Phillips County precipitated a profound transformation in the lives of Ulysses Bratton and the members of his family. Ulysses Bratton didn't dare go to Helena to see about his son, because he was the "rascally" white man who had sent him. The talk in Helena was that there was a thousand-dollar reward for his capture, should he be found in Phillips County, and that H. D. Moore, the county judge and one of the Committee of Seven, would himself pay nine hundred of that amount. To get his son Ocier home, Bratton knew he had to prove he had done nothing illegal in sending him to Phillips County. He proposed the following to the Committee of Seven: "I will waive all my Constitutional rights, the right of an indictment, the right of a jury trial, the right of a Circuit Court proceeding and allow you to submit anything that you have to the Supreme Court [of Arkansas] and give me an opportunity to answer it and to disprove anything. . . ."[29]

This grandiose scenario, outlined in a letter on October 15, was a measure of the desperation Bratton felt in not being able to get his son released, but it is also a sign of how seriously he took himself. In many ways, Bratton's oldest son was an unlikely representative for his father. Ocier, who would turn thirty in jail in Helena, was not a lawyer like his father or his brother Guy. A stenographer and a clerk, sometimes he worked in his father's law office and sometimes not. He had a wife, Nora, and two children under six years old. Smaller than his father and brothers, he had almost a pinhead in place of regular features. He was remembered by his family as a dapper dresser and as having a playful nature in contrast to his serious father. However, his passion was playwriting. Author of the play "The Creation," he had it copyrighted in 1913, when he was twenty-two. This play, one of several allegorical plays he wrote, is concerned with the spiritual transformation of a morally bankrupt businessman. It is full of angels and terrible dialogue, but it reflects the idealism of the elder Bratton in its concern for morality.[30]

In the course of the next month, before Ocier Bratton was released, his brother Guy, his wife, Nora, and his mother, Mattie, would make pilgrimages to Helena, bringing him clothes, books, and personal items, but his father could only stew in Little Rock. Compared to his coconspirators, Ocier, as a white man, received preferential treatment. In a letter to his father after his release, he wrote, "Mr. Seamon was very friendly and generally let Nora come into the cell—in fact, from that time forward an air of friendliness came over all whom I came in contact. The jailer was very courteous, explained that it was through misunderstanding, the further fact that he was worried, overworked, afraid of desperate Negroes he had to pass thru the room, etc. that caused him to speak too gruffly."[31] This treatment occurred after the federal troops had arrived. Still, on the very day of his release, Ocier would be marched into the grand jury room, where one last attempt would be made to have a black to identify him.

Ocier makes no mention of torture of blacks in his correspondence that has survived, though he makes clear that he is omitting some details. Despite his proximity, his contact with black prisoners was limited. In Arkansas during the Jim Crow era custom more than the law dictated segregation. In fact, there were only a handful of statutes mandating segregation. One of them dealt with separation of the races in the penitentiary. The jail was crammed with 285 prisoners.[32] It had space for about forty-eight.

One can almost feel the bitterness and anger growing in Ulysses Bratton on a daily basis as he futilely tried to convince his fellow Arkansans to help him get his son out of harm's way. In the space of a few hours, Bratton had gone from being a respected and successful attorney to being seen as a traitor and pariah. The alienation would have a profound effect. Shortly, he would begin to get a measure of revenge, but the month of October was a nightmare because of the treatment and threats he and his family began to receive. Attorneys who were on cases with Bratton requested that he withdraw and said that otherwise they would. At one point he went so far as to point out that he didn't favor social equality for blacks either.[33] He claimed to know nothing of Hill's sharecropper union, which seems unbelievable but is understandable given the circumstances of his son. In a state whose ruling class breathed the pure oxygen of white supremacy, Bratton's passion for justice for blacks was quite real but must have seemed as doomed to him as his attempts to help his son.

Bratton tried to use his contacts in Little Rock to free Ocier. Among his friends was a gregarious and well-placed Democratic lawyer by the name of Edgar McHaney, who would play a major role in the defense of the Elaine Twelve. "Mac" McHaney, whose superb political connections would later get him named to the Arkansas Supreme Court in 1927, was the kind of man who had friends in every part of the state. Originally from Tennessee and one of fifteen children, McHaney crossed the Mississippi River into Arkansas and, like many men of his era (including Ulysses Bratton and Scipio Jones), taught school, first serving as principal in DeWitt in eastern Arkansas. He was also the principal in Piggott in the northeast corner of the state, where he met his wife Gail, who was the daughter of a well-to-do stave-mill owner. Ambitious and extroverted, McHaney made his way to Little Rock, where he eventually got a job in the secretary of state's office and went to night law school.[35] By 1919 he was in practice with a former attorney general of the state, George Murphy (who would become lead counsel for the Elaine Twelve until his death in 1920), and Edwin Dunaway. A member of the Little Rock Country Club, McHaney knew everybody worth knowing, including governors past and present and state legislators. As a Democrat, he was as establishment as one could get in Arkansas.

He went to Helena to see what he could do, but his friendships and connections could not secure the release of Ocier Bratton, a failure that Ulysses Bratton, in his growing bitterness, would hold against him. McHaney was told by the Committee of Seven that Ocier Bratton's safe passage out of Helena could not be guaranteed even if he was released on a writ of habeas corpus.[36] Thus, there was no point in even trying to go to court to free him.

According to his great-niece, Ulysses Bratton might well have harbored ambitions of one day being governor of Arkansas. That he truly expected to accomplish this in the most solidly Democratic state in the country is doubtful, but the story does suggest that he saw himself before October 1919 as being well within the mainstream of Arkansas culture and politics.

In fact, however, Bratton had committed the one unpardonable sin for a white man in Arkansas. By agreeing to represent blacks who had joined a labor union, he had placed himself in diametrical opposition to the planter interests in the Arkansas Delta. More fundamentally, he was now seen as helping blacks challenge white supremacy. Initially, however, Bratton didn't see himself as a radical. To Bratton, he and his sons had been simply helping clients to get their fair share of money owed to them. Indeed, this part of his practice could hardly have been a major revenue producer, since the cases were difficult and at the time there were no statutes requiring defendants to pay successful plaintiffs' attorneys their fees in civil rights cases. Yet his firm was doing well enough for him to have recently had a large home under construction in North Little Rock. Bratton did not see himself as a radical, but in the lexicon of the day, he would soon become one. Walter White had recognized his potential in their conversation about peonage. Bratton could do the NAACP a lot of good in New York. But first he had to get his son out of jail.

By the middle of November the disillusionment felt by the Bratton family was complete. In a letter to his father, Guy Bratton, who had been a captain in France, sarcastically describes the visit of a client. Guy had gone in on a Sunday to their law offices "to talk with one of our clients who had been the victim of 'safe democracy,' here in this land, Obie Carrell, an ex-slave eighty years old. He had been beaten up by the Chief of Police in Pine Bluffs [*sic*] without any provocation."[37]

This snide reference to the Democrat Woodrow Wilson's pledge that the last world conflict had been the war to end all wars, waged to make the world safe for democracy, was not a political barb. By this time Ulysses Bratton was already letting his family know that he was ready to leave Arkansas for good. The anger and sense of estrangement that Bratton felt would be put to good use by the NAACP. Immediately after Ocier Bratton's release in November, Bratton was on a train to New York to meet personally with NAACP officials.

CHAPTER 7

The Trials Begin

[John Miller said] that he did what he did to appease the mob, but that enough
was enough.
    —*Letter from Guy Bratton to his father, November 9, 1919*

October–November 1919
Helena

From the beginning there had been tension among the factions within Phillips County about the disposition of the blacks who were taken into custody. These differences were papered over in public, but they existed nonetheless. Nothing would be done about the massacres. Whites acted as if they hadn't happened and insisted that only those blacks who had resisted had been killed. Though in theory the Committee of Seven had taken responsibility for investigating the disturbances, the transcripts of the trials would bring out that many others were involved in questioning the defendants. The planters themselves took a hand in the interrogation of blacks. Each naturally wanted to know about the participation of those families on his plantation in the union.

In Phillips County the fiction that blacks had been about to revolt was a unifying principle for all whites, but it caused its own problems. Instead of satisfying the bloodlust of the residents of Phillips County, the massacre, for some, had whetted it. This group wanted the blood of all the blacks who had dared to resist whites and also the blood of any whites who were believed to have supported them. The fear that this group's anger would erupt, the white power structure's efforts to appease that fear, and the political ramifications involved in these efforts would dominate the decisions of those in control of Phillips County for the next four years.

There had been talk of lynching Ocier Bratton. As plans for lynching him were being debated, Ocier Bratton later wrote his father, "Men came in from Helena, including Judge Jackson, and they also informed me that they were going to protect me and take me to Helena."[1] The trial judge of the Elaine cases, J. M. Jackson, age thirty-eight at the time of the massacre, was no Johnny-come-lately to Phillips County. His maternal grandfather had come to Helena from Mississippi in 1856, making his way in real estate and the mercantile business. "He [John P. Moore] owned considerable land at the time of his death," observes the writer of the biographical piece on J. M. Jackson in the *Centennial History of Arkansas*.[2] The family had done well enough to send the future judge off to the University of the South (Sewanee) for his legal education. At the age of twenty-four Jackson was serving in the state legislature. He gained an appointment to the circuit court from Governor Joe T. Robinson, who himself would go on to the United States Senate. In 1918, Jackson was elected to the bench in his own right. Knowing Ocier Bratton had committed no crime, Jackson released him from jail without bond. It was Judge Jackson who personally saw that he was gotten safely out of town. Ocier wrote his father, "When I was ready to leave the jail I found him at the door and he directed me to go with a fellow a back way to the hotel and remain there 'till three when he said he would get a car and take me to West Helena to catch a train. When we arrived at West Helena, some four miles out, he came in person, and remained till the train left, bidding us a very friendly good bye."[3]

So long as the beneficiary was white, the judge showed unusual courage for a public official during this period. His treatment of the black defendants in the Elaine cases, however, would be considerably different. As the judicial officer for the county, Jackson, along with the prosecuting attorney for the Phillips County judicial district, John E. Miller, had to be concerned with observing the formal trappings of judicial procedure, but as elected politicians, both Jackson and Miller had a constituency to satisfy. Originally from Missouri and with no roots in Arkansas, Miller, who practiced law in Searcy, in White County, would prove to be the more enduring politician of the two, going on to the U.S. House of Representatives, the U.S. Senate, and a federal judgeship. Jackson would be defeated for reelection by a candidate from neighboring Lee County, E. D. Robertson, who would also figure in the story of the Elaine Twelve.

According to a letter written by Guy Bratton to his father after Ocier's release, John Miller privately expressed his own misgivings about Ocier's treatment. In the letter written just after his return from Searcy, Guy Bratton wrote that John Miller had said that "so long as he is P. A. [prosecuting attorney] that no trial will ever be permitted in those cases [of barratry, or stirring up litigation] against any of us. He says, which is logical, and we know is true, that he would have been run out of the county himself. And because of the strong pressure which the so-called commit-tee of seven brought to bear on him he said he thought the best way to meet it was the way that he had and that he was determined that it would go no further. That he did what he did to appease the mob, but that enough was enough."[4]

There would be other ways in which John Miller would appease the mob. However, one decision of his would have been nonnegotiable for any politician in Phillips County: no white person would be charged with so much as a misdemeanor, despite the fact that four members of a promi-nent black family had been killed. "My investigation [of the events in Phillips County] failed to show that a single negro was killed unneces-sarily," Miller wrote in a report to Thomas McRae, who succeeded Brough as governor in 1921 and was considering clemency for the Elaine Twelve.[5] There is no indication that Miller conducted any investigation of deaths of blacks, nor would he have had any intention of doing so. From the beginning, the "investigation" was in the hands of the Committee of Seven and, in fact, in the hands of planters and other self-appointed quasi-prosecutors of Phillips County, who conducted interrogations in a drag-net fashion. Had Miller wished to do so, the time to insist that no committee of citizens would usurp the function of the sheriff and the prosecuting attorney would have been before Brough put his seal of approval on the Committee of Seven. However, there is nothing to sug-gest that Miller was even consulted in advance about the committee's for-mation. He was not from Phillips County and may have been viewed with some suspicion by Allen and his committee. With the governor of the state capitulating to a vigilante approach to justice, it would have been political suicide for Miller to protest that Frank Kitchens, the duly elected sheriff of Phillips County, had no authority to turn his office over to a group of citizens. Miller was not a man who was going to commit politi-cal suicide.

In public the whites spoke as one; in private their handling of the Elaine crisis was clearly not without its difficulties. Planters wanted their blacks back in the fields. And while it was one thing for the Committee of Seven to conduct an investigation and announce its findings that there had been plans for an insurrection, as it did on October 7, it would be another thing entirely to prove in a court of law that union members had planned to murder planters on October 6. Normally, the sheriff of a county and the prosecutor work together. In Phillips County, until the grand jury met, the investigative arm acted independently of the prosecuting attorney, who had to try the case. Though the results at the trial level were a foregone conclusion, John Miller ultimately faced a much harder job than his constituency thought: in order to fulfill the Committee of Seven's promise to the mob that justice would be done—in other words, that blacks would be appropriately punished by death—Miller would have to prove murder charges that would be able to stand up on appeal. That would be no easy task because there were no white eyewitnesses who saw the shots fired that killed the three Phillips County residents, Will Adkins, James Tappan, and Clinton Lee. Obviously, only so many individuals could be charged with murder anyway. Most essential would be the charge of "aiding and abetting" in the murder of Phillips County residents.

First, the grand jury had to meet and charge the defendants, which it began the process of doing on October 27. Since two of its members, T. W. Keesee and Sebastian Straub, were serving on the Committee of Seven, its results were not unexpected. On October 31, it charged 122 blacks with crimes ranging from murder to night riding, a crime that had its own ironic implications, since in Phillips County it had been brought on behalf of planters against whites who tried to run off their black labor.[6] Since grand jury proceedings are secret, it can only be surmised how active a role John Miller played in deciding which blacks would be charged. Normally, a grand jury proceeding is the prosecutor's show, and jurors willingly indict whomever the prosecutor wants. Perhaps this was John Miller's finest hour, since the decision was made to release twenty-one blacks for lack of evidence. But perhaps, understandably, Miller simply didn't want to make his job any harder than it already appeared to be. With as much attention as the NAACP and other African American papers like the *Chicago Defender* were paying to what was occurring in the Arkansas Delta during this period, appeals would not come as a surprise. It would be expected that if the first few trials produced first-degree murder convictions, which carried an automatic death penalty, then others would plead to lesser charges. Still, it seems astonishing that by November 7, only a handful of cases would remain to be disposed of, so rapidly was justice dispensed in Phillips County.

Though there were others still at large, there were two men especially whom the grand jury wished to put on trial: Robert Hill and Ed Ware, the secretary of the Hoop Spur union. During the weeks after the massacres, blacks who had any connection with the union were tracked down and arrested even if they hadn't been within fifty miles of Elaine on

October 1 and 2. The charges stretched the imagination. The *Helena World* reported solemnly on October 10 that the sheriff of Desha County had arrested four blacks on charges of being officially associated with the Progressive Farmers and Household Union of America.[7]

Law enforcement had also found G. P. Casey, the Bratton associate who had manned the Helena office. He was charged with barratry, granted bail, and released, his only crime guilt by association. The charges of barratry, made against Ulysses Bratton and Ocier Bratton, were dismissed a year later, as promised, when the heat had died down.

Decades after the events in Elaine, it seems particularly outrageous that the trials of men charged with murder would have begun immediately after the grand jury had returned indictments and would have moved so fast. In Arkansas, however, such haste was sanctioned by law. Such was the problem of lynchings in the state that "in the case of a crime calculated to arouse the passions of the people to an extent . . . [at which] mob violence would be committed," the county sheriff was authorized to notify the judge, who was then required to start the trial within ten days.[8]

Judge Jackson did even better. The grand jury finished its deliberations on Thursday, October 31. Jackson began the trials on Monday morning, November 3, appointing local Helena counsel as defense attorneys, with the exception of the two black lawyers who practiced there.[9] Another reason for such speed on Jackson's part would have been the fear that out-of-town attorneys might be hired by the NAACP to represent some of the men. By starting the trials immediately, that possibility was averted.

As was typical, there was once again an attempt on the part of the white power structure in Phillips County to pretend that all was normal. The *Helena World* reported that Judge Jackson began the trial of the first defendant (Frank Hicks) but adjourned court at 11:00 A.M. to attend the funeral of a member of the bar, Oscar Thweatt, and then resumed after lunch. In fact, the tension surrounding the trials could only have been a high-voltage affair because so much was riding on them. As evidence of this, a detachment of soldiers from Camp Pike was guarding the Phillips County courthouse, but the *Helena World* neglected to mention that fact in its coverage.[10] The mob had been promised this day for a month. It was time to collect on the IOU made by the Committee of Seven.

In many ways, the first trial would set the stage for the rest. Miller allowed his assistant, P. R. Andrews, who was from Helena, to try the first case, though he would personally try most of the other cases of the men who would be sentenced to die in the electric chair. Jackson appointed Jacob Fink to represent Frank Hicks in his trial for the murder of Clinton Lee. Hicks, understandably, was reported by the *World* to be nervous during the reading of his charges, when he "shifted from one foot to another, his fingers clinching the seams along the sides of his overalls."[11] He had good reason to be nervous. He had everyone in the Phillips County criminal justice system working against him, including his own attorney.

Knowing that his professional career in Helena and perhaps his life and those of his family were at stake, Fink set the tone for the defense of the Elaine Twelve by accepting without a murmur the first twelve men (all white) called to be on the jury. One can only imagine how long the process would have taken had he questioned each member of the jury panel about what he (no women were allowed to serve on juries) had heard about the case. That kind of vigorous advocacy was clearly not available. Fink told the twelve men during his opening statement that he had not "had time to talk to the witnesses in the case," but he managed to ask for a fair, impartial trial. Fink then sat down.[12] Thus, from the beginning the trials were a travesty of due process. Prosecutor Andrews began his opening statement by telling the jury that the "principles" of the union of which Frank Hicks was a member "were to kill the white planters if they failed to meet the demands of the negroes at the settlement for the crops in the fall of the year."[13] In contravention of all the rules of ethics and trial procedure, Andrews would fail to put on a single witness who could testify about the plans for such an insurrection. The transcript does not show that Jacob Fink moved for a mistrial or that Judge Jackson instructed the jury at the close of the trial to disregard that part of Andrews's opening statement. Fink called no witnesses and did not even make a closing argument. Since he had practically made no opening statement, his defense of Hicks was limited to cross-examination, which for the most part, as we shall see, merely reinforced the testimony of the prosecution's witnesses or helped the prosecution's case. He did make a few hearsay objections, briefly keeping out a map of the area, but it was later introduced. None of his objections had any effect on the prosecution's case.

The transcripts of the cases would be crucial in more ways than for the purpose of making a record on appeal. They would be used by the defense to try to persuade Brough and his successor, Thomas McRae, that they should commute the death sentences the Elaine Twelve received.

Though the Arkansas Supreme Court would affirm the trial court on the question of whether the evidence was sufficient in this first trial, even if one accepts the testimony of individuals who may have been coerced to testify, it is debatable whether the prosecution, even with coerced witnesses, presented enough evidence to convict Frank Hicks of the murder of Clinton Lee. In the era before forensic ballistic tests, this would have been a difficult case for any prosecutor since Clinton Lee was shot from a distance too great for any of the whites to identify his attacker. Since there were no white witnesses who could testify that they had seen Frank Hicks fire in the direction of Clinton Lee, who was sitting in a car at the time he was shot, the prosecution mainly relied on two black witnesses to establish that Hicks had shot Lee.

After first establishing Lee's death through white witnesses, Andrews called George Green, who testified that he had joined the Elaine lodge only days before the violence began at the Hoop Spur church. The next morning he had been rousted out of bed and told to go to the house of Frank Moore, who was now, along with four other men, charged with "aiding and abetting" in the death of Clinton Lee and would be tried after Hicks. At Moore's house about seventy-five men had been organized into a squad and marched two-by-two to a public road that ran by the railroad. Green testified that he had been twenty yards from Frank Hicks when he had seen him fire his rifle down the road in the direction of Helena. Previous testimony by whites had established that cars had been in the road and that one of the vehicles had been occupied by Clinton Lee.

Q: Now from the point where you say you saw Frank Hicks fire a gun up the road—did you see up the road in the direction in which he shot?
A: I couldn't see nothing but cars.[14]

Solely based on Green's testimony, it is arguable whether Hicks was shooting at a human being. On cross-examination Jacob Fink helped the prosecution's case that Hicks was the only one doing the shooting by asking the following:

Q: How long before he fired—had there been in [sic] shooting in the gang before he fired?
A: No sir.
Q: In no other gang?
A: No sir, if it was I didn't hear it; that was the only shots made in the gang I was in.[15]

John Jefferson, who resided near Hoop Spur on the plantation of K. P. Alderman, testified after Green. He too said that he had just joined the union right before the violence began. And he too had been gotten out of bed in the early morning hours on October 1 and told to go to Hoop Spur:

Q: Now who was in command of that squad of negroes when they marched away?
A: This fellow Frank Moore was the fellow I heard; he was on the bridge, he—
Q: What was done with the crowd?
A: He says don't you all hear them shooting, he says come on and let's go help them people out.[16]

Since Jacob Fink called no witnesses, the question of which individuals were doing the shooting and why was never followed up. John Jefferson was much more certain about what he had seen than Green:

Q: Did you get to where you could see the automobiles?
A: Yes sir, I could see them.
Q: Before the shooting could you see them?
A: Yes sir.
Q: Do you know where Mr. McCoy's house is up the road from where the shooting occurred?
A: Yes sir.
Q: How far was it from where the shooting occurred up to the automobile?
A: I guess it is a quarter of a mile.
Q: Could you see the men up there in the automobile?
A: Yes sir.[17]

This would have been the length of four-and-a-half football fields, but Jefferson was not done:

Q: What did he did do when he raised up his gun?
A: He raised up and made one shot.
Q: Then what did he say?
A: I didn't hear him say anything; he taken down and unloaded, and he raised up again and somebody in the crowd hollered don't shoot, he says, yes I'm going to shoot, and he made the second shot.
Q: Then what did he say?
A: He says I would have got that guy if it hadn't been for that horse.
Q: Did you see anybody on a horse up there?

A: There was a loose horse in the road, between him and the car.
Q: What time of day was that as near as you can come at it?
A: I guess one or two o'clock.[18]

On cross-examination Jefferson said that he had been told to bring his gun to every meeting:

Q: What for?
A: Just told to bring it, because they was looking for trouble, looking for them to come down there and break the meeting up.
Q: Who told you that?
A: This fellow Hill. He was there that night.[19]

With his cross-examination Fink seemed to be trying to discredit the union by making it appear to be trying to accomplish its aims through violence:

Q: What did you all understand your Union was going to do?
A: I understood it was for the good—to help us out, that is what they told me in the meeting, the night I met them.
Q: Who was going to help you out, how were they going to do you good?
A: Give us legal rights and everything, and we would have justice in the law and everything.
Q: Was that the way you were going to get it with your guns and pistols?
A: No sir; we was going to get along better in this world but it might cause trouble.
Q: And then if you had any trouble you wanted to have your guns with you?
A: Yes sir. He told everyxx [sic] body to come and bring their guns to the meeting.[20]

The prosecution called a white man named Tom Faulker, who testified that he had been fifty to one hundred feet from Clinton Lee when he was shot. He said he had seen three men in the road, one of whom fired two shots. He could not identify him, nor could he give the time when the two shots had been fired.

The trial ended with the testimony of Sid Stokes, the mayor of Elaine, who told the jury that Frank Hicks had been questioned by himself, J. C. Crow, K. P. Alderman, Mr. Nelson, C. W. L. Armour, and J. M. Countiss. According to Stokes, Hicks had voluntarily told them of his involvement, basically repeating the testimony of the two witnesses as to how he had come to be on the road near the McCoy house:

Q: Who do you mean when you say he?
A: Frank Hicks. He said when he got to the road he thought he
   would just take a shot into the crowd and maybe get some of
   them and he said he borrowed Sweat Coleman's rifle to make
   the shot, and he shot once, I am not positive whether he shot
   once or twice, he said he shot into the crowd and the crowd
   scattered.[21]

Since the defense called no witnesses, the trial was over but for the
reading of the jury instructions on first-degree murder. Neither attorney
chose to make a closing argument. The next day the *Helena World*
reported that the "jury took 8 minutes to return a verdict of guilty in the
first degree against Frank Hicks."[22] The first trial had taken a total of
three-and-a-half hours from arraignment to verdict.

The judge, however, was not done for the day. He empanelled a new
jury and tried Frank Moore, Ed Hicks (the brother of Frank Hicks), Joe
Knox, Ed "Sweat" Coleman, and Paul Hall together for "aiding and abetting" Frank Hicks in the murder of Clinton Lee. John Miller personally
handled this case. John Moore and Greenfield Quarles were appointed to
represent the defendants. Based on the evidence presented in the courtroom, it is difficult to see how the Arkansas Supreme Court sustained the
convictions.

The prosecution began by establishing Clinton Lee's last moments
through the same witnesses called in the first trial. As before, none of the
white witnesses could identify the individual who had fired the shot that
killed Lee. The state then again called John Jefferson, who stated that he
had been a member of the Elaine lodge and knew the men who were
charged with aiding and abetting Hicks. Confusingly, he identified both
Ed Hicks and Joe Knox as president of the Elaine lodge. He identified
none of the other three charged as leaders in the union. Asked by John
Miller why members carried their weapons to the meetings, he responded:

A: Said they was looking for them to come down there and pick
   them up.
Q: Looking for who?
A: Looking for the White folks to come down there and break the
   meeting up.
Q: Well, what did they have their guns for?
A: They had their guns for protection, to fight with. The first night
   I went there I didn't have no gun, and they asked me who [*sic*]
   [what] did I bring to fight with and I told them I didn't—nothing

and this fellow says well a couple of fellows come here and broke us up.

Q: How many meetings of the lodge did you attend when these fellows were there?

A: I met only one meeting after I joined.

Q: Do you remember the night that meeting was on?

A: The meeting I j-ined, I j-ined Friday night before this racket come up there.

[defense counsel]: We object to any testimony two or three nights before this transaction.

Court: That will be admissible for the purpose of showing a conspiracy.

Mr. Miller: That will be the purpose of it, your honor.

Court: If they do not show that it is admissible, that is if they do not connect it with this affair, the jury will be instructed to disregard it.[23]

Conspiracy to do what? At this point, Miller had established absolutely nothing.

Jefferson then proceeded to tell the jury that he hadn't even seen Knox and Hall at the meeting he had attended. He had seen Ed Hicks, Frank Moore, and Sweat Coleman. Miller didn't ask him anything about what had happened at the meeting or what had been said. The only exchange about the meeting was the following:

Q: Did these fellows have guns there that night?

A: Yes, sir.[24]

This was the sum total of the state's evidence in this trial that there had been a conspiracy to revolt against the planters. If anything, Jefferson's testimony proved that the only purpose of carrying guns had been self-defense. None of Jefferson's testimony showed an intent or effort to "aid and abet" Frank Moore or anyone in the commission of a murder.

As in the previous trial, the state showed through John Jefferson that men had gathered at the home of Frank Moore the next morning:

Q: Now, what did you hear Frank Moore saying there during the morning?

A: I heard him say later up in the day, I guess it was about 12 or 1 o'clock: that was on the bridge in the road, he hollered for all of us to come on up there: he says don't you hear that shooting, he says come on and let's go up there and help them people out, and everybody come on up there, and he paired us all up.

Q: What do you mean by pairing you up?
A: Two and two.
Q: Who did that?
A: Frank Moore.
Q: Who was helping Frank Moore?
A: It was Frank Moore, Hicks and Knox.[25]

This answer would prove significant because this witness did not even mention Paul Hall or Sweat Coleman as "helping." When asked directly about them, all he said was that they had been present with the other men. As far as proving that any of the men had aided and abetted Frank Hicks when he shot down the road toward Clinton Lee, Jefferson's testimony proved just the opposite. Miller got the witness to say he that had seen Frank Hicks fire two shots and then asked the following:

Q: Where was Moore then?
A: Moore, he was out there in the road, too, he wasn't so far from Hicks.
Q: What was he saying?
A: I ain't heard him say nothing.
Q: But he was right there?
A: Yes sir.
Q: That was the man who led you there?
A: Yes, sir.
Q: Where was Ed Hicks?
A: He was across the road, he was over in the field.
Q: How far was he from you?
A: From the fellow that shot—I guess he was 25 or 30 yards.
Q: Where was Sweat Coleman?
A: I don't know where he was, but he was in the gang there somewhere.
Q: You know how close he was to Frank Hicks?
A: Sweat Coleman?
Q: Yes.
A: No, sir.
Q: Where was Joe Knox?
A: Joe Knox. I seen him he was on the side of the railroad.
Q: How close to Hicks?
A: He was about 15 or 20 yards from Hicks.
Q: Do you know where Paul Hall was?
A: No sir, I don't know where Paul Hall was.[26]

Again, the cross-examination by the defendant's own lawyer (though not the response) seemed designed to help the prosecution. In the first trial Sweat Coleman had been identified as loaning his rife to "make the shot":

Q: When did these fellows make up their minds to kill somebody?
A: I don't know when they made up their minds to kill somebody.
Q: Whose gun did Ed Hicks use in shooting at Mr. Lee?
A: I seen him with it when I first seen him. I ain't seen him get it from nobody else.
Q: You didn't see him get it from anyone else?
A: No sir, he had it when I seed him.
Q: Did Sweat Coleman have a gun at that time?
A: Yes sir, he had a 45-72.
Q: He didn't give that to Hicks to do the shooting with?
A: No sir, I ain't seen him give it to him, Hicks had one.[27]

Any defense attorney who had the interest of his client at stake would never have brought up the issue of a borrowed gun at this time. And the effort in cross-examination to do what the prosecutor had not done continued:

Q: Did you hear any talk about killing anybody that morning when you met there before daylight?
A: No sir. I didn't hear no one say they were going to kill somebody else.[28]

Walter Ward, another black man, testified next for the state. He testified that he was a union member and that he knew the men on trial were in the union, too. Both defense counsels let it be brought out on hearsay that Knox was vice president of the union. Ward testified that he had been awakened early on the morning of October 1 by Paul Hall. This was the first mention of Hall's involvement.

A: Paul Hall woke me and told me to go to Ed Hick's [*sic*] house.[29]

Ward then testified that once he had arrived at Frank Moore's house, Moore had given him a gun to carry. He identified Frank Moore as the leader, testifying that Moore had said that if anyone broke ranks, "he was going to turn loose on him; and if they find a man picking cotton in the field, that is where they were going to kill him at, right there."[30]

Though Ward was asked about the other defendants, like the witness before him he did not say that they had done anything at the time Frank Hicks had fired down the road:

Q: Where was Paul Hall?
A: Paul Hall was over in the field on the other side of the railroad.
Q: Where was Coleman?
A: Old man Coleman was over on the other side of the road—I don't know which side.
Q: Where was Knox?
A: Up on the railroad.
Q: What happened there?
A: Frank Hicks made two shots.
Q: How close were you to him?
A: I was over inside the field, about 10 yards from him.
Q: Who was the closest man to Frank Hicks?
A: Frank Moore was sitting down close to him as from here to that gentleman.[31]

The prosecution then put on its final black witness, Dave Archer, who testified that he was not a member of the union but had been forced to join Ed Hicks's squad that morning:

Q: How long did you stay there?
A: Just about an hour before I got away.
Q: How did you get away?
A: Hicks was pointing the way for us men to go to watch for the white people—
Q: What were they going to do?
A: He said they were going to kill the white people when they come down there.[32]

Archer worked for Sid Stokes. He testified that Frank Moore had also said that they were going to kill all the white people that came down there. Since he had run away, he had not been present at the time Frank Hicks fired down the road. All he could testify to was that the defendants in this trial had been present in the early morning.

At this trial the only white witness was J. Graham Burke, who testified that he had questioned Coleman, Knox, and Ed Hicks. This "conversation" had taken place in the county judge's office at the courthouse. According to him, each of the men had admitted to being present in the area where Hicks fired two shots. They had admitted to marching to the area.

With this testimony, the state rested its case. The defense called no witnesses, and the case went without closing arguments to the jury, which was again back within minutes with a guilty verdict.

When this case went to the Arkansas Supreme Court on appeal, the court summarily dismissed the argument that the testimony had not proved that Frank Moore, Paul Hall, Ed Hicks, Sweat Coleman, and Joe Knox had aided and abetted Frank Hicks in the murder of Clinton Lee: "According to these witnesses those appellants were all armed, and before leaving the place from which they started the purpose of going to Elaine to fight the white men found there was announced, and we think the testimony warranted the jury in finding that Hicks' act in firing the fatal shot was done pursuant to a conspiracy previously formed, which contemplated violence, and the possible killing of white men."[33]

Even if one credits the testimony of Dave Archer that Frank Moore had said that they were going to kill white men (testimony not corroborated by other prosecution witnesses), it does not implicate the other defendants. Aside from Frank Moore, it was not even alleged that the other defendants had said that they were going to kill whites. The testimony proved, in fact, that they had not done a thing to assist Frank Hicks. The prosecution, not able to prove its case, had succeeded in showing the opposite, but the supreme court of Arkansas brazenly rubberstamped the jury's decision, which had been a foregone conclusion.

Counsel made other arguments on appeal that were ignored as well. They will be explored in chapter 8.

After the November 3, 1919, conviction of Frank Moore, Ed Hicks, Joe Knox, Sweat Coleman, and Paul Hall, the race to conclude the Phillips County trials was on. Judge Jackson began the next trials at nine o'clock on Tuesday morning. If it should have been difficult to convict Frank Hicks of the murder of Clinton Lee, the case against the union members who had allegedly killed Will Adkins should have been twice as difficult, since the shooting at the Hoop Spur church took place in the middle of the night. The men standing trial for murder for this crime were two of the guards outside the Hoop Spur church, Alf Banks Jr. and John Martin. William Wardlow was originally to have stood trial with them, but the prosecution changed its mind and tried him the next day as "aiding and abetting" in the murder.

As mentioned earlier, it has long been debated why Will Adkins, Charles Pratt, and Kid Collins were parked outside the Hoop Spur church when the shooting began. In its early accounts, the *Helena World* reported that their car had broken down at the church. In the paper's report of the trial of Banks and Martin, the reporter, J. R. Miles, wrote that the three had been on their way to Elaine to arrest a bootlegger: "As they reached a bridge near Hoop Spur something went wrong with their car, and they stopped by the roadside."[34]

In fact, Charles Pratt, a deputy sheriff, would start the trial with a potentially damaging contradiction of these earlier reports under questioning by John Miller:

Q: Why did you stop [at Hoop Spur]?
A: We stopped the car. . . . Mr. Adkins was driving the car, and we came to the bridge, right up to the bridge, and right up to the bridge I called Mr. Adkins' attention to it and I said let's go around the side of the bridge instead of going over it, and he says very well, we will get out and take a leak.[35]

The significance of the contradiction lies in the fact that any defense attorney able and willing to do his or her job would have raised self-defense on behalf of his or her clients. Any contradiction as to why law enforcement had appeared in the middle of the night at the church would have been a potential weapon in the hands of competent counsel. As it developed, W. G. Dinning, the appointed counsel for Banks and John Martin, did not even request that Jackson instruct the jury that if the men were acting in self-defense, the jury could acquit them. Nor did he object to the judge omitting such an instruction. Though an instruction on self-defense would have made no difference to the jury, this argument would have been properly preserved for appeal.

Pratt, surprising no one, testified that possibly a dozen blacks had approached them and fired first, killing Adkins and wounding himself in the knee. He was not able to identify anyone, and once again the prosecution was forced to rely on black witnesses to identify Martin and Banks as two of the guards who had killed Adkins.

The first black to testify was John Ratliff, who admitted that he had been to three union meetings but said he was on his home from the meeting because Robert Hill, the union's principal organizer, was supposed to be there and had not shown up. Ratliff, who then claimed to have been leaving the meeting to go coon hunting, said he had seen flashes from their guns:

Q: Where from?
A: Looked like to me from every which a-way, you couldn't tell whether them on that side or them on that side started it, but it was all around.[36]

Whether intentionally or not, John Ratliff with this answer had placed the prosecution in a precarious position. Since he had said that he couldn't tell who had started the firing, his answer could cast doubt on others who followed him. As the defense counsel had the day before, however, Dinning rescued the prosecution about midway through his cross-examination:

Q: Who were the three men that passed the car and then came back?
A: Alf Banks and the two Becoe boys.
Q: And they were the ones who started the shooting?
A: Yes sir.[37]

Whatever his motive, Dinning seemed to be trying to establish that Ratliff had been too far away to see John Martin that night, but in his questioning he implicated his other client, Alf Banks. If that in fact was his strategy, there was a serious conflict of interest in his representing both Martin and Banks at the same time. In any event, with his question and Ratliff's answer, Dinning undermined his clients' argument that they had fired in self-defense. As before, no closing argument would be made on behalf of either.

Two other blacks, Sykes Fox and Joe Michon, were called to testify against Martin and Banks, but in fact the most damaging testimony was again from J. G. Burke, who said he had been part of a committee that had interrogated both men in the county judge's office. He said that both men had confessed to firing three shots each at the automobile.[38]

John Martin took the stand in his own defense:

A: Well, I was there that night, they put me out to guard, and I didn't much want to go out there and they told me I had to go, well I went. When the shooting come off I was down under the trestle about 50 yards from that bridge, from the car, and when the shooting come up, I didn't shoot narry one until mighty nigh the last, I made air shots, and the reason I made air shots I was under an obligation not to rebel against anything like that, I had to make them air shots for a sham; I was scared they would kill me if I didn't.[39]

Martin claimed he had been ordered to shoot by Ed Ware, who was still at large.

Alf Banks did not testify. The jury was out for nine minutes. Both men were found guilty as charged.[40]

The trials of Albert Giles and Joe Fox for the murder of James Tappan, near Yellow Banks plantation just outside of Hoop Spur, got underway shortly before noon. Again, John Miller represented the state. Greenfield Quarles represented Giles and Fox. Originally, Milligan Giles, the fifteen-year-old brother of Albert Giles, had been indicted for Tappan's murder. Why he was dropped from this particular prosecution is not known.

The first witness was Herbert Thompson, who testified that he had led a group of ex-servicemen on the morning of October 1 on a search for blacks thought to be in the Hoop Spur area. Thompson said that the men in his group, as part of the larger posse from Phillips County, had approached a thicket near a bayou, where blacks were known to be hiding. He testified that he had called in a loud voice for them to surrender and they wouldn't be hurt. If they didn't, Thompson and his men would come in and get them. Miller asked Thompson the following:

Q: Did you speak those words loud enough for them to carry any considerable distance?
A: I would say that it could easily have been heard 125 yards.[41]

Whether anyone hiding in a thicket could have understood these words (assuming that they were actually spoken) at this distance may have been a moot point to the individuals hiding there: they had no faith in the word of the whites. Thompson stated that the only answer he had received was a shot from a rifle. Between five and fifteen minutes later, according to Thompson, James Tappan had been shot in the face and neck and taken to the McCoy house, near where Clinton Lee had been shot. Miller asked what weapon had been used:

A: To me it appeared to be buck-shot.

Miller then called to the witness stand two physicians who had seen Tappan before he died. Dr. O. Parker testified that he had found both shot and a rifle ball in Tappan's face:

Q: You know whether it was a pistol ball or from a rifle?
A: No sir, I couldn't say.[42]

Dr. J. B. Ellis also testified that he had attended Tappan as he was dying:

Q: Did you make an examination of the wound to see the nature of it?
A: Some of the wounds were so large . . . there were two or three larger than a buck-shot, but most of the wounds looked about the size of buck-shot.[43]

At no point did any of these three witnesses establish that Tappan had been shot with a pistol. This evidence should have been crucial because of the testimony of the next witness, Alf Banks Jr., whose appearance must have surprised the spectators in the courtroom, since he had just been convicted as one.of the guards outside the Hoop Spur church along with John Martin. He now testified that he, Joe Fox, Albert Giles, Milligan Giles, Jim Miller, Arthur Washington, and another man whose name he didn't know had been in the thicket together when the soldiers came:

Q: What was your business in there, what were you doing there?
A: You see I run up on this gang, I had been looking for my father and they stopped me at the little bridge right at the little thicket. Jim Miller he was placing them all about, telling them which a-way to get, he said the white people was coming; me and Jim Miller first went together.

. . . .

Q: Alf, did you see the white men when they came down there?
A: We never seed them, but we heard them talking . . . when they started on across [an opening in the thicket] Joe Fox and Washington started to shooting at them, and afterwards Albert shot that way with a double barrel shot gun and it jumped all to pieces, it jumped from the stock, and he jerked out his 32 special pistol and went to shooting it, but Joe Fox was shooting a 38 Colts pistol; when he shot this fellow that had on this striped shirt, I was looking right at this fellow when he fell, and this boy [Joe Fox] made five shots with this Colts.[44]

Later in his testimony, Banks said that Joe Fox had told him that he had killed two men:

Q: Who did you say killed one?
A: Joe Fox, I know he killed one, but after we got in the corn field he said he killed both of them.
Q: He said he killed one coming this way and the other from the corn field?
A: Yes sir. One was coming across the corn field; both of them was coming across but they wasn't together, one was away from the other about as far as from here to the door. Well, the tall one, I saw him, Joe Fox shot him down, and after he shot him down, well he run back to me, his pistol had gone to snapping, wasn't but one bullet left in it.
Q: What kind of a pistol was that?
A: It was a 38 Colts. Then he run back to me.

Q: What kind of a pistol ws [*sic*] it that this other fellow had?
A: Albert Jiles [*sic*] had a 32 Special.
Q: Do you know how that gun of Albert Jiles [*sic*] was loaded?
A: No sir, but I know when he shot through the cotton field, the barrel jumped off the stock and he was trying to get it back on the stock and he couldn't get it like he wanted, and he jerked out my pistol and he shot right over my side, powder or something hit me in the eyes.[45]

The testimony of Banks at this trial is suspect, even before one considers the allegations he later made that he was tortured and forced to testify against his fellow defendants. The whites reported only one death resulting from this incident, that of James Tappan. Thus, Banks's statement that Joe Fox told him that he had killed two men is not credible. Had there been another member of the posse killed, it surely would been reported by the group of men from Phillips County. In addition, as noted before, the whites, including two doctors, did not note that Tappan had been killed with a pistol. Assuming Albert Giles's shotgun stock came off his shotgun the first time he fired it, there was no evidence that either Giles or Fox had fired anything but a pistol.

Both Fox and Giles testified in their own defense. In some respects Fox confirmed some of Banks's testimony:

A: I was there, Jim Miller told us to go in the thicket; there was a woman come running down there and told us the white folks was coming, and Jim Miller told us to go in the thicket and we went in the thicket, he scattered us around in there, he told us if they didn't bother us don't bother them, let them go by, and the white people started to shooting a little before they got to us . . . this white fellow what got killed when he come in the bushes.[46]

Fox claimed that Washington, Jim Miller, and Alf Banks had shot six or seven times, knocking the white man (apparently Tappan) off his feet. He said that he had shot no one.

On cross-examination, however, he admitted to having fired a "pistol 38 Colts":

Q: Who was you shooting at?
A: I wasn't shooting at nobody, when the fellow started to shooting, when Miller told us to shoot, I held my pistol up and shot four times.[47]

Upon further questioning he implicated himself further:

Q: You shot just to show he [presumably Tappan] was coming in there?

A: No, sir, the reason I shot they was hollering shoot, shoot, this fellow Washington, and Banks and Miller, telling all of us to shoot, and I was down on my knees, I had my pistol laying across that way; I shot four shots.

Q: When did you hear Albert Giles shoot?

A: I don't know, sir, I couldn't tell whether he was shooting or not on account of the fellows on the other side of where he was shooting. Albert was next to Jim Miller's house.[48]

Albert Giles was lucky to be alive. The *Helena World* reporter described his court appearance for the paper matter-of-factly: "Giles, with a bullet hole in each side of his head, and an arm wrapped in splints, was very nervous when he took his place on the witness stand. He claims to have been hit with a rifle bullet on the right side of the head, the bullet coming out near the left ear."[49] As the others had, Giles tried to blame Jim Miller, who at that time was still at large:

Q: How come you to get into the thicket?

A: Jim Miller ordered us to.

Q: Why did he tell you, what authority did he have?

A: He was head of the lodge, the Secretary of it; he told us the white people was coming and kill everybody.[50]

Giles claimed he had never fired a shot. According to him, he had fallen unconscious and had awakened hours later and then walked out of the thicket to a house that afternoon. Given his wounds, that account is possible.

Q: Who commenced the shooting in the thicket down there?

A: It commenced from the people on the outside, they shot before they ever got to us.

Q: Did you shoot your gun?

A: No sir, I didn't make narry shot.[51]

However unlikely it may be that Fox fired into the air, there was no evidence introduced at the trial that Tappan had been killed by a pistol. Given the defendants' circumstances, it would not have been surprising for them to have fired at Tappan, just as it seems likely that Alf Banks and John Martin at some point fired at the men who came upon the church at Hoop Spur. Tappan may indeed have been killed by Fox and Giles.

However, the proof of this arguably fell far short of what was necessary for a murder conviction that could withstand appellate review. Apparently, what was assumed throughout, as the trials progressed, was that none of these defendants had a right to defend himself. It was given that these men were part of an insurrection and had to be hunted down. So long as they admitted to belonging to the union, no proof was apparently needed that they had broken a law and thus forfeited their right to self-defense.

Certainly no proof was offered. It is not evident from the *Helena World* that after the opening statement in the trial of Frank Hicks the prosecution even mentioned the insurrection theory during the rest of the trials. Because opening statements and closing statements are generally not reported in trial transcripts, one has to rely on what is reported in the press. Since the prosecution apparently had no proof to offer of an insurrection plot (the trial of Ed Ware, who was captured and tried a couple of weeks after the others, would be the only exception), it can be assumed that the *Helena World's* failure to mention such a plot as part of the prosecution's opening statements, after the Frank Hicks case, means that the prosecution was no longer talking about insurrection in opening statements

Immediately after the trial of Fox and Giles, Jackson assembled another panel, and the trial of William Wardlow got underway. As mentioned previously, the prosecution had decided to charge Wardlow with "aiding and abetting" in the murder of Will Adkins. Given the testimony of the prosecution's witnesses, it is easy to understand why Charles Pratt, who had testified in the trial of Alf Banks and Joe Fox, returned to the stand and responded to questions about the shooting that killed Adkins:

Q: Which volley was it that killed him?
A: The first, he didn't know what hit him.[52]

As before, Pratt, who had been injured, did not identify any one of those who were doing the firing.

The next witness was a black man named Dave Hays, who testified that he knew Wardlow and had had a conversation with him the day after the shooting. On direct examination by John Miller, Hays said that Wardlow had told him he had been in the shooting the night before. On cross-examination by L. A. Semmes, the following exchange took place:

Q: And he said he fired a shot?
A: Yes sir.
Q: Did he show you how he held his gun when he made that shot?
A: In that position. (Illustrates)

Q: Almost straight up?
A: Yes sir.
Q: And he told you he fired his gun one time.
A: He fired his gun, he said he held it in that position.
Q: Did he say he was shooting at any body?
A: No sir, he didn't say he was shooting at nobody.[53]

Alf Banks appeared again to testify and said he had seen Wardlow firing his gun:

Q: Where was he when he first saw him?
A: He was in the road coming right direct up to the bridge and had a double barrel shot gun, and John Martin was with him. He emptied his shot gun, and he had a little bright handled Smith & Wesson pistol with no hammer and he jerked this pistol out and emptied it.
Q: Which direction was he pointing this pistol?
A: Right toward the car.[54]

On cross-examination it quickly became apparent why Wardlow had not been charged with killing Adkins:

Q: How long after the first shot was it before you saw William?
A: When the first shot fired, in about five minutes him and Martin come past.

. . . .

Q: There were at least 100 shots fired in the direction of the deceased before you saw William Wardlow?
A: Yes sir, about that many any how.

. . . .

Q: As a matter of fact Adkins was killed and dead before you ever saw this defendant make a shot, wasn't he?
A: Yes sir.[55]

On re-direct Banks amended his testimony to say that he didn't know if Adkins had been dead:

Q: You know whether Mr. Adkins was dead before they shot him or not?
A: I don't know, but he was lying down.
Q: And the shooting began just as soon as these fellows came up there and couldn't give the pass word?
A: You are right.[56]

Semmes, who appeared to try at times to do his job as a defense attorney, then asked a series of questions that should have made it clear to the jury that Wardlow had no authority in the union:

Q: Did this defendant ever give any orders?
A: I didn't hear him give no orders.
Q: He was not one of the leaders in the lodge?
A: No sir.
Q: And he was not an officer in the lodge?
A: No sir.
Q: He had nothing to do with the management of the lodge?
A: No sir, all he had to do was to follow their commands, when they told him what to do he went and done it.[57]

It of course made no difference to the jury that John Miller had proved absolutely nothing that connected Wardlow to the death of Adkins. It was enough that he had been there and fired his gun. The jury was out for two minutes before returning a verdict of guilty of first-degree murder.

As had surely been hoped by the bar in Phillips County, the eleven convictions made an impact on the remaining defendants. In many of the cases, the only point of a trial was to invite a death sentence. On November 5, the morning after Wardlow's conviction, shortly before ten o'clock, the defendants began pleading guilty by the dozens. The *Helena World* reported, "In accord with rumors the pleas of guilty began to come thick and fast, lasting until 11 o'clock, up to which time 24 negroes had been sentenced to serve 5 years in the State Penitentiary on 2nd degree murder charges."[58] Three other defendants pleaded guilty that morning, making a total of twenty-seven, including a fifteen-year-old boy, Milligan Giles, the brother of Albert Giles, who had been convicted of first-degree murder and thus sentenced to die in the electric chair. Milligan Giles was given a five-year sentence for the second-degree murder of James Tappan and then accepted an additional five years for attempting to commit the murder of Ira Proctor, a posse man who had been wounded. "Giles showed no sign of emotion and took his sentence very much as a matter of course," reported the *Helena World*.[59]

John Miller was not pleased with the sentences being handed out by Jackson. The *Helena World* reported his dissatisfaction:

It was at this time [11 o'clock] that Hon. J. E. Miller, Prosecuting Attorney for this District, arose and stated to Judge Jackson that with all due respect and deference to the court he felt that the prisoners had been given too short a term in the penitentiary. He later announced that indictments had been returned against all the prisoners sentenced this morning for nightriding, and he would later arraign them on this charge. The maximum penalty for nightriding is confinement in the penitentiary for some period of time, not to exceed five years. Whether the negroes will enter a plea of guilty to this charge has not been learned, but it is understood the majority of them will so plead.[60]

Whatever moved John Miller to protest these sentences can only be a matter of speculation, but it had the desired effect. In the afternoon Jackson began imposing the maximum sentence for second-degree murder. The *Helena World* reported that of ten blacks arraigned in the afternoon and pleading guilty to second-degree murder, nine drew sentences of twenty-one years each and one was to serve five years.

The haste with which Judge Jackson acted in taking the guilty pleas became embarrassing on the afternoon of the November 5, when it was discovered that John Jefferson, charged with first-degree murder, had already pleaded guilty in the morning. The *Helena World* reported that, "Jefferson was in the crowd of the negroes who were given 5 year sentences this morning."[61] At this point Jackson slowed the process down slightly, saying that he wanted to investigate the cases of twenty-seven blacks who were ready to appear before the court on the charge of nightriding. Forty-eight men had pleaded guilty in one day.

Among those who were sentenced on November 5, some familiar names appear. George Green, Walter Ward, Sykes Fox, and John Ratliff had testified against the Elaine Twelve.

The afternoon session was expected to be prolonged by the decision of a group of blacks that morning to demand a trial after they had initially agreed to plead guilty to the charge of assault with intent to commit murder. Nineteen of them, from the Lambrook plantation, had come to the Hoop Spur area to join up with Frank Moore's group. They had been notified by one of the so-called Paul Reveres, who had been dispatched to tell them that the union was under attack at Hoop Spur. John Miller told the court that "the prosecution would be able to show that these negroes all went to Frank Moore's house armed and that they had contact with the posse, firing several shots at them. He also stated that the Prosecution would be able to prove that this band of Negroes had determined to kill Mr. B. J. Cunningham of Helena. In conclusion, Mr. Miller asked the court to give each of them who pled guilty at least 10 or

15 years, saying that the evidence in the case would warrant such a penalty."[62]

As it developed, one of the trials reported on by the *Helena World* involving a black defendant from the Lambrook plantation resulted in the only acquittal of an individual during all the prosecutions. The *World* reported on November 6 that a black man named Cornelius Morgan had demanded a trial, contending that he was unarmed during the march to Hoop Spur and while he was there. Jackson appointed R. B. Campbell as counsel for Morgan, and thus began the only trial in which members of the jury panel were excused. The paper reported that "over an hour was consumed in the selection of the jury. The defense excused a number of jurymen, while the prosecution only excused one."[63] Brief opening statements were given. J. R. Moseby represented the state. Apparently, no evidence was presented by the prosecution regarding Morgan, and Jackson, at the request of Campbell, directed the jury to acquit. While six others pleaded guilty to night riding and three others were tried and found guilty on November 6, this acquittal may well have had an effect on Miller's decision to dismiss charges against ten other blacks on November 7 for lack of evidence.

It will never be known how many blacks were innocent and pleaded guilty out of ignorance or fear or how many would have been acquitted had they been defended aggressively. By Friday, the *World* reported that sixty-five men had been convicted. Twelve would be continued over for the next grand jury. Jackson accepted a plea from Sam Wilson of second-degree murder for the killing of Corp. Luther C. Earles, the Army's only fatality. Wilson would have been tried, but an alleged eyewitness from the contingent of soldiers could not be present, and thus Miller agreed to a plea bargain. The seven blacks who acted as "Paul Reveres" were given one-year sentences for the crime of night riding.

The one big trial remaining was that of Ed Ware, who had been apprehended in New Orleans. Ed Ware was perhaps the most prosperous of the Elaine Twelve. Not only did he own and farm his own land, he hired himself and his Ford out as a taxi service. Because he could read and figure, he had been chosen secretary of the Hoop Spur union. He clearly had no chance. "Not before yesterday has the prosecution presented a more clean-cut case of murder in the first degree," crowed the *Helena World* the day after Ware's trial, on November 17.[64]

Since the transcript of Ed Ware's trial has been lost, the *Helena World* must be relied upon for an account of the trial. The prosecution had a new star witness; Suggs Bondsman appeared in the trials for the first time. He had previously been identified in the *Arkansas Democrat* as "Sugg Bondman," one of six leaders of the union who had been captured with Frank Moore before noon.[65] He claimed, however, that he had "slipped" into a board meeting where "Ware with other members of the Elaine lodge, were putting down names of white men at Elaine on a piece of paper and then after they were read off a vote would be taken by them as to whether they were to be killed or not. Among those who were to be thus murdered were J. N. Moore, J. M. Countiss, S. S. Stoaks [*sic*], and a number of others."[66] Bondsman, whose name does not appear in the list of blacks either released for lack of evidence or found guilty, portrayed Ware as one of the primary leaders of the union movement: "He said Ware went there [Elaine] to show the Negroes at that place 'how he run his lodge at Hoop Spur."[67] During the board meeting it was Ware who "was heard several times to remark 'I am 'fraid there are some snitches and white mouths in this bunch, and we had better be careful as to what we say while they are here.' It was then that all the members of the lodge were dismissed and the Board members went into session."[68]

Who Bondsman worked for and what induced him to testify will remain a mystery, since the *World* does not report any questions asked of him on cross-examination. Whoever he was, it must be said that Bondsman was certainly a convenient witness, having just happened to have overheard Ware tell the Elaine lodge how he ran things at Hoop Spur and to have overheard a crucial vote being taken that indicated a plot. Unexplained in the article is why Ware would have been permitted to be present and vote at another lodge's meeting. Unmentioned too is the fact that the Hoop Spur lodge had its own president, who presumably ran its affairs. Ware's words concerning any of this are not reported by the *World:* "When Ware was placed on the stand, he was plainly nervous. He was quite willing to talk but continued his tactics of 'beating around the bush' before he would answer the questions asked him by the prosecution. When asked why he left Phillips County, and assumed the name of Charles Harper, he said, 'I thought these people would kill me if I stayed here."[69]

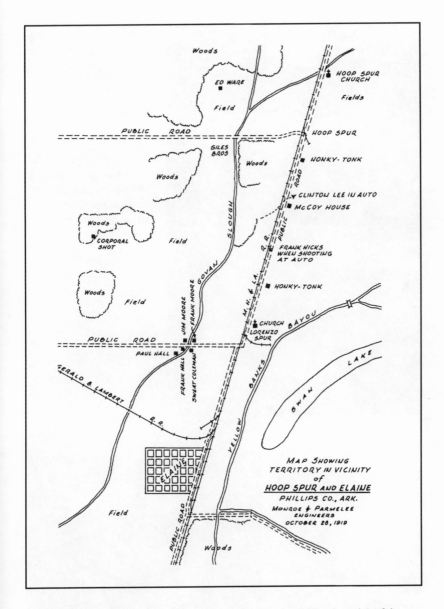

The map that was introduced into evidence at the first trial (of Frank Hicks) of the Elaine 12 by the prosecution in November 1919. *Courtesy of Butler Center for Arkansas Studies, Central Arkansas Library System.*

John E. Miller, prosecutor of the Elaine defendants, who later became a congressman and then a federal judge. *Courtesy of Butler Center for Arkansas Studies, Central Arkansas Library System.*

Ulysses S. Bratton, former Republican state legislator, assistant U.S. attorney, and postmaster of Little Rock, had agreed to represent black sharecroppers in the Elaine area to gain better settlements for their cotton. *Courtesy of Virginia Lee Crossier.*

Ocier S. Bratton, oldest son of U. S. Bratton, was taken prisoner by Phillips County authorities after meeting with sharecroppers on the morning of October 1, 1919. *Courtesy of Virginia Lee Crossier.*

Louis S. Dunaway, author of the 1925 *What a Preacher Saw through a Keyhole in Arkansas,* which alleged that 856 blacks were killed in Elaine. *Courtesy of Butler Center for Arkansas Studies, Central Arkansas Library System.*

Walter F. White, NAACP field secretary, and later head of the NAACP, came to Arkansas to investigate the massacres and was nearly lynched. *Courtesy of Butler Center for Arkansas Studies, Central Arkansas Library System.*

Scipio A. Jones, defense lawyer and son of a southern Arkansas planter and his house slave, ultimately gained the freedom of all the men who were convicted in Phillips County. *Courtesy of Butler Center for Arkansas Studies, Central Arkansas Library System.*

The *Helena World* reported that the prosecutor Andrews "entered witness after witness who had seen Ware at the church the night W. A. Atkins [*sic*] was killed. Some who had seen Ware fire his rifle three times, one who had seen him lying on his stomach behind a log with his rifle pointed toward the automobile in which Atkins [*sic*] was killed, and Charles Pratt severely wounded, and one or two witnesses who had been placed on guard outside the church by Ware with instructions to 'shoot anything white you see, whether it is a dog or a man.'"[70]

Not a single witness for the defense, other than the accused, had testified in any of the previous trials of the Elaine Twelve, and the *World* article would have surely commented on the fact if witnesses had appeared for the defense in the Ware case. Any minimal defense of Ware would have shown that Adkins had most likely been killed by one of the thirty or so guards outside the church in the first volley of shots, as was admitted in the Wardlow case. By the time that Ware (and any others inside the church, for that matter) would have picked up a weapon and gotten outside and begun firing, Adkins was already dead, if the testimony in the trials of William Wardlow, Alf Banks, and Joe Fox has any meaning. Even if it was proved that Ware had killed Adkins, Ware could have argued self-defense. As mentioned earlier, there was no credible reason for Adkins and the others to have been out at the Hoop Spur church at that time of night. Just as there were too many coincidences and holes in Suggs Bondsman's story (and he reappears in chapter 10, this time subject to vigorous cross-examination), it strains logic to think that the trip out to Elaine when there was a union meeting going on nearby had come about by sheer chance.

There were many arguments that could have been made for the defense in the cases of all of the Elaine Twelve. Other than his calling Ware to the witness stand, whether L. A. Semmes tried to show Ware's innocence is doubtful. What is clear is that any effort wouldn't have made a bit of difference.

As he had done for the others, Judge Jackson set the date for Ware's electrocution. Now there were twelve executions planned for late December and early January. Justice had been served.

CHAPTER 8

Colonel Murphy for the Defense

The Governor saw that I had him in a box.
        —*Letter from Ulysses Bratton to the NAACP, December 5, 1919*

November 1919
New York

As sour as his life had become in Arkansas, Bratton was a star in New York. The national office of the NAACP had invited him to come to New York to consult with it about Arkansas peonage, and once Ocier Bratton had been released from jail and was out of Phillips County, his father wasted no time in getting there. He arrived by November 5. Bratton probably didn't realize it at first, but he was being auditioned as soon as he walked in the doors of the NAACP's headquarters in the middle of Manhattan. He was an instant hit. Here was an articulate Southerner who knew the truth about the South and now was anxious to tell it to the NAACP and its supporters. "'What makes it so immensely interesting is that we have testimony from a Southern white man . . . it is very wonderful to have a southerner who is such a splendid radical on this matter [peonage]," Mary White Ovington, the chairman of the board of directors, wrote contributors.[1]

Bratton's first assignment in New York was to write a long letter to the Justice Department describing how peonage had worked in the past and was employed in the present. As a white former assistant U.S. attorney who had prosecuted peonage cases in the Delta and had then had ongoing cases as a private lawyer, Bratton had credibility that no other Arkansan could or would supply the NAACP. It was his precise description and firsthand examples of peonage that would be used over and over by the NAACP in a variety of ways to persuade the public outside of Arkansas and ultimately the United States Supreme Court that blacks had legitimately organized against oppressive conditions in the Arkansas Delta and had not engaged in an idiotic scheme to kill whites. In a long letter dated November 6, he wrote about his lengthy involvement with the system that existed in Arkansas. This letter bears extensive quotation here because of Bratton's intimate knowledge of the subject. Regarding the time that he spent serving in the U.S. attorney's office, beginning in 1897, Bratton notes:

> At that time it came to our knowledge in the southern part of the state that a condition of peonage was being practiced whereby the colored people were being held under the pretense that it was a violation of the law for them to leave their landlord while they were indebted to them, and the landlord, having absolute control over the situation—both the charging and the price-paying end of the products raised by the Negroes—always saw to it that at the end of the year, instead of the Negro having money come to him, he received a statement showing "balance due"; this being the only statement that he ever received, never being permitted to have an itemized statement of his account or anything of that character.
>
> Under the directions of the Department of Justice, an investigation was had which established the fact that these conditions existed to a very large extent. The persons were indicted, entered pleas of "Guilty," and paid heavy fines for thus violating the law. This resulted in breaking up of the open system of peonage, but another system followed in its wake, which an investigation will show to exist throughout the entire "black belt" of that country, which is this:
>
> The planters have inaugurated a system among themselves whereby one of them in any particular locality will refuse to take a Negro tenant or share-cropper from the plantation of another person as long as the Negro is indebted to the other person, unless the taking planter is willing to pay whatever indebtedness the planter on whose place the Negro is located claims that the Negro owes him. In this way the system of peonage is as effectually practiced as it was under the old system, and, (excuse the suggestion) in my judgment an investigation will show that under the law as complete a system of peonage is maintained in that country now as it was prior to the prosecutions as I mentioned in the outset.[2]

Bratton's letter goes on to describe his perception of what occurred if a black decided to leave his employer. He was not permitted to take anything, nor was his family. Bratton wrote that he knew of situations in which "fictitious" charges had been made against blacks in order to prevent them from leaving.

The possibility of obtaining an itemized statement is unthinkable with those who are engaged in so dealing with the Negroes, and an investigation will show that this system of dealing with them prevails in a large majority of cases.

When the crop is gathered, the Negro is permitted to haul it to the gin. From that time he has nothing more to do with it than a rank stranger. The cotton is ginned, and such part of it as they see fit is put into the bales which are theoretically to be accounted for to him. The landlord proceeds to take the cotton at whatever price he sees fit. Less than two [weeks?] ago a Negro was in my office who had cotton which was selling at $.53 and .54 a pound in the market. The landlord told him that he would only allow him $.43. This landlord declined to allow him to take samples of the cotton and get bids in the open market; but reserved to himself the absolute right to take the cotton at an arbitrary price to be fixed by himself.

These conditions have resulted in the Negroes, in large numbers, coming to us in an effort to get relief, and we have attempted to obtain relief for them and have been able to obtain judgments in the courts in some of their cases. It having been known that we did not hesitate to take their cases, they have come to us from distant parts of the state.[3]

Bratton backed up his "testimony" with letters he had received from clients whose lives had been devastated by the practices he described. "These fiew lines is in the respect of thim things that i writen to you about on May 20. Sir what i want to know is this what will you get my things for what is the charges on thim. My wife went and ask for thim and he told her wasent goint to give her a thing and she had to leave thim down there. It is getting cold now and we need our things he took all of our house good and our hogs 4 head of hogs i have had so much of sickness until i coulden get up there But please send me word at once what you can do for me," wrote Arthur Henderson of Gould to Bratton on August 30, 1919.[4]

Walter White had been right about Bratton. Now Ovington and the entire staff of the NAACP knew that Bratton could provide the kind of details that made involvement in the Elaine cases attractive to supporters. The question of whether planters were routinely cheating black sharecroppers was at the heart of the economic debate about the conditions that existed in the South generally. Bratton also described the inflated prices that his clients had to pay. One client had to pay $3.50 for a pair of "sea-grass plow lines." Forty cents, he said, was a fair price. One had to pay eight dollars for a sack of oats. In Little Rock the highest retail price was five dollars.

The work of Bessie Ferguson shows that prices charged on credit in Elaine were substantially higher than cash prices. For example, work shoes cost $2.50 if the buyer had the money. If not, the shoes cost $4.00.[5] At a minimum, the credit price was usurious, since the Arkansas Constitution set the interest limit at 10 percent. Such economic exploitation cut across racial lines, but because the Arkansas Delta was so heavily black, this was a natural issue for the NAACP.

With his firsthand knowledge of the facts and his sense of outrage, Bratton was perfect for the NAACP's fundraising campaign. If the NAACP was going to defend the Elaine Twelve, it would take a substantial sum of money, and with execution dates being set in December, there was no time to lose. In the two weeks Bratton was headquartered in New York, Mary White Ovington and the staff of the NAACP had him on the go constantly. For Bratton's own safety, his dealings with the NAACP had to be kept a secret from his Arkansas enemies. Thus, Ovington arranged confidential meetings in the homes of wealthy supporters such as Mrs. Henry Goddard Leach of New York City. Bratton traveled to Boston and Philadelphia to tell his stories of exploitation, again in private venues. He also journeyed to Washington, D.C., with Walter White to meet with the Justice Department and sympathetic members of Congress.[6]

Bratton was not only good for information and fundraising, but he also knew the lawyers in Arkansas. On November 14 the NAACP's anti-lynching committee met in Boston at the home of Moorfield Storey, a former president of the American Bar Association. The committee recommended legal action and agreed that Bratton should recruit a law firm in Arkansas to bring it. His choice would have to be approved by the board of directors.[7]

Bratton recommended George Murphy, a former Confederate colonel who even at the age of seventy-nine was recognized as one of the best criminal defense attorneys in the state. Lecturing part-time at the Law Department at the University of Arkansas, Murphy, it was claimed, "could have rewritten the entire first volume of Greenleaf on Evidence from memory." Since Murphy had been the attorney general for the state of Arkansas from 1901 to 1905, his reputation had been established for years. Yet he was more than a good lawyer, having once run for governor on a third-party reform ticket. Months later, Bratton would write John Shillady, "Col. Murphey [*sic*] is one of the most courageous and noble men I have ever known."[8]

By November 24 the deal with Murphy had been made, and the board met in emergency session to ratify it. Murphy was to get three thousand dollars and incidental expenses and be responsible for representation of all the blacks convicted in Phillips County if necessary, up to but not including the United States Supreme Court.[9]

Bratton's view of the African American bar in Arkansas and, in particular, of Scipio Jones is not known, but the NAACP's attitude toward Southern blacks did not escape class bias. In the *Chicago Daily News* article describing his investigation in Phillips County, published on October 18, Walter White, seeking to counter reports of an insurrection, wrote that Hill "is an ignorant, illiterate country farm hand."[10] In fact, though Hill was not educated, he was neither stupid nor illiterate, and in the course of the next year he would write several letters, including some to the NAACP.

The NAACP did not routinely trust black lawyers either, preferring to use white attorneys as local counsel. When Thomas Price, Scipio Jones's law partner, initially contacted the NAACP for assistance in the cases, James Weldon Johnson, who would replace Shillady as executive secretary, wrote the executive director of the Memphis NAACP in order to check out Price: "You can see that there is a possibility of come [*sic*] colored lawyers going of [*sic*] on a tangent to raise money and, of course, to figure in the cases, thereby messing up the whole matter."[11]

The choice of a well-known white attorney to represent blacks in a criminal case of this nature (involving charges of insurrection and murder) would have made tactical sense to Bratton and the NAACP alike. White juries in the South would naturally have been hostile to a black attorney when the deaths of whites were involved. In criminal cases, the art of cross-examination is a major tool for the defense, and Southern white judges, given the prejudices of the day, would not have given the same latitude to a black attorney whose case required that the credibility of a white witness be impeached.

December 1919

While the NAACP may have followed Bratton's advice in hiring the colonel, it wasn't averse to asking someone else to watch him. In the above letter to Robert R. Church of Memphis, James Weldon Johnson asks him "to undertake the task of keeping a check on Colonel Murphy as best you can. . . . Will you write us a confidential letter telling us what you know and what you can find out about Colonel Murphy's standing as a man in the state and as a lawyer, and as to his attitude toward colored people?"[12]

At the same time, the NAACP was playing cat and mouse with its own Little Rock affiliate and with the partner of Scipio Jones. Johnson continues his letter to Church by informing him that he had heard from a Thomas J. Price, who was asking for assistance in helping the men convicted in Phillips County:

> Mr. Price, I think, is a member of our Branch at Little Rock. We have judged it best for Mr. Price to know that the Association has already employed Colonel Murphy, but we do not wish to say this in black and white because, as you fully understand, the Association wishes to keep its hand hidden in this matter until we get results. We feel certain that if the people of Arkansas knew that we were raising funds to set aside the verdicts already rendered by the courts of Arkansas, there would be aroused opinion on the part of the public, if not on the part of the courts, which whould [sic] be prejudicial to the cases of the men on trial. We do not want Mr. Price to "gum up" the case. We do not know how good a lawyer he is. But if Colonel Murphy wishes Price or any other lawyer to associate with him on the case, that is all right with us.[13]

The arrogance of the NAACP notwithstanding, this was an equally busy time for Scipio Jones and for others in the black community in Little Rock, who also saw it as their responsibility to try to save the Elaine Twelve. Price's letter to the NAACP in late November stated that he and Scipio Jones had begun to work on the cases of the men slated for execution. Besides themselves, "the firm of Murphy and McHaney (white) are in the case with the understanding that a fee can be raised."[14] Price asked for ten thousand dollars.

In an undated letter to Ovington (probably from late November), Bratton, who was at this stage surely acting with Murphy's knowledge and was also involved in the defense of the convicted men, wrote: "I went over there and made an investigation and was very fortunate in being able to have a conference with the wives and mothers of all the accused. Their story was heart rendering to say the least. Attorney Jones had them there on that very day to have a conference as to evidence. I had a talk with Attorneys Jones and Price, and I found from their conversation that they are not aware that the National Association has advanced any money or contracted for the same. They are associated with Colonel Murphy in the case and from their point of view the association is harmonious. I inquired particularly as to Mr. Murphy's interest in the case and they claim he was employed by Mr. Bratton and themselves."[15]

What Bratton meant by this last phrase is unclear, but it seems likely that Scipio Jones and the black legal community knew that Murphy was already on the case and had approached him to work with them. In his letter to Ovington, Bratton mentions that he was told that Murphy was already getting paid out of a fund the black community had started. The administration of this fund would become formalized in January. In the beginning, Arkansas blacks would raise more money for the defense of the Elaine Twelve than the NAACP.[16] Further, Bratton mentions a meeting at the governor's office that a number of leading blacks had attended, at which Sheriff Kitchens had assured Scipio Jones that he would not be hindered in his attempts to get information. Jones, Bratton said, had already gone to Phillips County and was satisfied with his ability to conduct his own investigation. By the end of November, then, Scipio Jones and his partner, Thomas Price, had begun to work with Murphy.

However the first meeting between Scipio Jones and Colonel Murphy came about, in the eyes of the black community in Little Rock the defense of the men convicted in Elaine was a local effort, with regards to not only the money to support it but also the talent. From the amount of work they did and the money they raised from the very beginning, Scipio Jones and the black community saw the colonel and his law firm as necessary partners, but only as partners. To be successful in the defense of the Elaine defendants, Scipio Jones knew that white allies would have to be involved. Scipio Jones and Thomas Price obviously realized from the beginning that the NAACP had hired Murphy. However, the black community in Little Rock felt that *it* had enlisted, if not employed, the colonel to work with them. The significance of this local effort has never been fully understood or recognized. It was an important indication of the strength and vitality of the black community in Little Rock and of its desire and ability to protect the interests of blacks throughout the state.

As merely one marker of the extent to which Scipio Jones was already involved with the Elaine defendants, he had already met with Brough. Almost as an afterthought, Bratton, in his letter to the NAACP, drops what surely was welcome news to the staff and board: "The governor has informed the Attorney [Jones] that he is willing to commute sentences to imprisonment of all the accused with the exception of one."[17]

The battle for the soul of Charles Hillman Brough was underway.

If whites were putting pressure on Brough, so were blacks, and not just a group of polite blacks from the middle-class black section of Little Rock. Brough claimed to have received angry letters from blacks threatening dire consequences if the twelve blacks were executed. In public Arkansas blacks might support Brough, but they were upset by Elaine—which became a jumping-off point for other long-held grievances—and expected him to listen. They had a laundry list that included lack of political representation, Jim Crow laws, all-white school boards overseeing their schools, inferior schools, and even "the attentions of the lower class of white people to negro women. . . ."[18]

Brough did listen, up to a point. His initial plan was to convene a meeting of black and white leaders in the "reception room" at the state capitol on November 24. It is tempting to be cynical about Brough's motives in calling this meeting, but one has to remember that this was the first time in the twentieth century when large numbers of blacks (all men, apparently) were asked to come to the state capitol to do anything but clean it up. Brough had his own agenda, of course. The *Arkansas Gazette,* on the morning the conference was to meet, suggested that one of its probable accomplishments would be that "steps will be taken by the conference to answer the attacks made in the newspapers of the north and east against the whites of the South."[19] This could have only come from Brough, who surely was still seething inwardly over his deception by Walter White.

In his initial remarks to the conference, Brough was reported by the *Gazette* to have said that the "conference was primarily a heart-to-heart discussion of race differences. The governor said relations have become strained during the past few months. He emphasized the Phillips County affair, which he branded as a 'damnable insurrection.'"[20] Brough told the gathering that he was "on the ground [in Elaine] the day after" and knew what had happened there: "He said he did not need any assistance."[21] This curiously defensive remark about not needing assistance suggests a man whose armor was sealed vacuum-tight. If there had ever been a time in the almost two months since the massacres that Brough had woken up in the middle of the night and let himself think about the actions of the white mobs and soldiers, it was well behind him: "Governor Brough commended Sheriff Frank Kitchens and the white residents of Phillips County for the manner in which they broke up the insurrection. He said the matter could not have been handled more wisely."[22]

The emperor was wearing no clothes, and there was no child present to raise the point. None of the blacks present stood up and responded that the governor was a liar. Why? For the first time in the century, black men were being treated almost as equals (though ever so briefly), and it was too much to expect that those present would become immediately confrontational with the governor who had invited them to participate. When Brough brought up the topic of Elaine, it must have caused the kind of anxiety that makes hearts pound and bowels weaken. But he said what everyone wanted and needed to hear before the conference could go forward: nothing horrible had happened. On the contrary, whites had responded magnificently and the sheriff had risen to the occasion. Now that the main issue was off the table, there were problems that could be discussed so long as everyone tiptoed around the corpses in Phillips County. The trials of the Elaine blacks, for one. Brough was not prepared for the anger that spilled out from the blacks during the morning session as they detailed their grievances. In typical fashion, that afternoon he appointed a more manageable biracial commission of eight blacks and eight whites—adding himself as the chairman to ensure white dominance—to study the problems of blacks in the state.

Brough, of course, was not about to pick any blacks for the commission who would call for radical change or make radical charges. Thus, he appointed men he knew he could rely on, including college presidents James Monroe Cox and Joseph A. Booker and Bishop J. M. Conner, all of whom had signed the letter of support in October. Other black appointments included Pastor E. C. Morris from Helena and Scott Bond of Saint Francis County, probably the richest black man in the state. The white members were typically sympathetic conservatives—for example, John Hugh Reynolds, president of Hendrix College.

Cox later would claim that "we have discussed the Elaine trouble again and again and the Negro members have expressed fearlessly their views concerning the whole affair."[24] To a man, Cox said, none of the black members believed that there had been an insurrection or that the trials had been fair. He did not write that blacks had been massacred or that not a single white person had been arrested, nor did he write that not a single black person had confronted the governor with these facts.

Though the commission would accomplish little, the body did pass unanimously a resolution endorsing the view that the cases should be appealed to the Arkansas Supreme Court. This was no small achievement, but as was usual when dealing with a handpicked conservative body of Arkansas blacks, Brough was able to ignore the larger issues such as the failure of the white power structure to arrest a single white man in Phillips County despite the deaths of black citizens like the Johnston brothers. His biracial commission was a reprise of the commission that Brough had headed in 1914. Its objectives were lofty: "Justice before the law, including the prevention of lynching and other denials of legal justice to the negro."[25] In theory, the plan sounded like nirvana. In practice, predicated as it was on total white control, the commission accomplished nothing. In truth, no governor before Brough would have even bothered to appoint a biracial commission. Typically, blacks everywhere were then appointed to auxiliary commissions that were allowed to offer suggestions to the white commissions, which held the power. Appointing blacks at all to a commission that had white members implied a measure of equality that was unheard of in Arkansas or elsewhere in the South. Bishop Conner pronounced the initial meeting on November 24 a success: "The Negroes of the state express themselves as absolutely satisfied with the explanation of the governor regarding his position, and believe his position is safe and sound. They have expressed confidence in his leadership. Everything said at the conference leads me to believe that the whites and negroes will better understand each other in the future and less friction is sure to follow."[26]

As much as it infuriated the advocates of equality outside the state to hear it, Charles Hillman Brough was the only game in town. The idea of a biracial commission sounded so appealing that even a man as sophisticated and outspoken as Ulysses Bratton fell for it. On December 5, he wrote Mary White Ovington, "I think you will be interested to know just how I am planning to put Gov. Brough and his Committee on record and make them show just what can be depended upon from them." He then described taking a black man up to the governor's office:

> He has raised a crop worth $3600. The landlord insists that his indebtedness will consume it all and still declines to give him a settlement, itemized statement of account or anything of the kind. The negro is afraid to return home without some kind of protection or relief. Now Governor, what is this man to do under these circumstances.
>
> The Governor saw that I had him in a box. After a little hesitation, he inquired of me as to what I thought of putting it before his Racial Committee which meets on the 15th. I fell into his suggestion readily. . . . In that way we are going to make the committee know the facts.[27]

In fact, nothing came out of the biracial commission, and Bratton grew more disillusioned than ever.

The focus of the NAACP and Arkansas blacks would always be on the Elaine Twelve. This was the only battle they could possibly win. The first order of business for the colonel and Scipio Jones was to prepare motions for new trials for the twelve men. These motions, they knew, would be routinely denied by Jackson, but they were a precondition to appeal. At this point in the association between white and black attorneys in the defense of the Elaine Twelve, Scipio Jones and other black attorneys who worked with him were very much junior partners. Because of his reputation and expertise the colonel had no equals, white or black. Yet Murphy would have respected the legal ability of Scipio Jones if for no other reason than Jones had beaten him in *Castleberry v. State*, which had raised the issue of jury discrimination. That issue, more than once, would be raised again.

The colonel's forte was the courtroom, not necessarily constitutional law. It was said of him that he was a genius at drawing inferences from the evidence favorable to his client that other lawyers missed and at presenting them to the jury. Like many great trial attorneys, he also was a showman. Injured in the battles of Shiloh and Murfreesboro, he was said to have "exaggerated his limp many times to gain sympathy for his clients from the jury. He is also reputed to have had a trick watch with a hinged cover which he would open at a strategic moment during a trial. The inner workings of the watch would fly all over the courtroom, naturally drawing the jury's attention away from the prosecutor's summation while Col. Murphy searched the room for all the pieces."[28]

Yet as good in the courtroom as he was, the colonel, perhaps trying to placate the sensibilities of the bar in Helena (he certainly did not want to offend Judge Jackson), made a tactical error almost immediately after taking on the cases. Acknowledging publicly his entry into the case, he told the press that though he wasn't yet up to speed on the facts: "From what I can gather no exceptions were made and no witnesses were summoned for the defense. *Able lawyers were appointed to defend the 12 men,* I am informed, but the trial was held in the same county where the uprising is alleged to have occurred and there seems to have been a great deal of excitement and possibly prejudice. I am in favor of granting the 12 men every possible chance before the law."[29]

In giving this statement to the press, Murphy indicated that he had already made up his mind that he was not going to directly attack the performances of the attorneys appointed to represent the Elaine Twelve. This was a mistake that would come back to haunt the defense.

Preparing motions for new trials was labor intensive in those days, before word processing and copying machines. At least the Elaine Twelve were no longer in Helena, having been transported on November 22 to "the Walls"—as the penitentiary then outside of the city limits of Little Rock was unofficially called—to await execution.

Each of the motions was identical. Their thrust in general was that the defendants hadn't gotten a fair trial. The motion for Frank Hicks alleged "that the excitement and feeling against the defendant among the whites of said county was such that it was impossible to obtain an unprejudiced jury of white men to try him—and that no white jury, being fairly disposed, would have had the courage to acquit him, regardless of the testimony."[30]

The facts supporting the allegations that a mob atmosphere had prevailed during the trial were disturbingly scanty in these pleadings. The Franks Hicks motion stated that Clinton Lee had been killed

> in a deadly conflict following a disturbance between the white and black races. . . .
>
> That at the time of the returning of said indictment said excitement and bitterness of feeling among the whites of said county, against the negroes, especially against the defendants, was unabated and still at the height of intensity.[31]

There was an allegation that a mob would have stormed the jail had not United States troops prevented it, but there were no allegations concerning the behavior of Helena residents during the trial.

The motion in the Frank Hicks case set forth in general terms that no witnesses had been called, that the case had gone forward without any preparation, and that no evidence had been submitted on his behalf. It alleged that he had been tortured but provided no specifics.

Attached to each motion were the affidavits of Alf Banks and William Wardlow. It is in these affidavits that the specifics of torture first appear. After reciting that he was put in jail with more than a hundred other blacks, Banks swore:

> I was frequently whipped with great severity, and was also put into an electric chair and shocked, and strangling drugs would be put to my nose to make me tell things against others that they had killed

or shot at some of the shite [*sic*] people and to force me to testify against them. I had not seen anything of the kind, and so told them, at first; but they kept on, and tortured me so'that I finally told them falsely that what they wanted me to say was true and that I would testify to it. They would have me blindfolded when torturing me. Once, they took me up-stairs, put a rope around my neck, having me blindfolded, pulled on the rope, and one of them said, 'Don't knock the trick out yet, we can make him tell,' or words to that effect. . . . During the trials, at one or two of them, they took me from the jail to the Court-room to testify against them; I think it was the trial of Joe Fox and Albert Giles, and I think also against one or two others. As they were taking me to the Court-room, they told me if I changed my testimony or did not testify as I had said, when the [*sic*] took me back, they would skin me alive.[32]

Banks alleged that generally blacks were used to torture him. One of them was Kid Collins, the trusty who had accompanied Adkins and Pratt to the Hoop Spur church the night of September 30.

The affidavit of William Wardlow was similar in content. Neither man was literate, and they signed their affidavits with marks. Both affidavits were signed on December 18, just two days before the hearing on the motions for new trials in Helena (thus accounting for the excessive number of typographical errors). They were notarized by J. R. Booker, one of the attorneys helping Scipio Jones.

Other legal arguments included the absence of negroes on the grand and petit juries: "[F]or more than thirty years it has been the unbroken practice of said courts to appoint only white men on such commissions, and of such commissioners to select only white men for grand and petit jurors for the succeeding terms,—constituting a discrimination in the administration of the law against the negroes, on account of their color and of their being members of the African race."[33]

Though both Scipio Jones and the colonel journeyed to Helena to file the motions and to appear at the hearing to ask for new trials, the decision to deny them had already been made. The state wasn't even expected to respond to the motions. Jackson entered orders denying them the same day they were filed—December 20. He granted the defense sixty days to perfect an appeal to the Arkansas Supreme Court. As promised, Brough issued a stay of the executions to allow an appeal, which was docketed on January 9, in the Arkansas Supreme Court.

CHAPTER 9

The Retrials of the Ware Defendants

The South has always been the negroes' best friend. . . .
     —Charles Hillman Brough

January–March 1920
Little Rock
    Until Robert Hill's capture in Kansas on January 20, Brough had every reason to be generally pleased with the way the public was reacting to the insurrection at Elaine and the state and local response to it. Except he wasn't.
    He couldn't muzzle the *Crisis* or the *Chicago Defender,* but criticism from Northern black publications, while infuriating, was only an irritant. Blacks inside the state had supported him. His biracial committee was functioning. An article on November 14 in the *Arkansas Gazette* by a white Methodist minister, A. C. Millar, from Little Rock, had gone a long way toward straightening out the story of what had really happened in Phillips County. Reverend Millar had attended the trials, investigated the facts, and concluded, "In Phillips County there was a deliberately planned insurrection of negroes, which, if it had not started prematurely, would have resulted in the wholesale slaughter of the whites in the vicinity of Elaine and an attempt to take possession of the property of the white owners."[1] In Millar's version, D. A. E. Johnston, along with Robert Hill, had been the mastermind of the union. Millar had preached to the blacks. They were now penitent, admitting that they had been "grossly deceived and misled by their own crafty leaders."[2]
    All that was remaining was the supreme court's review of the cases. If the court affirmed the convictions, as it was expected to do, Brough would have to decide whether to commute the sentences. The appeal had bought some time on that decision. He knew he would get pressure to commute the sentences. He already had, if Bratton's letter to the NAACP is correct; Scipio Jones had already been to see him.
    Almost equally as important to him as Arkansans' view of the riots

was the fact that much of the rest of the country also seemed to have the proper perspective on the riots. Clare Kennemore, a reporter for the *New York World,* had come south and conducted his own investigation, and his November 16 article had captured the events perfectly. Brough couldn't have written a better headline himself: 11 NEGROES TO PAY FOR THE GREED OF ONE. (Ed Ware had not yet been convicted.) Kennemore had listened to the planters, to the Committee of Seven, to the Helena American Legion, to the Phillips County bar: "Prompt and vigorous action of citizens and soldiers has left no trace of the trouble, and serious men, who hope to prevent a recurrence, wonder whether the sore has been cured or its virus driven inward to reappear elsewhere. One of the reasons for fearing a recurrence is that the principal germ, Robert L. Hill, by name, has not been isolated."[3] In Kennemore's view, the South was, well, the South. As the "ruling race," whites "accept the responsibility and they manage the affairs. They care for the negroes in their employ, advance them money a year ahead of crop time, advise them, manage for them and govern them. It is the custom of centuries, and whether good or bad is not for me to say."[4]

Here was the kind of newspaperman Brough had thought he was getting when Walter White had shown up in his office and so shamelessly deceived him. If people wanted to know the real Robert L. Hill, all they had to do was read Kennemore's article: "Robert L. Hill was projecting around trying out his powers over his people, and on the lookout for some way to make a living without working. The southern part of Phillips County was just made to order for him."[5] It was all there: how Hill had set up the lodges, bamboozled ignorant darkies, and then set up his final scheme: "By September, Hill had dealt out sensations to the union members so liberally that it required some pretty strong stuff to furnish the needed thrill, so he told them it was getting close to time to strike. He told them of the army of 500 trained men he had at Winchester, which was going to help the Phillips County negroes when the time came. He told them to pick the white men who were to be the first to die."[6] When the fighting was over, fifteen or twenty blacks had died, and the ringleaders were put on trial: "The leading members of the bar and the officers of the law all believe that the evidence was such as would have convicted the men in any court in the country."[7]

Poor Robert Hill. Judging from his letters while he was in hiding, all he wanted to do was come home and tell his side of the story. Beginning in November he began writing a series of letters asking for help—to

Bratton, Thomas Price, the NAACP, and even the chief executive of the state of Arkansas. The *Arkansas Gazette* reported on December 1 that he had written the governor saying that he would come back to Arkansas if he got a fair trial and if the money being offered for his capture went to his family.[8]

On November 26, he wrote the NAACP:

> I am a detective on the case for the farmers in Phillips Co., and hope you all will get up for my help. Course we didn't have anything to do with the trouble. I was only rendering legal service, I was helping out the Bratton law firm on others on the case. Mr. Bratton was expected down Wednesday morning, October first and the people met Tuesday night somewhere about Hoop Spur in Phillip [*sic*] County and the trouble started. We come to Ratio, Arkansas, six or eight miles from where the trouble had started. . . a crowd of armed men come up and arrested Mr. W. L. [*sic*] Bratton and I fled for my life. . . . After they found I was detective helping the law firm they charged me for inciting trouble. It was a fact that the people could not get statements of their accounts and their cotton was being shipped and the custom in that section was the landlord would take the cotton and seed and ship them away and didn't ask them no odds and the people had decided to put their money together and get legal help. . . . I can't say how the shooting started but it shows the Negroes were harmless, they went back into the wood according to Newspaper that says the soldiers had to go into the Cone Brokes [canebrakes] and get them. Please get up at once for my help because if they get me, they will kill me, just like they are doing, sentencing all leaders of the Union to death they say that blacks was planning to kill whites. Course the union was in about 25 or 30 counties, and it seems that it would be awful foolish for me to go to Phillips County only to plan killing whites of that county.[9]

Hill's letter to Bratton asked for help and denied any evil intent: "They are trying to accuse me of inciting that trouble but Dear Sir I didn't even dream of such a thing."[10]

Although asked by Hill to keep his letter to him confidential, Thomas Price sent it on to Walter White, explaining that he had advised Hill to make his way to the offices of the NAACP in New York. Hill, who at one time had been in an all-black community in Boley, Oklahoma, went to South Dakota before ending up in Kansas. He never made it to New York.

Picking up Robert Hill in Kansas and returning him to Arkansas for trial on state murder charges should have been a routine manner. After all, Robert Hill also faced federal charges for impersonating a federal officer (his badge said "U.S. detective"). As if to accomplish some poetic justice, Deputy Sheriff Charles Pratt was dispatched to bring back Hill, only to find out that the authorities wouldn't turn him loose.

The titanic struggle over the extradition of Robert Hill back to Arkansas had begun. The legal machinations that ensued in Kansas have been exhaustively covered in Richard C. Cortner's superb constitutional study, *A Mob Intent on Death: The NAACP and the Arkansas Riot Cases.*[11] The battle to extradite Hill foreshadowed the difficulty the white power structure of Arkansas would encounter over the Elaine affair once it had to deal with forces outside the state's borders. When it became clear that a legal challenge was shaping up, the honor of the state was involved to such an extent that Attorney General John Arbuckle personally went up to Topeka for the hearing on January 27 in order to bring Hill back. He returned empty-handed. Henry Allen, the governor of Kansas, had granted a postponement of the hearing in order to give Hill's attorneys an opportunity to prepare to rebut the evidence given by Arbuckle.

Upon his return on January 28, Arbuckle noted the large number of blacks at the hearing and the bitter feeling against the state of Arkansas, but was confident of eventual success. After all, Governor Allen had said, "Kansas cannot be recognized as a mecca for negroes fleeing from Justice."[12]

What Arbuckle didn't know was that the NAACP was already gearing up for an all-out effort to keep Hill from returning to Arkansas and, not incidentally, to continue to expose the conditions of peonage in the state and by implication the entire South. Upon the recommendation of U.S. senator Arthur Kapper, from Kansas, John Shillady secured the services of the Topeka prosecuting attorney, Republican Hugh Fisher, who was about to make a run for the state senate. Seeing votes and a popular target, Fisher agreed to work for nothing but expenses. Following the pattern of the Arkansas cases, three black attorneys from Topeka worked with Fisher: James Guy, Elisha Scott, and A. M. Thomas, all members of the Topeka NAACP. Now that he had a postponement until March 22, Fisher, with the national NAACP's guidance and assistance, set about gathering the information that he needed to convince Governor Allen not to return Hill to Arkansas. As they had in November, once again the NAACP turned to Ulysses Bratton.

An embittered Bratton by this time had given up on Arkansas and left the state. First he had relocated in Saint Louis for a short time, apparently associating himself with the Brotherhood of Maintenance of Way Employees and Railroad Shop Laborers, and then he had permanently moved to Detroit.[13] The decision to leave the state could not have been easy for a man as proud as Bratton. He felt he had been driven out. In a May 11 telegram to John Shillady, to be used by the NAACP in the extradition fight, he explained: "Open threats that if I dared go into certain portions of state to represent clients would be killed. Clients intimated [*sic*] rather than take my life in my hands and be murdered or quit practicing law and for protection of my family necessary to leave state."[14]

Bratton, who must have felt like an exile, was eager to help. In a letter dated February 10, Fisher wrote John Shillady, starting off by saying that what he was about to tell him was so confidential that he hadn't told the lawyers working with him: "I received a letter from Mr. Bratton from Detroit, suggesting that I have Governor Allen listen to his story and he would come to Topeka if necessary. He further suggested that Governor Allen send an investigator to Arkansas and that he would assist in seeing that the expense was paid."[15]

Rather surprisingly, the governor of Kansas agreed to meet with Bratton and Hugh Fisher alone, the only other person present an unnamed clerk. Fisher wrote Shillady on February 13:

> No one in the City of Topeka aside from the two men mentioned know he has been here. I told the other lawyers the substance of his talk but did not intimate that it was Mr. Bratton. I will expect you to keep this matter secret as I pledged Mr. Bratton my word that the matter would not be released to anyone.
>
> I put Mr. Bratton on the same train that Governor Allen took, going to Kansas City, and the Governor said he would talk with him further on the train.[16]

This off-the-record chat between Bratton and Allen may have been crucial. Bratton was in a unique position to tell the governor of Kansas about the union and its purposes. As it so happened, Allen was interested in farm tenancy, and on this point, he undoubtedly got an earful from Bratton. He also was visited by James Weldon Johnson, who came away encouraged by his interview.[17] What neither Bratton nor Johnson could tell Allen was whether Hill had *ever* encouraged union members to resort to violence. Hill himself would have to testify about that.

In fact, the NAACP was going to need all the help it could get with the governor of Kansas, because three black members of the executive committee of the governor's biracial commission had just joined with the white members in signing a letter to Allen on February 2 calling for Robert Hill to be returned to stand trial in Arkansas. Not surprisingly, the three were Cox, Booker, and Conner, who had all joined with Scipio Jones in October in publicly writing of their support to Brough: "The citizens of Phillips County and the Governor have assured us that Hill will be guaranteed a fair trial and the right to change of venue. We believe the return of Hill is in the interest of justice to the negro and will materially strengthen this biracial commission in the work of promoting interracial justice."[18]

Short of Robert Hill now saying that he thought he could get a fair trial, it was hard to imagine a more severe blow to the NAACP's extradition fight. If the leading blacks in Little Rock were saying that a Negro could get justice in Arkansas, what was all the fuss about? "I was satisfied that we would be successful before the Governor until I saw this statement," wrote Fisher to Walter White.[19] There would be nothing else in the Elaine affair that would so effectively highlight the differences between middle-class blacks in the South and their Northern counterparts. The reaction from the *Chicago Defender* was one of stinging, almost hysterical denunciation. Calling the three men "rattlesnakes" and "animals," the *Defender* raged, "The names of Conner, [Cox] and Booker henceforth will be as a stench in the nostrils of self-respecting men and women and they should be shunned as a pestilence and hated as traitors of a type that would have made Benedict Arnold blush with shame."[20]

The NAACP could not afford to be quite so vitriolic, since these same men were helping to raise thousands of dollars to defend the Elaine Twelve, but the staff was horrified by this show of support for Hill's extradition. Why would these men who had lived in Arkansas all their lives under a judicial system that included no blacks—with such disastrous results for their race—be willing to trust whites now?

Cox tried to answer that question in a letter to William Pickins of the NAACP: "Yes, I signed the petition to Governor Allen for the return of Robert L. Hill, signed it of my own accord and knowing at the time that I would be criticized by many Negroes who live in Arkansas and by many who do not live in Arkansas. . . . Not a Negro on the commission believes that the Negroes got a fair trial, not a Negro believes that Mr. Hill's order was organized for the purpose of killing white men and taking their property. In our meetings we have discussed the Elaine trouble again and again and the Negroes have expressed fearlessly their views concerning the whole affair."[21]

Once again, it came down to unwavering faith in Brough: "Mr. Hill, if returned, will get a fair trial, he will not be molested. Governor Brough is one of the fairest executives in the country. The leading Negroes of Arkansas believe in him and he believes in the Negroes in Arkansas. The trial of Hill will bring to light facts touching the Elaine trouble that ought to be known and facts that will materially affect the case of the condemned men."[22]

It was Cox's sincere belief that the biracial commission would be able to save the day for the Elaine Twelve. He wrote that he, Booker, and Conner had spent four hours interviewing the Elaine Twelve and planned to go to Helena to conduct their own investigation: "We shall insist also that the white members of the commission go and interview the men that are in the penitentiary. If they see what we saw and hear what we heard, in case the supreme court fail to grant a new trial, we will be able to lay facts before the governor that will weigh mightily in our plea for pardon, and my word for it, the white members will support us to the man."[23] Cox pointed to his thirty-four years in education and said that he knew the conditions in the state: "In nearly all sections the most friendly feelings exist between the races."

He claimed that the blacks on the committee had talked to all the "leading Negroes" in Little Rock, and with just two exceptions, they had supported their action: "Attorney T. J. Price, who knows as much about Mr. Hill's order as any other man in the state and who is Mr. Hill's representative, thinks it best for him to return. Attorney S. A. Jones, who is making the appeal to the supreme court for the condemned men, believes Hill should return. . . ." Cox concluded by saying that he believed in the "good people of Arkansas" and believed that somewhere in the state, a black could get justice. If Arkansas were such a "regular hell," he said, then "we would be the biggest fools possible to remain here."[24]

Of course, Arkansas was not a "regular hell" for the black elite in Little Rock, so long as they accepted white domination. They had depended on white support and approval all their lives and weren't going to change now.

Was it true that Scipio Jones supported the return of Robert Hill? There is no evidence to suggest that he didn't. Though it may dismay civil rights advocates and historians who want to see in Scipio Jones an early militant who saw clearly that Arkansas was indeed a "regular hell" for blacks, his entire career before this point and afterward suggests that Cox's letter fairly represents his sentiments. Above all, Jones was a pragmatist. As a lawyer, he would have wanted Hill's testimony in case of a retrial of the twelve men (hopefully in a different venue) or to try to convince Brough that there had been no planned insurrection and that thus he should commute the sentences. For his entire career, he had gone to the white man when there was trouble. He would do so again and again.

Somewhat curiously (since it would have affected a possible retrial of the Elaine Twelve), Colonel Murphy did not appear to be at all involved with the Robert Hill extradition proceedings. Yet he would have been concentrating on the briefs and oral arguments to be presented to the Arkansas Supreme Court in March. In any event, there is no evidence concerning his position on the matter.

There was much to be done in Arkansas to get ready for the extradition hearing. Hugh Fisher needed the help of Arkansans, and he got much of it from another black lawyer. "Most of the help we received in the way of affidavits and depositions came through Mr. Hibbler," Fisher wrote the NAACP.[25] "Mr. Hibbler" was John Hibbler, who had joined with Scipio Jones and the others in writing the letter expressing support for Brough. Though Scipio Jones carried the primary load in the black legal community throughout the Elaine affair, Thomas Price, J. R. Booker, and John Hibbler did important work as well: "It was he [Hibbler] that appeared at the taking of the testimony of the witnesses at the penitentiary and it was also his efforts that procured a certified copy of the constitution of the Farmers and Laborers Household Union of America."[26]

Scipio Jones agreed to represent Robert Hill on the federal charges if it should come to that. First, there was the hearing. If Allen sent Hill back to Arkansas to stand trial as an accessory to murder, the federal charges would be irrelevant.

Once the state of Arkansas got an inkling of the fight that the NAACP was making, it got itself in gear. The issue, Brough said, was stopping violence, not prohibiting legitimate activities of blacks to organize. "The authorities of Arkansas, both local and state, will take steps at any time to suppress any organizations arming its members to take possession of land belonging to bona fide citizens, who are guilty of sending out incendiary propaganda, or plan murder of both whites and blacks who have the courage to combat this very dangerous type of Bolshevism," he told the *Arkansas Gazette* on March 16. Despite the bellicose tone of this statement, Brough also promised "competent counsel, and change of venue, if necessary."[27]

The night before the hearing Topeka blacks came together en masse and passed resolutions against the extradition of Hill. The hearing began the next day at 2:00 P.M. in the Topeka courtroom of the Kansas Court of Industrial Relations, which was packed with blacks. From Arkansas appeared Attorney General Arbuckle with his witnesses, which again included Charles Pratt and Sheriff Kitchens. It was the South against the North, but instead of being led by the likes of Robert E. Lee, the former Confederate side made do with one of its least savvy generals. Arbuckle was easily flustered and stupidly insensitive to his surroundings, referring to blacks as "niggahs," which caused considerable resentment, according to a local paper's account the next day.[28]

His primary evidence was material from the trials, but Robert Hill undercut it by acting as a good witness for himself. As he had been explaining for months, he had had nothing to do with the violence. He recounted what had happened on the morning of October 1. He had been with O. S. Bratton, "helping him to sign up about 30 contracts with negroes to start legal proceedings to get an accounting on their cotton."[29] It was one thing to answer questions from your own lawyer, but quite another to be cross-examined by a hostile one. Inexplicably, however, the attorney general refused the opportunity to cross-examine Hill. Though the hearing went on until two in the morning, it was over when Arbuckle failed to challenge Hill on a single point.

Governor Henry Allen tersely announced the next afternoon that the state of Kansas was refusing to extradite Robert Hill. He didn't provide reasons.

Predictably, Brough and many in the state were furious. Brough should have been angry. The state of Arkansas had been publicly humiliated and shamed. Now it wasn't just black radicals and their sympathizers who were questioning the justice system in Arkansas. It was a fellow governor, a white man who should have accepted the solemn promise that the state would provide a fair trial. Doubtless, Brough took Allen's refusal personally. Allen's rejection was a slap in the face. If Brough could have offered to duel Allen, he might have. Instead, he said that Robert Hill was "universally recognized as having been one of the leading spirits in the whole damnable conspiracy to murder white citizens and take possession of their property" and accused Allen of playing politics.[30]

If the governor of the state felt this way, why would anyone have expected Robert Hill to get a fair trial in Arkansas? Surely, the governor's black supporters in the state had to have been chilled by these words. If anything demonstrated that the NAACP had been right to mount the battle to keep Hill out of Arkansas, it was this reaction. Furious, Brough once again blamed the "northern press" and "other radical negro-phile publications."[31] This was Brough at his most pompous, but he believed every word of what he said: "The South has always been the negroes' best friend. . . ."[32] If anything, this public slap hardened Brough. To take a different posture after this toward the Elaine Twelve might have been construed as an admission that he, Arkansas, and the South were wrong. He was still the governor and would be until January 14, 1921. Certainly, this was a victory for the NAACP and Robert Hill. But the blacks who knew Brough best, among them Scipio Jones, must have wondered if in fact Governor Allen's action was not another nail in the coffins of the Elaine Twelve.

In fact, with the federal charge hanging over Hill's head, he was not out of danger; once he was back in Arkansas, he could be charged with state crimes. But nimble lawyering on Fisher's part and a sympathetic federal judiciary in Kansas eventually resulted in the charge being dismissed. As long as Robert Hill stayed in Kansas, he was going to be safe.

Robert Hill would be safe but not the Elaine Twelve, and certainly not the six who would later come to be known as the Moore defendants. On March 29, 1920, the Arkansas Supreme Court handed down its decisions.

One by one the court knocked down the arguments made by the colonel and Scipio Jones. Defense counsel had not raised the issue of racial discrimination in the grand and petit juries in a timely manner. How the court expected that error to have been raised in a timely manner, given defense counsel, was not explained. However, as stated earlier, the colonel had conceded this issue. "It is admitted, however, that eminent counsel was appointed to defend appellants, and no attempt is made to show that a fair and impartial trial was not had, except as an inference from the facts stated above," stated the Arkansas Supreme Court in *Hicks v. State*.[33]

The United States had not yet ruled that this specific guarantee of due process applied to state court proceedings, yet this issue could have been argued, and given the actual performance of most of the attorneys, it would have made it much more difficult for the Arkansas Supreme Court to have concluded that the defendants had enjoyed due process of law. At a minimum, an incompetence of counsel argument would have skewered the court's reasoning that the defendants had waived such issues as jury discrimination.

The reasoning in the other cases of the Elaine Twelve was the same, with one exception. In the briefs and at the oral argument the week before, the colonel, arguing the kitchen sink—as lawyers call the shotgun approach of making all the arguments, strong or weak, one can think of—had thrown in one more: Judge Jackson had failed to require the jury to state specifically on each verdict the degree of murder. This was required by law, the colonel had told the seven members of the supreme court.

In fact, it was plain as day. The jury had failed to specify the degree of murder in six of the cases—of Ed Ware, Will Wardlow, Albert Giles, Joe Fox, John Martin, and Alf Banks Jr. This technicality (everyone in the state over the age of six knew that each jury had intended to convict each defendant of murder in the first degree) was enough. The court found that previous cases had held that a remand for a new trial was required where the "verdict was so defective that no judgment could be entered."[34]

From this point on, Murphy and Jones would deal with two separate sets of cases: those of the Moore defendants, whose convictions had been upheld and who again faced execution, and those of the Ware defendants, who were getting a new trial. The consequence for the Moore defendants was that Brough could set new execution dates at any time, and the governor was angry. If Brough had once said privately that he would commute the sentences of all but one of the twelve, that commitment had been made before the governor of Kansas had rejected his solemn promise that Hill would get a fair trial. It would be back to square one in persuading the governor to commute the sentences.

The "best and brightest" of all Arkansas governors could have reacted to Allen's decision by engaging in some genuine soul-searching. Perhaps it was time to question the criminal justice system in the "Wonder State" as it pertained to its African American citizens. Though he may not have intended it (Brough was far from a real demagogue), Brough's reaction to Allen's decision was a signal to the rabid racists in the state. Hate mail from Arkansas rained down on the governor's office in Topeka, thus confirming the decision he had made in March. When a black man was lynched in Kansas in April, Brough couldn't contain himself and again demanded Hill's extradition, despite his earlier outburst that Hill was guilty.

Allen, who perhaps had not stated his reasons at the time for not allowing Hill to return in an effort to avoid embarrassing Brough and the state, now did so publicly in a letter to the *Arkansas Gazette:* "The immoderate messages I have received from Arkansas before the hearing and the tirades since the hearing, convince me that the temper of that community made it impossible for anyone to guarantee a fair trial." He added that he regretted that Brough had seen his decision as a "discourtesy to yourself or to your state."[35] Republican politics, huffed the *Arkansas Gazette.*

For the NAACP staff in New York, the extradition proceedings had raised further questions about the reliability of working with Scipio Jones and the colored community. The "best Negroes" had supported Brough, thus demonstrating how thoroughly they were in denial about what conditions were like in Arkansas. And in truth, it was a mutual nonadmiration society. Yet just as Brough was the only game in town, so too were the "best Negroes," since, as mentioned earlier, they had raised more money than the NAACP. And if the NAACP staff had worries about Scipio Jones and what he was doing on the case, their fears should have been allayed by a letter from Monroe Work of the Tuskegee Institute, who had conducted his own investigation of the massacres. He wrote John Shillady on April 19:

> I note what you state relative to Mr. Scipio A. Jones. I have had some knowledge of conditions and affairs in Little Rock before the Elaine trouble arose. The best information which I have supported by my own personal investigation is that Mr. Jones is an able lawyer and is the heart and center of the defense which is being made of the alleged Elaine rioters. This may not agree with your own information but I feel that it is never-the-less correct. What I am trying to say is that you should not discount the influence of Mr. Jones and the part he is playing in the defense, which I am sure is just as important as what Mr. Murphy is doing. In fact, you may not know that Mr. Jones is in a position to do a number of things which Mr. Murphy cannot do.
>
> The main thing is that all the agencies should work in cooperation and in harmony to get a just decision in the Elaine cases.[36]

They had better work together. The Ware defendants had been transferred back to the Phillips County jail in early April. On April 26, Scipio Jones traveled to Helena to argue for more time to prepare for the trials, which were to begin on May 3. Judge Jackson denied this request.[37] They needed much more time, because one of their primary motions was to ask for a change of venue to get the cases out of Phillips County. They were desperately trying to find blacks who would be willing to testify that they couldn't get a fair trial in Phillips County. Only four came forward. Blacks were going to have to live in Phillips County afterward, trial or no trial.

The Elaine massacres had shaken blacks to the core. No longer in Arkansas could they hope that whites would content themselves with sporadic lynchings. Whites had shown themselves to be fully capable of mass violence on an increasing scale. Some kind of political alliance with whites had to be maintained, yet this was increasingly difficult. The state Republican Party, sick of defeat after defeat, periodically wanted blacks out, and in 1920 the Pulaski County Republican boss, A. C. Remmel, was particularly active in making known his own desires for exclusion. Barely four months after the massacres, Scipio Jones wrote Remmel a letter asking if blacks were "to be treated as citizens and granted the right of representation, or are the conventions to be held in hotels for white people, where colored voters are not expected to come?" Jones reminded Remmel that blacks had recently done their part in the war "by cheerfully complying with every call of the government, from the giving of their sons on the battlefield, to the purchasing of bonds, and the contributions of funds for war activities."[38]

Ultimately, the answer in Pulaski County was that the Republican county convention to select delegates to district and state conventions was to be held in a segregated hotel. On the evening of April 13, black Republicans, known as the "Black and Tans," met at the Mosaic Templars Building on Ninth and Broadway to consider what to do. Finally, at eight o'clock, the time the convention was to start, Bishop Conner made a motion that the Black and Tans should walk down to the Marion Hotel, which they did. They entered the lobby and proceeded to the ballroom, which was deserted. Then someone turned out the lights on them, and they "filed solemnly out."[39]

Their contention that they had met at the appointed time and selected their own delegates naturally fell on deaf ears. At the state convention on April 28 the "Lilly whites," as they were called, were seated. The blacks, led by Camp Morris, left the hall, went back to the Mosaic Templars Building, conducted their own convention, and selected their candidate for governor, Josiah H. Blount from Forrest City, who had once been a school principal in Helena. Scipio Jones was selected to be a delegate to the National Republican Convention. Thus, for the first time in Arkansas history, a black candidate ran for governor. This was a doomed enterprise, of course, one that blacks didn't expect to win. Given their loyalty and prior dependence on whites, it was a singular sign of their frustration.

May 1920
Helena

The retrials in Helena of the Ware defendants were the biggest cases in Scipio Jones's life. Even Colonel Murphy must have been nervous. With every white person in Phillips County knowing who he was and watching his every move, Scipio Jones had to be alert at every moment. He wasn't just anxious about how well he would do in a hostile environment; he was afraid he would be murdered and thus slept in a different bed every night during the trials.[40]

Despite all the hopes placed on the colonel's legendary ability in the courtroom, it was going to be an uphill battle. In retrospect, no trial attorney, however skillful, could have won an acquittal for any of the Elaine Twelve in Phillips County in front of an all-white jury. The best any lawyer could have done was to make a record for appeal, and Murphy and Jones had begun the process of accomplishing this well before the trials started by filing a motion objecting to the composition of the grand jury on the basis of racial discrimination.

The fate of the Ware defendants was essentially decided at 2:30 on the afternoon of May 3, when Judge Jackson denied a motion for a change of venue and a motion to transfer the cases to federal court. What had been accomplished for the defense, however, was that it had timely raised the issue of equal protection—there were no blacks on the grand jury or petit jury. Despite this, the ego of the colonel was such that he actually thought he might be able to win the cases, and he set about trying to get a jury that would view the facts fairly.

The transcripts of the retrials of the Ware defendants, unfortunately, have been lost. However, the appellants' legal brief to the Arkansas Supreme Court has been located. The legal brief contains a voluminous abstract of the defendants' testimony and physical evidence, as well as the legal arguments by Jones and Murphy. An abstract of the testimony is required by the rules of appellate procedure to include an unbiased and fair recapitulation of all relevant testimony of both prosecution and defense witnesses. As in the first trials, the *Helena World* was not a neutral reporter of the testimony, failing to report any negative information brought out on cross-examination by Jones and Murphy. For its part, the

Arkansas Gazette, though placing the retrials on its front page each day, barely mentioned the testimony.

The significance of the abstract is two-fold. First, it provides a more complete picture of the shoot-out at the Hoop Spur church, because in these retrials an actual defense was made. Second, and more importantly, it allows the evidence of whether blacks were planning an insurrection to be addressed further, since Suggs Bondsman, the only prosecution witness on this point, was recalled in the second round of trials to testify again against Ed Ware.

Murphy and Jones tried valiantly to get juries as unbiased as possible. For example, in the trial of Joe Fox and Albert Giles for the shooting of James Tappan on May 6, ninety-nine jurors were struck.[41] Of the three Phillips County residents who were killed, Tappan was the most popular. "Jimmie," as the *World* referred to him, was a "young business man" and had been a lieutenant in World War I. Many had watched his first trial and honestly admitted during jury selection that they had already formed an opinion as to the defendants' guilt. Of all the indicators that a change of venue was necessary to give the defendants a fair trial, the striking of scores of jurors for "cause," as lawyers say, is the most telling.

The first man to be tried for the death of Adkins was John Martin, one of the guards outside the church at Hoop Spur. Originally, he had been tried together with Alf Banks Jr. Though a conflict was again perhaps unavoidable, given the circumstances, Jones and Murphy should not have represented both John Martin and Alf Banks, because the evidence in this trial (as well as in the first one) tended to show that that it was Alf Banks, along with two others never apprehended (the Becko boys), who had fired the shots that killed Will Adkins. During the first trial members of the union who had been previously convicted had named Martin as one of the guards who had fired his gun that night, but the testimony of John Ratliff and Sykes Fox in the second trial was vague about Martin's involvement. Martin's testimony from his first trial, in which he admitted that he had fired his gun, was read into evidence.

When the defense began to present its case, Murphy called numerous witnesses to try to establish that the first shots fired had passed through the church. Lizzie Wright, a member of the union, testified that she had been inside the church when the shooting started: "When the shooting commenced, it came in the windows, threw splinters of glass over the [church] house."[42] In fact, as Murphy and Jones generally argued in their brief on the issue of self-defense for all the six defendants, "nine

. . . [witnesses,] three of whom were the State's witnesses, testified to the effect, or in direct terms, that the first shots were fired into the glass windows of the church."[43] The defense also tried to establish that the church had been burned shortly thereafter to destroy any evidence that the blacks had been attacked. For example, in Martin's case, Sam Walker, who lived at Hoop Spur, testified: "Three white men, apparently two soldiers and one civilian got out, walked around the church house, went back to the car in a minute or two, and by that time it was burning,—flashed up around the roof, and the car sped away."[44]

Lit Simmons, the "doorkeeper" at the meeting in Hoop Spur the night of November 30, was also called in Martin's case to further establish that the union members had acted in self-defense. He testified, "Those who carried guns there did it for protection, in case anything occurred [sic]. They had heard they were going to kill us out. I saw an automobile come up and stop. . . . I saw three shots from the automobile. . . . It was a white man that fired the first three shots."[45] Simmons claimed to have been able to see Adkins, testifying that he could see "by the flashlight and by the light of the pistol. He fired very rapidly,—from an automatic pistol, and was about 21 or 22 yards from the church."[46] On cross-examination, Simmons testified that he had given a different statement earlier because of fear. He had been arrested and put in jail: "I would have said anything to please you all."[47] However, a list of individuals who were convicted for their participation in the disturbances does not include his name.[48]

Simmons's further testimony on cross-examination was extremely damaging to Alf Banks, who was to stand trial again on May 8: "Alf Banks and one of the Becko boys were disputing, each claiming to have killed the man; one had the pistol and the other the flashlight, and each claimed that it was his, saying he had killed him."[49] With this information becoming available, Simmons was later called as a prosecution witness against Alf Banks at his trial, three days later.

Lit Simmons (and other witnesses for the defense) mentioned another car that had come by after the first round of shooting had died down: "I had to run to get away from there, because another crew came, and went to shooting, just after I got out a little piece,—another crew of white men. They fired on the church,—looked like the flashes were going right at the church. They must have left their car up the road. I didn't see any of the second crew; I was gone."[50]

The question of whether there were whites besides Pratt and Adkins (and other than W. K. Monroe) who were present at Hoop Spur that night seems destined to remain a point about which the evidence is too conflicted to make a judgment.[51] The defense brief of Murphy and Jones that went to the Arkansas Supreme Court in the second Ware cases makes no argument that other whites were involved. After Jones's and Smiddy's affidavits became available, the argument would be made that "armed men surrounded the church and fired upon them, killing several."[52] However, whether in fact other "armed men" attacked the church the night of September 30, 1919, will always be a subject of debate.

There was even less evidence to convict Martin in this first case because the prosecution chose not to call J. G. Burke, who had testified in the first trial that Martin and Banks had confessed to firing their weapons. In fact, only one white witness was called in any of the second round of trials to testify that any of the defendants had confessed to anything. One can only speculate as to the reason for this. Since the prosecution knew that there was going to be testimony that the men had been beaten, it chose, for the most part, not to make the confessions a part of its case, perhaps to avoid making torture and intimidation more of an issue. The whites who had questioned the blacks had been treated with kid gloves by the Helena defense attorneys in the first trials. They would not have been treated so gingerly by the colonel or Scipio Jones the second time around. The defense brief noted, "Why did they [the prosecution] not call some one or more of the Deputy Sheriffs, if it [torture] was not true? The trouble about it was that it was all true, and there were more yet that might be brought to light, if the perpetrators were subjected to cross-examination."[53]

Not only did J. G. Burke not testify against Martin, but two of the prosecution witnesses from the first trial, John Ratliff and Sykes Fox, also recanted their testimony implicating Martin. Fox said he had been beaten; Ratliff said he had lied out of fear of being beaten.[54]

John Martin testified in his own defense and said that he "was in the church at the time of the shooting and had nothing to do with the shooting." Asked on cross-examination why he was testifying differently this time (he had testified previously that he had made "air shots"), he said that he had been beaten to make him testify as he had. Though Sykes Fox testified at this trial that he had seen John Martin "inside the [church] house," he did not testify as to when this was in relation to the time the shooting started.[55]

No witnesses called by the defense placed Martin inside the church when the shooting began. On balance, despite the changes in testimony, it seems likely that Martin had been outside as a guard and had fired his weapon, though it will never be clear when he started firing.

At the end of the testimony in Martin's case, the colonel was in an ethical bind. The most logical and strongest argument (besides self-defense) to make to the jury was that regardless of where Martin had been or whether he had fired his weapon, the testimony had shown that Alf Banks and the Becko brothers had shot and killed Will Adkins. The problem was that the colonel was representing Alf Banks too. Perhaps this dilemma explains his willingness to waive making a closing argument, as was reported by the *Helena World*. Yet, by not making a closing argument, he violated his ethical duty to represent his client John Martin zealously. In hindsight, one has to wonder what efforts, if any, were made by Murphy and Jones to avoid the conflict of representing both Banks and the others. Surely a comprehensive interview with Lit Simmons by one or both of these very experienced criminal defense attorneys would have revealed the information about Banks. Yet perhaps this information was overlooked. By agreeing to represent all the defendants, the colonel and Scipio Jones had boxed themselves into a corner that neither they nor the NAACP had thought to avoid. All they managed to do in this regard at the second trial was to get Martin and Banks tried separately.

Although the *Helena World* reported that the trial of Will Wardlow on May 5 was essentially a reprise of the Martin case, in fact it was not. Though the white witnesses (Charles Pratt, W. K. Monroe, Amos Jarmon, and H. F. Smiddy) testified substantially the same as before, none of their testimony (as before) could link Wardlow to Adkins's death. As already noted, the charge against Wardlow had been changed before his first trial from murdering Adkins to "aiding and abetting." In the second trial of Will Wardlow, J. D. Moseby, an assistant prosecutor, who had not testified in Wardlow's first trial, testified that while the first trial of Ed Ware was going on Wardlow had told him that Ed Ware had ordered him to act as a guard that night and "that he took his gun, and did so act as a guard."[56]

This time Will Wardlow took the witness stand and testified that he had been whipped to make him say what he had at the first trial. It was not Moseby who had whipped him or threatened him. It was Kid Collins, who had beaten him: "Well, they stripped me naked, and two men stretched me out, and they whipped me across my back; if you don't believe I have any scars on me, I will let my clothes down and let you see it."[57] Wardlow in his second trial denied having been one of the guards. He admitted that he was a union member and had been to two meetings but said, "If they put guards out there I don't know it. When the car came up, I was standing in front of the church."[58]

Though there is no doubt that Wardlow and others were whipped to make them testify against themselves and others, it seems likely that Wardlow was one of the guards and did fire his weapon at some point. His story that he happened to be out in front of the church and was unaware that guards had been placed around the church seems as improbable as Pratt's story that he, Adkins, and Collins happened to stop in front of the church to "take a leak."

Even though Wardlow (and the others on trial) probably fired their weapons, the question will always remain as to whether it was in self-defense. Certainly, there was evidence to suggest that the shooting at the church was begun by whites, and more evidence would be coming in 1921 with the affidavits of T. K. Jones and H. F. Smiddy.

For Will Wardlow, as for the others, there was no mystery about the outcome of his trial. The jury had been chosen the night before, and the trial was over in the afternoon. Again, there were no closing arguments. The same ethical problem existed as before. The verdict was guilty.

It may well be that the failure of the colonel to make closing arguments was due to his failing physical condition. He became ill on May 5 and had to be taken to the Helena hospital. According to B. Boren McCool's account, Murphy suffered a "severe heart attack." McCool interviewed J. W. Butts, whose father, a physician, treated the colonel. Butts "told Murphy that as a doctor he would do everything he could to save his life but that as a man he could not care less whether Murphy died."[59]

The rest of the trials were conducted by Scipio Jones, who was assisted by J. R. Booker, a black attorney from Little Rock who had done some work on the cases.

On May 7, Albert Giles and Joe Fox, who had hidden in the thickets near Hoop Spur the day after the fighting at the church, were convicted again. In the November trial, there had been little credible prosecution evidence that these men had fired the weapon or weapons that had killed James Tappan. Alf Banks, who had provided the bulk of the eyewitness testimony at the first trial for the prosecution, now changed his story completely, saying that he had been "whipped up" to give false evidence against Giles and Fox.[60] Now he testified that it was not true that he had seen Joe Fox shoot Tappan. None of the blacks in the thicket had started the shooting, nor had he heard whites call out for them to surrender. In fact, according to Banks, "The white men hollowed [sic], 'look out, we are killing our own men.'"[61]

In the May retrial an effort was also made to show that the men had acted in self-defense. Scipio Jones called a number of witnesses who testified they had heard that whites were coming to kill Negroes that morning after the shoot-out at the church. For example, Ed Ware testified that he had been told that "a gang of white people . . . were coming to kill me and every Negro they saw. . . ."[62]

As in the first trial, Albert Giles again testified on his own behalf, but interestingly, Joe Fox did not take the witness stand in the second trial. Usually, an individual who might incriminate himself will be advised by his lawyer not to testify. Giles, who had been wounded, testified that he had "got shot in the first shooting" and that he had not fired his weapon.[63]

Though Giles and Fox were again convicted, after two trials it is not clear who shot James Tappan. Given the mayhem that was occurring that morning, self-defense was obviously an issue, but not one that would find favor with a Phillips County jury composed entirely of white men. However, the later affidavit of H. F. Smiddy casts further doubt as to the culpability of the defendants. Smiddy, it turns out, had been part of the Phillips County posse that morning when James Tappan was killed and claimed to have been no more than twenty feet from him when he was shot. He stated in his affidavit, "I feel perfectly sure that he [Tappan] was accidentally killed by a member of our own posse on the other side of the thicket from us. About the time he was killed somebody hollered from both sides of the thicket, 'Look out, we are shooting our own men.' I know that this is possible because I was shot in the right shoulder by a stray shot of some kind by a member of our posse, and also Mr. Dazell was shot over the left eye." Smiddy stated that the shot or shots that had killed Tappan could not have come from the blacks in that part of the thicket because after Tappan had been killed, "we searched it thoroughly after the shooting . . . and found no negroes near anywhere he was shot."[64]

Further, Smiddy swore, "I did not hear Mr. Herbert Thompson or anybody else holler out to the negroes to come out of the thicket and surrender. . . . When we started down that thicket it was the understanding with all of us that we would shoot the negroes as we came to them which we did." Perhaps to illustrate that the posse was in a "take no prisoners" mode, it is in this affidavit that Smiddy admits to shooting and wounding an unarmed Milligan Giles (the brother of Albert Giles).[65]

On May 8, as previously mentioned, Lit Simmons was called as a prosecution witness and implicated Alf Banks, whose trial had been severed from John Martin's: "I saw him there, after the first shooting. He and the two Becko boys came in the church. He had a flashlight and the other had a pistol. One of them would say, 'I killed him,' and another one would say, 'I killed him.' Alf said, 'I killed him,' and each of the Becko boys said the same. They were arguing over a flashlight and pistol. They said, 'carry on your meeting; I have done killed him.'"[66]

On cross-examination, Lit Simmons would not back away from his testimony, and since he had originally been a defense witness in the John Martin case, there was nothing that could be done to minimize the damage done by him. Thus, inadvertently, the defense had provided the most reliable evidence for the prosecution of any of the six Ware defendants. Scipio Jones called some of the same witnesses who had testified in the John Martin trial to try to establish that the first shots fired had come into the church, but their words fell on deaf ears. Alf Banks was convicted again.

On Tuesday, May 11, Ed Ware, the last of the six, was tried for the second time. Ware had originally been the prosecution's strongest murder case. Witness after witness had placed him in the church, setting guards out. He had been seen firing his weapon. However, as had occurred with the other retrials, this time evidence of his involvement was sparse until the final rebuttal witness. Again, Charles Pratt and Kid Collins testified that the first shot had been fired by the guards. Since Kid Collins was now available for cross-examination, Scipio Jones forced him to admit that he had been in jail for second-degree murder and that at the time of the second trial he had been released and was living in Hughes, a small town in Saint Francis County in the Arkansas Delta. Attempting to show that Kid Collins had received favored treatment, Jones got him to disclose that he had been in Memphis for a week before Christmas. Collins denied that he had gone to Hoop Spur to "break up a Negro meeting."[67]

John Ratliff testified that Ware had fired his weapon "two or three times" but that this was after the first round of shooting had taken place. In response to W. K. Monroe's testimony that he had come along the road at midnight and been wounded, Ratliff testified, "There wasn't anything going on at that time. There had been shooting before that. A car had come up and shooting had occurred, but it was all over."[68]

Joe Machon (Michon in some accounts) testified that he had been in the church with Ed Ware when a car had come up with whites in it. Ware had said not to let them in: "Ware said we had a guard out there at the door, and if he can't hold it, 'I will go out there.'"[69] However, Machon also testified that Ware had not left the church until after the shooting started. Dave Hays placed Ware outside the church during the shooting, but he testified that he hadn't seen him firing or seen that he even had a weapon: "Ware was sitting on the upper end of the log, the same log the Becko boys were sitting on."[70]

Again, witnesses testified that the shooting had been started by individuals in the car and that Ware had been inside the church.[71] Ed Ware testified that he had put no guards out that night and had not carried a gun to the meeting, nor had he shot one, testimony that conflicted with John Ratliff's. He said that Dave Hays was mistaken and that he hadn't seen him that night. Asked why he had fled to New Orleans and assumed a new name, he testified, "Because threats have been made that they were going to kill me."[72]

On cross-examination he was asked a series of questions about Suggs Bondsman and about his claims that he had overheard Ware and others at a meeting at the Elaine lodge planning to kill a number of white planters. Bondsman said that Ware had taken over the meeting and told how he put out guards at meetings at Hoop Spur. Ware said that he hadn't known of Bondsman until the first time he had testified against him and that he had never talked about killing planters, nor had he taken over a meeting at Elaine.[73]

The prosecution then called Bondsman, who again testified, as he had in November, that Ware had come to the meeting in Elaine on the Thursday before the shoot-out in Hoop Spur the following Tuesday: "He took charge of it [the meeting]." Ware had showed Ed Hicks, the president of the Elaine lodge, "how to handle the men, what to do, and send out guards."[74] He had said "to kill everything that come by, white."[75]

The transcript of the November trial reveals nothing about Bondsman, but in the second trial, Bondsman testified that he had been living in Elaine for three years and was a member of the union. He testified that Ed Ware and Ed Hicks "said they were going to kill Mr. Countiss, Mr. Crow, Mr. Craig, Mr. Barnard and Mr. Stokes. Then they held the conversation up, and said there were some white mouths in there, and he had better be particular. They then began to write it off, show it to each other, and asked how about him."[76]

This time Bondsman was subject to cross-examination. Scipio Jones asked him to name some of the people who were there that night: "Well, there was Ed. Hicks, another Ed. Just really I didn't know the people."[77] Scipio Jones bored in on this point, but Bondsman could not name another person who had been at the meeting:

Bondsman: I would have to get after that; there were about 300 men; lots of them I didn't know, the biggest ones. . . .
Jones: Name those you did know. . . .
Bondsman: The biggest members of the union from all places.[78]

Again, Jones asked him again to name another person who had heard Ed Ware:

Bondsman: All around and about Elaine.[79]

Whether Bondsman was too nervous and genuinely could not remember or wasn't telling the truth obviously cannot be known, but to impair his credibility further, Scipio Jones called two witnesses to rebut Bondsman's testimony. Joe Machon testified that he had been at the Thursday meeting in Elaine but that it "was an open session," meaning that nonunion persons could attend. He said that he hadn't been seated far from Ed Ware but hadn't heard him discuss killing anyone: "He [Ware] wasn't present much. He was running a jitney and hauling passengers."[80] On cross-examination he said he had seen Ed Ware "sitting around a table helping fill some blanks. I had one of them. That was directly after he got there. I didn't go out of the house."[81] He said that he had gotten to the meeting before Ed Ware, who, once he got there, made two trips. He "went to Countiss . . . and to Hoop Spur."[82]

Will Curry testified that he was a member of the Elaine lodge and had gone to the Thursday meeting: "Hill presided over that meeting. There were no armed guards out that night. It was an open door session; anyone could attend. I didn't hear Ed. Ware say anything about how he conducted the Hoop Spur Union, nor about having anyone or any white people killed, nor about putting about any guards."[83] On cross-examination, Curry stated that he had left before Ed Ware, who, he said, "was up [at a table] helping with the finances."[84]

Suggs Bondsman's testimony remains the only evidence adduced at the trials of the Elaine Twelve that blacks were ever planning to kill planters. Taken into custody and identified as a leader of the union back on October 2, 1919, by the *Arkansas Democrat,* Bondsman was unable to name a single other person at the meeting besides Hicks and Ed Ware, which weakens his credibility. Most interestingly, Bondsman testified on cross-examination that he "wasn't a big Nigger, wasn't among the board," and hadn't been put in jail in Helena.[85] He was at least lying about having gone to jail, however briefly. Whether he was a union leader is not known, but he does not appear to have been convicted; this fact, coupled with his false testimony, raises the distinct possibility that he made a deal with the prosecution he did not want to disclose. Too, one would suspect that any plot to kill individual planters would not have been discussed in a meeting of three hundred people. Ware's other activities that night (running a taxi service, filling out forms, helping with the finances) do not indicate that he was a man who was bent upon murdering planters. As Will Curry testified, he hadn't heard any speeches that night except by "Robert L. Hill; he lectured."[86]

As expected, the jury once again convicted Ed Ware. The evidence suggests that Ware was likely involved in the shooting at Hoop Spur but that he did not fire the shots that killed Will Adkins. He may well have "set the guards out" that night. His claim that he intended to resign from the union that night is not credible or particularly relevant.[87]

Anyone who looks at the picture of the automobile driven by Will Adkins the night of September 30 has to conclude that there was a fierce battle at the Hoop Spur church. Though on balance, with the additions of the affidavits of Smiddy and Jones, it appears that the whites were intent on disrupting the meeting that night, exactly who fired the first shot simply can't be determined from the available evidence.[88]

In any event, Jackson sentenced the defendants to die on July 23.[89]

Governor Brough again agreed to stay the executions so that the defendants could appeal once more. Though the issue of blacks being excluded from the grand and petit juries waved about like a Confederate flag on Robert E. Lee's birthday, Brough solemnly intoned that "absolute justice" had prevailed at the trials.[90] Brough was back in control once more. Content to wait, he had set no execution dates for the Moore defendants, who on May 24 had filed a writ of certiorari to the U.S. Supreme Court. No one expected it to be successful, but it was felt to be a prudent step before filing a writ of habeas corpus in federal district court, which, if it came to that, would be the final bullet in the legal arsenal.

Shortly after the retrials, Scipio Jones and Edgar McHaney made a trip to New York to discuss strategy with the NAACP. Colonel Murphy did not go, and from a letter written by Ulysses Bratton, it can be inferred that he thought the trip a waste of time. In a letter to John Shillady in August, Bratton wrote that his son Guy had written him "sometime ago" that he had seen the colonel, who expressed "regrets that they were disposed to go."

It is in this letter that Bratton's antipathy toward his former friend Edgar McHaney is revealed: "The Col is a sincere fighter but his partner McHaney has absolutely no interest other than to get the money. . . . McHaney was grumbling all along as to the cases and the fee. He was scared to death for fear of the local feeling, and besides said the bunch at Helena were his special friends."[91]

The depth of Bratton's bitterness at having been forced to leave Arkansas had no bottom. He had referred to McHaney earlier as a "friend" when he had gone to Helena in October to free Ocier from jail, without success. McHaney did indeed care about the fees. He had five children to feed, the cases were taking huge chunks of time, and the end was nowhere in sight. After his trip to New York, he wrote the NAACP that he thought "$25,000 will be a very moderate compensation for the service which we will be compelled to render if we go through with all these cases to the end."[92] If Murphy couldn't be bothered about money at his age, McHaney, speaking for the firm, could. The cases were taking up nearly all of the colonel's time. They were driving away other business because of the ill feeling they engendered. The cases, McHaney believed, weren't going to be finished for another two or three years. But McHaney was wrong. They would take almost five.

CHAPTER 10

The Changing of the Guard

He was ready to cut through anything that seemed to stand in the way of justice.
—Biographical sketch of Chancellor John Martineau

October 1920–June 1921

On October 11, 1920, disaster struck the defendants again. The colonel, who had just days earlier tried a case in Pulaski County circuit court in Little Rock, died at Saint Luke's Hospital in the city. Almost at the same moment, the defense team got notice that their petition to the United States Supreme Court for a writ of certiorari had been denied. Ironically, the day brought one bit of good news: the Robert Hill extradition saga ended with his release from jail in Kansas. He was free, but with the denial of the writ of certiorari, there was nothing now to keep Brough from setting execution dates for the six Moore defendants.

The first item of business for the NAACP was to figure out who was going to replace the colonel, whose death produced flowery obituaries and editorials in the *Arkansas Gazette* and the *Arkansas Democrat*. Had the colonel been more successful with the Elaine cases at the time of his death, it is doubtful the editorials would have been as kind. "Fearless . . . tender . . . sympathetic. . . . [H]is name was everywhere held in the highest respect," gushed the *Gazette*. Referring to the Elaine cases, the *Democrat* purred that the colonel was "devoted to the right as he saw it."[1]

Ulysses Bratton wanted a new team to work with Scipio Jones. Walter White wired James Weldon Johnson (now secretary of the NAACP, following Shillady's resignation in August) from Detroit that Bratton "strongly recommends that McHaney be not allowed to continue cases."[2] Bratton suggested sending his son (presumably Guy) to Arkansas to find lawyers he thought would be acceptable. White was ready to jump on a train himself, but cooler heads in New York prevailed. McHaney was fully up to speed on the cases, and the NAACP was fully aware of his abilities. In July it had already agreed to pay the firm of Murphy, McHaney and

Dunaway an additional five thousand dollars. It is not unlikely that James Weldon Johnson consulted Scipio Jones for his opinion. Jones would have known that McHaney was not only a good lawyer but also had superior political skills Bratton could no longer appreciate. From his long history in dealing with whites, Scipio Jones knew from the beginning that criminal cases involving blacks ultimately had more to do with politics than justice and that he and his new partner would ultimately have to deal with Brough or whoever was governor. If the money issue could be settled, McHaney would be fine. Another factor would have entered into it: from this experience he knew he could work with McHaney. With another white attorney, he couldn't be sure what the relationship would be. Others writing about the Elaine massacres has mistakenly claimed that at this point Scipio Jones basically soldiered on alone, but in fact Edgar McHaney played a crucial role in the defense of the Elaine Twelve for another two years.[3]

Back in Little Rock, the pressure on Brough began to mount immediately to commute the death sentences. Brough liked to please everyone if he could, but this was an issue whose resolution could not make both sides happy. The question of his own political future was not at stake. His biographer writes that during much of 1920 Brough was considering making a run for a United States Senate seat but that by October he had accepted a job, which was to begin when his term was over in January 1921, as a one-man traveling road show for an unofficial state chamber of commerce.[4]

The decisive moment was approaching, and clearly Brough was torn. The black community in Arkansas had backed him to the hilt. He had always seen himself as the protector of Arkansas blacks. And Arkansas blacks had seen him as their protector. In the face of scathing criticism, they had insisted that Northern blacks were wrong. Certainly, a state like Arkansas was a dangerous place for black people, but you could trust a man like Brough to do the right thing. Hadn't Scipio Jones worked with him for years? If anybody knew white men, it was Scipio Jones, and Scipio had said that the governor would at least commute all but one of the sentences, if it came to that. In a very concrete way, the middle-class black community's entire approach to race relations was on the line. From the beginning of the trouble, Brough had acted to protect blacks. Hadn't he sent the troops? And if there were stories about how the troops had been a part of the massacres, that wasn't Brough's fault. He had said he would let the law take its course, and he had made good on that promise. And if in the case of the Moore defendants, the law had been a joke, that wasn't his fault either. In addition, Brough had appointed a biracial committee, and the very best blacks on it had promised that the whites on the committee would investigate and see things from their point of view.

But it wasn't quite working out that way. Despite the fact that nobody had ever produced the actual list of planters to be killed and that nobody in Phillips County had believed beforehand that such an insurrection was about to occur—and in fact, didn't—Brough couldn't be persuaded that perhaps the blacks had been acting in self-defense. Yet he let it be known that he was still troubled by the fact that the transcripts in the Moore cases revealed practically nothing about the involvement of Ed Coleman, Paul Hall, and Joe Knox.[5]

As soon as word got out that Brough was considering commuting the death sentences, he heard immediately from the organization that had lost two of its members. "When the guilty Negroes were apprehended, a solemn promise was given by the leading citizens of the community, that if these guilty parties were not lynched, and let the law take its course, that justice would be done and the majesty of the law upheld," read a resolution from the Richard L. Kitchens American Legion Post number 41 in Helena.[6]

Brough was reminded over and over again that Phillips County whites had fulfilled their end of the bargain—no lynchings. Five members of the Committee of Seven wrote him a letter stating that "this Committee gave our citizens their solemn promise that the law would be carried out."[7] He heard from the Lion's Club and the Rotary. No commutations. Since the trial record was bare, he wanted to hear from the Legionnaires themselves. They were happy to oblige: first, Joe Knox had been vice president of the Elaine lodge, so he had been involved in planning the deaths of whites; Ed Coleman had loaned his rifle to Hicks "immediately prior to the time that Hicks fired the shot that killed young Lee"; Paul Hall had helped select the death list and "stood by and aided, abetted, and encouraged Frank Hicks to shoot and kill young Clinton Lee."[8]

The "best Negroes" might have believed in Brough, but at bottom he was ruled by race and said as much on November 15, when he released his decision not to commute a single death sentence: "Every business, civic, and other organization in the community which refrained from mob violence, has taken a strong stand for carrying out the decree of the court to the letter."[9] Thus Brough at a defining moment in his career honored his racist roots. The evidence was not there to convict any of the men of first-degree murder, so he went behind the evidence to justify his decision. The mob wanted death, and he gave it to them.

For probably the first and only time in his life Scipio Jones gave vent to public anger at a white man. Being Scipio Jones, however, he would make comments that were muted and veiled. He released a statement to the press suggesting that Brough had announced his decision to sway the Arkansas Supreme Court's upcoming decision in the Ware cases: "Nor do we understand why the Governor should issue a statement . . . at this particular time, unless it might be possible that it was desired to give notoriety to this matter at this time, with the hope that it might possibly influence [the Ware cases]."[10] His press release was run by a single black-owned newspaper.

Perhaps concerned about his place in history, the governor set no execution date himself. Whether Brough heard about Jones's comments is not known. It wouldn't have mattered a bit if he did. He had less than two months left to serve as governor. In the November election, Thomas McRae, a Democrat in the most Democratic of states, got 123,604 votes in a contest that ignored the troubles in Phillips County as an issue in the campaign. The Republican candidate received 46,339 votes, and Josiah Blount, the black candidate, managed to get 15,627. If nothing else, the election sent a message to the Republican Party it chose not to hear, because in fourteen Delta counties, including Pulaski, Josiah Blount outpolled its candidate.

Significantly, however, the first crack in the unified front of the white power structure in Arkansas appeared within days of Brough's decision not to commute the sentences. In an editorial of November 17, the *Arkansas Democrat* advised that there was no reason to hurry up the executions, mentioning the "imperfections of human justice under which black dupes must die while their 'mastermind,' the mulatto they trusted, roams. . . ."[11] Embedded in this racist assumption of a "mulatto mastermind" was the germ of a belief even in Arkansans that perhaps the penalty of death was too severe for the apostles when the leader, Hill, had gone free.

In the first week of December, the Arkansas Supreme Court handed down its second decision in the Ware cases and again reversed Judge Jackson, this time on the issue of blacks being excluded from the grand and petit juries. "That sort of discrimination in the selection of both the grand and petit juries is in contravention of the Fourteenth Amendment to the Constitution of the United States and the Civil Rights Act of March 1, 1875," stated the court.[12]

If Brough's decision not to commute the sentences of the Moore defendants was "putting down lynching," as it was characterized by the *Arkansas Gazette,* someone forgot to tell Arkansans.[13] On Christmas Day 1920, Henry Lowery, a black tenant farmer in Craighead County, in northeast Arkansas, disrupted the dinner of a white planter named Craig by demanding a settlement. Outraged, Craig turned him away, and the man shot him and his daughter and his two sons. A mob began looking for Lowery, but when they couldn't find him, they went to the jail the next day and dragged out a black man by the name of Thomas, who had killed a police officer, and lynched him. After parading him through the streets, they hung him just outside the city limits of Jonesboro. This made the third lynching in Arkansas since the massacre in Elaine. Soon after the fighting, Marianna, in Lee County, had seen a lynching, and then in November a mob had killed the accused murderer of the Columbia County sheriff in southern Arkansas.[14] More grisly lynchings were to follow in 1921.

Scipio Jones may have had second thoughts about his press release, because he told the *Arkansas Democrat* on December 6, after the Ware decision came down, that "the governor's such a busy man that he has not been able to devote sufficient time, I think, to investigation of the cases." Yet he again accused the governor of bias: "He visited the scene during the Phillips County trouble and may be prejudiced against the negroes, though he may have no intention to be so."[15] Even after the governor had gone back on his word and had not commuted a single sentence, Scipio Jones seemed to be hoping he would change his mind before his term ended. The man he had trusted had failed him.

Again, it would be up to the governor, now a very different one. The personalities of Thomas McRae and Charles Hillman Brough were markedly different. Nothing could have illustrated their differences better than inauguration day, January 12. In the custom of the day, Brough made a vigorous defense of his two administrations and later stood in the receiving line, his phenomenal memory for names and faces working overtime as he introduced his own well-wishers to the new governor, who had turned seventy in December.[16] McRae had wanted to keep the ceremonies short and simple. Crippled by arthritis, his wife Amelia sat nearby in a wheelchair. If Brough had become governor as a result of his ability to dazzle (primarily Southerners) with his oratory, Thomas McRae became governor almost as an afterthought to his career as a professional politician who had spent a good many years of his life outside Arkansas. Brough loved to please his audience; McRae seemed not to care whether they were pleased or not. His chief assistant in the governor's office, C. P. Newton, said of him, "Rarely was he entertaining, but his personality could arrest and hold the unwavering attention of individuals and assemblages. He may not have been brilliant—and I don't think he was—and yet he was the wisest man I ever knew."[17] McRae was wise in the ways of experience. From Prescott, in southern Arkansas, he had spent eighteen years in Washington in the House of Representatives and had then come back to Arkansas, where he became a banker and did well enough to be elected president of the Arkansas Bankers' Association. At a meeting of the American Bankers' Association in Boston where Woodrow Wilson was pushing the creation of the federal reserve system, McRae spoke up in favor of it, the only banker to do so.

He had taken a stab at running for governor against Brough during his first campaign but had withdrawn. In 1917 he was elected president of the Arkansas Bar Association and was a member of the Arkansas Constitutional Convention. Running for governor, he had campaigned against granting pardons. In his inaugural speech he said it again: governors let too many prisoners go home. He wasn't going to do that.

His background didn't suggest a man who would have "advanced" views on race, nor did he have them (though he did continue Brough's biracial commission). As a thirteen-year-old boy he had acted as a runner for a few months for the Confederacy in Washington, in southern Arkansas.[18] After taking a law degree from Washington and Lee in 1872, he was admitted one year later to the bar in Arkansas. By 1876 he had been elected to Arkansas House of Representatives from Nevada County. Being elected governor didn't seem necessary to his ego. He had been to the nation's capitol, where real power was exercised. If he lost the race, he would go back to practicing law, which he did anyway, until his death a few years later.

One of McRae's first acts as governor was to proclaim "Law and Order Sunday," citing a "crime wave sweeping over the state."[19] But just a few days after taking office, McRae had to deal with another aspect of the criminal justice system. Henry Lowery had been caught in El Paso, Texas, and while being brought back to Arkansas, he had been taken off the train in Mississippi. He had then been brought to northeast Arkansas near the town of Wilson, on the banks of the Mississippi River, where he had been chained to a log. In front of hundreds of whites, he had been cooked inch by inch. "Every few minutes fresh leaves were tossed on the funeral pyre until the blaze had passed the negro's waist. As the flames were eating away his abdomen, a member of the mob stepped forward and saturated the body with gasoline. It was then only a few minutes until the negro had been reduced to ashes," wrote an eyewitness reporter from the *Memphis Press*.[20] Lowery, he related, had never begged for mercy during the thirty minutes of his agony, but at one point he had tried to stuff ashes in his mouth to kill himself. They were kicked away by the crowd.[21] Like Brough, McRae was appalled by lynchings and had tried to prevent this killing by telling the sheriff to transport Lowery to Little Rock. The offer had been refused, with predictable results. Furious, McRae had a bill introduced in the legislature requiring the removal of officers who didn't protect their prisoners. The bill went nowhere.

It was easy enough for the NAACP staff to rail against Arkansas blacks for supporting government officials who tried to maintain law and order. None of them feared that a white mob might be at their door. As in the past, the twenties throughout Arkansas were a time of constant fear. No place was safe. On March 12, 1921, in downtown Little Rock at approximately midnight, a white woman was allegedly raped by two blacks. The rumors began flying. Supposedly the night before a white woman had been propositioned near the rape scene. Once the allegation of rape was made in Arkansas, a black man, however prominent, however wealthy, became just another black face. On March 15 a black man named Browning Tuggle, accused of raping a white woman, was taken from a jail in Hope, in southern Arkansas, and lynched before a mob of two thousand people. In Little Rock, twenty blacks were rounded up and three were arrested, including one Emmanuel West, who was "positively identified" as the rapist on March 17. When the news got out, a mob of between five hundred and two thousand people assembled at the Little Rock jail and demanded justice. The police chief, Burl C. Rotenberry, had outfoxed the mob and had hidden the men at another site. The victim's brother was allowed to search the jail before the mob dispersed. By March 22, fifty men from the American Legion Post number 1 in Little Rock were patrolling the streets as auxiliary policemen, as reports of alleged assaults by black males continued. With hysteria reminiscent of the Salem witch trials mounting, the response of the black community was swift and predictable. Scipio Jones and his allies sent a letter to the local and county officials, thanking them for preventing a lynching and pledging their support.[22] It was a timely letter because on March 22, in Monticello in southern Arkansas, a thousand whites took a black man from the city jail and lynched him for entering the home of a white family and cutting off their daughter's hair while she was sleeping.[23] No story was too ridiculous. All it took was a white person to say it, and before long another black man was dead. Self-defense was tantamount to suicide. Recent history in Helena had taught blacks that. Thus, right in the middle of the increasingly frantic defense to save the Moore defendants, Scipio Jones was once again stroking the white power structure, hoping to stave off another massacre in the black community. Undoubtedly, he didn't give a damn how obsequious it looked to the NAACP in New York. Scipio Jones wrote that the purpose of the letter was to "preserve the happy, peaceable and prosperous conditions that distinguish Little Rock from every other city in the South."[24]

There was some truth to this, even if Scipio Jones was laying it on a little thick. Little Rock hadn't had a lynching since the late 1800s. It wouldn't be the last time.

Emmanuel West was tried and eventually executed, though in fact the first jury was hung at eleven to one. Emmanuel West had been given a real defense and had a blue-ribbon jury, including former governor George Donaghey and two ministers, one of whom, Reverend Hay Watson Smith of the Second Presbyterian Church, had a theology that was reputed to be quite a bit more liberal than the average churchgoer's. Edwin Dunaway, whose partner was Edgar McHaney, had been one of the attorneys appointed for West. The defense had called twenty witnesses to say that West had been in a real estate office in North Little Rock when the rape had been committed.

The criticism of Arkansas justice from the NAACP and others outside the state was beginning to have some effect. On April 9 the *Arkansas Democrat* ran a self-congratulatory editorial while the jury was out, praising its prominence: "And the next time somebody expresses doubt about the negro race getting justice in Arkansas, show them this jury. . . ."[25] There was more than a doubt, since the jury was all-white and more than one out of four persons in Little Rock was black. However, the *Democrat* had a point. At least the defense had called witnesses.

The spring of 1921 was a particularly stressful time for the black community in Arkansas. In retrospect, it seems to have been a peculiar moment to engage in a dispute with the NAACP over the lack of credit it was giving to the Citizens Defense Fund Committee. The CDFC complained that the NAACP was not presenting its financial role in aiding the men to the public; the NAACP was disturbed that the CDFC was rewriting history. Walter White saw fit to reprimand Scipio Jones on March 8 for publicly misstating the NAACP's role in beginning the litigation. Scipio Jones had released a statement to the press to the effect that the CDFC had learned in January 1920 that the NAACP was negotiating with Colonel Murphy. White wrote: "Your familiarity with the cases, without doubt, causes you to know that we were not negotiating with Colonel Murphy in January but had already retained him and that he had actively gone to work on the cases." White went on to say that the *Crisis* would report how much money the CDFC had contributed and then baldly stated: "The Association has always been willing to give full credit to the Citizens Defense Fund Commission and has no desire to minimize the splendid services which have been rendered to the cause by the Commission."[26] This assertion must have particularly galled Scipio Jones, for he knew better than anyone that the NAACP raised its budget precisely by taking as much credit as it could. In the year and a half he had been dealing with the NAACP, it would not have escaped his attention that the perception of its staff was that blacks in Arkansas were backward, uneducated Uncle Toms. All would be smoothed over in the fullness of time, but it was a bumpy ride.

Governor McRae set the executions of the Moore defendants for June 10. Judge Jackson had scheduled the third retrial of the Ware defendants for June also, so Jones and McHaney were about to enter a hellacious spring of nonstop preparation. Again attaching affidavits from local blacks, they had asked for a change of venue for the Ware defendants on May 10, but Jackson sat on their motion, which forced the defendants to prepare to try the Ware cases and seek commutations for the Moore defendants at the same time. If McRae denied their request, they would have to file a writ of habeas corpus in federal court and hope the federal judiciary would be responsive.

The same pressure that Brough had experienced began to build around McRae. With the executions drawing closer, a new voice entered the debate over whether to commute the sentences of the Moore defendants. On May 25, Col. Robert Kerlin, an English professor at Virginia Military Institute, wrote an open letter to McRae imploring that he not execute the men. It was not a spontaneous gesture. Walter White had vetted the letter but hadn't changed a word. It came from the man's heart. Kerlin wrote McRae that he should listen to a "still small voice . . . that bids you stand for the eternal right. . . . ."[27]

Here was another white man in the South daring to interfere with the established order. Kerlin, a socialist with a Ph.D. from Yale and a Methodist minister with experience as a chaplain in the Spanish-American War, held nothing back. He criticized peonage, the large number of black deaths, the trials, the torture of the defendants, and finally the death penalty: "It is a deed to be contemplated with horror. In the execution of these men a race is suffering crucifixion. I entreat you to take the matter into your private chamber and give it an hour's earnest consideration, as before the Eternal Judge."[28]

Telegrams poured in from all over the nation urging McRae to commute the sentences. On June 7, delegations favoring commutation— including Frank Moore's parents, his wife, and his sister—trooped to the state capitol and saw McRae. Jones and McHaney met with him and provided him with the affidavits of torture victims Walter Ward, John Jefferson, and George Green, who swore that their testimony at the trial had been false. Their plea was to at least delay the executions until after the retrial of the Ware defendants and any subsequent appeals.

June 8 was Phillips County day at the state capitol. In the delegation urging McRae to carry out the death sentences was John Moore, one of the attorneys who had represented the defendants! And Kerlin's open letter to McRae had been too much for Judge Jackson, who answered Kerlin with his own open letter to McRae on June 9. Outraged by Kerlin's letter, Jackson, who had presided over one kangaroo trial after another, wrote that the trials had been fair. Moreover, "the statement that the Progressive Farmers' and Householders' Union was a peaceful union founded for legitimate purposes is wholly untrue. The statement that the insurrectionists shot only in self-defense is false. The statement that the negroes were indiscriminately hunted, harried, and shot down is a wicked lie."[29] By responding, he was effectively ending his role in the cases, though he would not grant the motion for a change of venue until June 21. The Ware defendants' cases were to be transferred to neighboring Lee County (not a hotbed of liberalism) and heard in October.[30]

Unlike Brough, who flip-flopped on the issue of commuting the sentences of the Elaine Twelve, McRae did not tip his hand. It is not known whether his mind was made up from the beginning or whether, like a good politician, he simply appeared to consider both sides of such an emotional issue. There were sound reasons to act circumspectly in such a situation. He knew he and the state would be criticized if he failed to commute the sentences. If he simply announced that his decision to execute the Moore defendants was immutable, this would invite even more disparagement and certainly cause anger throughout Arkansas in the black community. McRae did not have Brough's standing among blacks, but he was not hostile to them in the manner of a Jeff Davis. In his two terms as governor, a sanitarium was built for blacks and named for him, an achievement he would mention in his farewell address.

Though at one time McRae was labeled a hard-bitten conservative by Arkansas historians, his reputation for following in the progressive steps of Brough and George Donaghey has recently been enhanced by a reexamination of his two terms as governor by Calvin Ledbetter in an *Arkansas Historical Quarterly* article.[31] In any event, McRae referred the affidavits given to him by Jones and McHaney to John E. Miller, who responded that it was hardly the first time prosecuting witnesses had changed their stories "under the careful leadership of some interested party."[32] However, John Miller went much further. He pointed out to McRae that he was not from Phillips County and that at the time of the trouble he had been to Helena for only one term of court. Thus, he was a neutral observer on the subject. As Judge Jackson had done, he completely vindicated the actions of the whites in Phillips County. Concerning the allegations of torture, he wrote, "They [the Committee of Seven] were not vindictive and used no cruel methods in their investigation."[33] As far as the charges that blacks had been cheated, "There had been no wrong committed, but the average plantation negro had been led to believe that he was being wronged by the white man."[34]

Clearly, according to Miller, there had been an insurrection: "The investigation showed conclusively that the entire county around Elaine had been organized by Robert L. Hill, and the men who are condemned to die, for the purpose of acting in concert to gain their fancied rights."[35] By accident the insurrection had been set off prematurely, and a good thing, too: "It is my honest opinion that there would not have been a white man, woman or child left in that part of the country to tell the story of their death and the devastation of the country."[36]

Assuming McRae had not already made up his mind, Miller's long, detailed letter surely would have carried some weight with him. Yet, as detailed earlier, almost fifty-five years after these events, in his remarkably candid interview taped for an oral history project, Miller, then a federal district judge, would seriously contradict his letter to McRae on several major points and confirm the defense's version of what had occurred in Phillips County in many respects. His characterizations of what had occurred would be the polar opposite of his conclusions in his letter to

McRae. Over a half a century later, Miller would portray himself as the sympathetic outsider who had tried to go easy on the blacks in Phillips County: "They [Hill and Bratton] started organizing the sharecroppers down there and the purpose of organization was legitimate. There is no question in my mind about it, but it progressed very fast. The purpose of the organization was to have an accounting settlement with all the land owners on what they were entitled to."[37]

Miller denied that there had been torture ("cruelty") during the investigations in his letter to McRae, but now he said: "I went in there and tried to uphold the law. But I didn't mince words with them either. I didn't miche [*sic*] words with the—I turned loose four or five niggers that they had whipped down there trying to make them confess. . . . I just stopped and I said, were [*sic*] whipping you? Were [*sic*] leaving scars? Yes sir. I said, Pull your shirt off. By g— they whipped the hell out of him and I just closed the case right then and there. I did it on four or five of them. Oh it was a hell of a place."[38]

Miller denied in his letter that any economic wrongs had been perpetrated against the blacks. Yet in the oral interview he said: "Never was a bigger fraud perpetrated on any set of people than was perpetrated on those sharecroppers. The deducts, as they called it, the niggers called it ducts. . . ."[39] Miller remembered that Ulysses Bratton had wanted to bring civil suits against the planters in Phillips County: "If any case had been tried by a Chancellor, with an end to [*sic*] view of purging the account of fraud and it was offered this [*sic*] charges, that the nigger would have come out emptyhandedly [*sic*]. I don't have the slightest doubt in the world about it. I see too much of these things. And hell, that used to prevail in any sharecropping counties."[40]

In his letter to McRae, Miller claimed there had been an insurrection. But fifty years later, he saw things differently:

Brown: Do you feel the Negroes were planning any more than a fair settlement?
Miller: Not a bit in the world. That was what made me—I was pretty lenient with most of those fellows, as much as I could be.
Brown: Because the officials [*sic*] opinion in the *Arkansas Gazette* and Arkansas newspapers was that it was an insurrection against whites.
Miller: Well, it had every appearance of that, until you got in and went to the bottom of it which I finally was able to do as I've told you a while ago. There isn't any question but what, there isn't

any question but was the sharecroppers were being xxx defrauded.

Brown: The planters, you fell [*sic*] the planters were really out to crush that union, don't you?

Miller: Oh yes. Well it was a union, that [*sic*] what it was. When that boy [Adkins] was killed they decided to crush it. I don't think they would have, had that unfortunate occurrence not occurred.[41]

Comparing his interview in 1976 with his actions and letter to McRae, one has to conclude that John Miller wanted to be remembered as being on the right side of history but that he forgot he had left a trail he wouldn't be able to hide.

Like Brough before him, Thomas McRae listened to the voices of the people he trusted most and in June 1921 refused to commute the sentences of the Moore defendants. The day after the Helena delegation visited him McRae announced that he would let the courts decide the fate of the defendants but that he would not interfere with the judicial process. It would be a promise the defendants' counsel would use to their advantage.

Since a man known to be as sympathetic as Brough had refused to commute a single defendant, McRae's decision didn't surprise Scipio Jones and Edgar McHaney. In fact, they thought they were prepared for it. They immediately filed a petition for a writ of habeas corpus in federal district court in Little Rock. Unfortunately, the federal judge Jacob Trieber, who would have heard the case, was in St. Paul, Minnesota, on temporary assignment to the Eighth Circuit Court of Appeals and was not due back in his chambers until after the scheduled date of the execution. It is not known why a substitute judge could not have been appointed to hear the case, but apparently one was not available. Now truly desperate, Jones and McHaney turned back to the state courts of Arkansas to get a stay until Judge Trieber returned from St. Paul.

McHaney and Jones knew one judge in Little Rock who might be sympathetic to the plight of the defendants. At first blush, John Martineau, the chancery judge of Pulaski County, might not seem as if he could have been bothered by the plight of six blacks who were about to be executed. A biographical sketch of him describes him this way: "Judge Martineau was not a man who cared about accumulating wealth. Living comfortably and pleasantly meant more to him. He was very immaculate in his dress and always had his clothes made to order. He belonged to the Country Club and a group of friends gave him a fine set of golf clubs . . . but [he] never could play golf."[42] A widower, Martineau had apparently made do on his judge's salary, but he had recently remarried, and it had changed his life. It would have been hard to resist gossiping about the judge's new wife, Mabel. The story was that as a young woman in widow's weeds, Mabel had gotten on a train in Little Rock and that by the time she got off in Pine Bluff, forty-eight miles away, she had changed her clothes from dark to bright and become engaged to be married to an older man she had met en route. The man was old Judge Thomas, a rich plantation owner from Clarendon, who allowed Mabel to entertain their guests on the banks of the White River with peacocks strutting about. After a successful and happy marriage, the judge had conveniently died, leaving Mabel a rich widow with no desire to stay in steamy eastern Arkansas. Now Mabel, her hair cut short and feather boas flying, could be seen driving her new husband to the Little Rock Country Club in her robin's-egg blue LaSalle. The judge didn't drive.[43]

But if Martineau had a reputation for living well, he was also known for having an expansive view of his judicial duties. "He was ready to cut through anything that seemed to stand in the way of justice," it was written of him after his death.[44]

At this point, with two days to go before the scheduled executions, Jones and McHaney needed justice in a hurry, because they certainly didn't have the law on their side. Nobody knew this better than Martineau, who had just been reversed by the Arkansas Supreme Court only a few years earlier in *Ferguson v. Martineau* for taking jurisdiction of a criminal case and trying to stop an execution.[45] Martineau's court heard divorces and other civil matters. He had no more authority to issue a writ of habeas corpus to stop an execution than Mabel did. The supreme court of Arkansas had slapped him down once. Most judges get the hint. A first-year law student would have known he didn't have the power to intervene in a criminal case. A judge who won't follow the law, especially on an issue like this one, doesn't help his chances of being reelected. Martineau, however, had a stubborn streak, not unlike Ulysses Bratton. Years later, when as governor he was about to appoint Edgar McHaney to the Arkansas Supreme Court and lawyers were joining together to oppose this appointment on the grounds that McHaney had not served as a lower court trial judge, a Pulaski County attorney who knew Martineau well said there wasn't any point in taking on that battle: "He will appoint E. L. McHaney if every lawyer in Arkansas is against it."[46]

Martineau, whose family had moved to Arkansas from Missouri when he was two, had a wider vision of the world than most Arkansans. Much of the Martineau family had settled in Canada, where they had become lawyers and priests. At one time in his life Martineau regularly corresponded in French with an uncle in Canada. The Canadian Martineaus "were devoted to God and to the welfare of the Indians," wrote Marcel Martineau in 1901.[47]

Though Martineau was stubborn and idealistic, for a man as ambitious as he was (he had served two terms in the Arkansas House of Representatives prior to becoming Pulaski County judge), helping out the Moore defendants was risky business. It would only buy some time. Still, he signed the writ and enjoined the state of Arkansas from proceeding with the executions, ordering the warden of the penitentiary, E. H. Dempsey, to show up for a hearing in his court on June 10, the day the men were to be executed.

Knowing Martineau didn't have a leg to stand on, the state attorney general, J. S. Utley, who had succeeded Arbuckle, filed a writ of prohibition with the Arkansas Supreme Court on June 9 to dissolve Martineau's order. A writ of prohibition would only be successful if a court was wholly without jurisdiction. And in actuality, Martineau's act was not even clothed by a fig leaf. Chief Justice McCullough voted to grant the attorney general's petition without further argument or a hearing. Had McCullough's position carried the day, the Moore defendants would have been executed, but the other members of the court agreed that they shouldn't grant a writ of prohibition without a hearing and allowed the postponement of the executions. Nothing was more crucial than this decision to follow the court's regular procedures, but even now the Moore defendants were not out of the woods. The *Arkansas Democrat* admitted that certain unidentified state officials had wanted to carry out "the executions on Friday," despite Martineau's order.[48] The *Democrat* pointed out how embarrassing it would have been to the state had the executions been carried out: "Here, the world would have said, and said rightly, was a state so thirsty for blood of a half-dozen wretched negroes that her own officials were not willing to let the law take its course, but must go ahead with execution, taking their own chance with the courts later. What a counsel of madness!"[49]

At the oral argument in the Arkansas Supreme Court chamber at the state capitol on June 12, Edgar McHaney barely got started on the contention that the defendants' confessions had been obtained through tor-

ture before Chief Justice McCullough thundered at him that this issue
was irrelevant. The only question was whether a chancery court had the
power to take jurisdiction over criminal cases. In his decision,
McCullough, on June 20, repeated language from *Ferguson v. Martineau:*
"Courts of equity have to do with civil and property rights, and they have
no jurisdiction to interfere by injunction with criminal proceedings."

But by then the danger of immediate execution of the Moore defendants had passed.[50] McRae, who by law could have set a new execution
date fifteen days after the decision, made good on his commitment to let
the issues be decided by the courts. Jones and McHaney filed a writ of
error and appealed the cases directly to the United States Supreme Court,
knowing this was doomed to failure as well. The appropriate way to
argue that mob violence had dominated the trial court proceedings was
through a writ of habeas corpus in federal court, but there was no point
in pursuing this until the United States Supreme Court had denied their
appeal.

McRae may well have been influenced by the point made by the editorial in the *Democrat*. There was only so much blood the state's citizens
could stomach without appearing to be utter barbarians. The "insurrection" had been put brutally repressed. The union was gone. Most of the
blacks thought responsible were behind bars. What was the hurry?
Whether the men who sat in the governor's chair cared to admit it or not,
they were influenced by how they and the state appeared to the outside
world. There would be plenty of time to execute the men. But unbe-
knownst to them, an event was about to occur that would change the litigation in the cases of the Elaine Twelve forever.

CHAPTER 11

Affidavits from Unlikely Sources

*It was not the money I did what I did for the Colored People in the South, I knew
the streight of the thing . . . I did this for them. . . .*
—H. F. Smiddy

August 1921

On August 4, the United States Supreme Court, as expected, denied
the writ of error. The Moore cases again seemed on track for the same
dramatic finale that had occurred in June.[1] Governor McRae set new execution dates for September 23. In fact, the drama was more on paper than
real. McRae had pledged to allow the courts to have the last word, and
all the parties now expected the Moore defendants to wind up in federal
court, where Edgar McHaney and Scipio Jones would fire their last legal
bullet—a writ of habeas corpus.

Jones and McHaney had changed their tactics for the upcoming
October battle on behalf of the Ware defendants in the circuit court of
Lee County in Marianna, some thirty miles from Helena. They felt it
would·do no good to try the case themselves. A Delta jury of all-white
men wasn't going to pay attention to them. The trick was to find credible local counsel who would fight tooth and nail for the defendants—an
unlikely prospect, it would have seemed. In an August 30 letter to Mary
White Ovington, McHaney asked for "authorization to employ local
counsel at Marianna, Ark. and promise him that he will be paid his fee
of $2500."[2] He also asked for five thousand dollars for additional
expenses.

The NAACP was, as usual, unhappy about McHaney's request for
more money and reminded him of the original deal. In a snit, McHaney
wrote back on September 16 that his firm was "tender[ing] its resignation and ask[ing] that you secure other counsel."[3]

This bit of pretended brinkmanship (McHaney knew he couldn't
withdraw from the cases with the executions scheduled for September 23)
was rebuffed by the NAACP, which told him it expected him to carry out

his obligations, which he did. His letter may have caused some historians wrongly to assume that he was no longer involved in the cases when in fact he continued to make significant contributions to the defense of both the Moore and the Ware defendants.

Ultimately, it would take the then-princely sum of ten thousand dollars to hire local counsel, money mostly raised by Scipio Jones. who was convinced they had found the right men for the job.[4] R. D. Smith, in fact, was from Marianna, and Burke Mann was from Forrest City, less than twenty miles north. Ten thousand dollars was a lot of money, but as Edgar McHaney had once told the NAACP, one had to take into consideration how much business a lawyer would lose by taking a case. Neither man had "advanced views" about blacks, but both were competent attorneys and were willing to put on an aggressive defense. The defendants were no more popular than they had been in Helena. Before they had been transferred to the Marianna jail on June 25, there had been rumors that they would be lynched on their way into town. Burned by his experience with the Lowery lynching, McRae himself had met with the Lee County sheriff and the penitentiary board to work out a successful plan to bring them into the county seat by special train.[5]

How Edgar McHaney found T. K. Jones and H. F. Smiddy is not known, but in a letter to Mary White Ovington on August 30, he wrote, "We now have two white witnesses who were in the trouble at Helena and Elaine from beginning to end and who are going to testify for us."[6] The inherent conflicts in helping witnesses (for prosecution or defense) with financial support were obvious but simply couldn't be avoided. "Mr. E. L. McHaney got me to make this affidavit and said I would be taken care of until I could get on my feet again," wrote Smiddy soon after McHaney contacted him.[7]

Yet the affidavits would be worth it. They were potent as two sticks of dynamite, for they were directly aimed at the testimony that had been adduced in the trials against the Elaine Twelve. A prosecutor might pretend to lick his chops in anticipation of cross-examining two turncoats like Smiddy and Jones, but since through their testimony they had already placed themselves directly in the middle of the events of October 1, one could not argue that these two men didn't have some direct knowledge of what they were saying.

The affidavits were significant for two reasons. First, they would have great impact on the majority opinion in the United States Supreme Court decision in *Moore v. Dempsey*. (The affidavits would be attached to the writ of habeas corpus filed in federal court.) Second, as already described, together with John Miller's admissions they provide independent verification of a massacre of blacks by white mobs on October 1 and of the routine torture of blacks to get false testimony in the Elaine trials. And though it will never be conclusively known who fired the first shots, they provide some evidence that Adkins, Pratt, and the black trusty Collins first fired into the church, thus provoking return fire from the guards outside.

In considering any affidavit to be used in a judicial proceeding, one has to remember that the person who draws up the document is the lawyer. This fact does not necessarily call its veracity into question, but it does account for its structure. First, the affidavit of T. K. Jones. "In charge of the Memphis Division," he had been taken by his job to Helena on the night of September 30, 1919.[8] At seven o'clock that night he was approached by deputy sheriff Dick Dazell, who requested the help of Will Adkins and Smiddy in going to Elaine with him and arresting a man named Clem, who "was charged with some kind of misdemeanor."[9]

Although it does not appear from his affidavit that this mission had anything to do with their jobs, it would not have been unusual for Missouri-Pacific employees to cooperate in local law enforcement matters, and Jones said they could go if they wanted to. In his affidavit Jones says that Adkins agreed to go with Pratt, but Smiddy did not. Jones says that when they left at about nine o'clock, he heard them say they were first going by E. J. Weyeth's house, though he did not hear them say for what purpose. Jones went on to bed in the Cleiborne Hotel. Smiddy had a room across from him. At two o'clock he received a telephone call from Dick Dazell, who said they "had gotten into some trouble down about Hoop Spur" and asked if he and Smiddy would go with a group of men to investigate.[10] Jones awakened Smiddy, and in two cars a group of nine left Helena to find out what had happened. When they got to Hoop Spur at around four o'clock in the morning, it was still dark. He immediately went over to the automobile in the road and found Adkins's dead body close by. Adkins's body was "about 30 feet north of the bridge across the slough which runs across the public road just north of the Hoop Spur church. . . . This bridge is about thirty-five or forty yards north of the church."[11] Jones does not describe how he felt, but it couldn't have been good. He was Adkins's supervisor, and the man had a family. He went into the church and saw the overturned benches but didn't examine it. They drove on to Elaine, where they called Sheriff Kitchens in Helena.

Then around sunup they returned to Hoop Spur: "I was more concerned about the disposition of Mr. Atkins' [*sic*] body than I was about the condition of the church house."[12]

Obviously, Jones wasn't willing to say that he noticed the church was full of bullet holes, as Smiddy's affidavit said, and his attorneys felt compelled to give an explanation. If in fact the church showed evidence of bullet holes, it would tend to suggest there had been an attack on it.

The affidavits of Jones and Smiddy both contain information that purports to show that the church at Hoop Spur was a target the night of September 30. However, they give quite different versions. Jones states:

> Along in the afternoon of the same day [October 1] while again at Elaine I heard some planters talking and from their conversation I understand that a number of white men had gone to the Hoop Spur churchhouse the night before for the purpose of breaking up the meeting of the negroes there and that the white people had shot into the church and started the shooting. Just who these men were I do not now recall. One of them said to the other, "My negroes don't belong to that blankety blank union." The other said, "How in the hell do you know they don't?" He answered and said, "I told my negroes about two weeks ago that if they joined that blankety blank union I would kill every one of them."[13]

The possibility that others besides Adkins and Pratt and the black trusty Collins were involved in the shooting has long been an object of speculation. The NAACP forwarded a letter to Scipio Jones from a resident of Oklahoma that said that Robert Hill's mother had said she had been told that whites had gone out to the meeting to break it up. Jones responded by letter that this was not one of the defense theories but that they would investigate it.[14] The difficulty with this scenario is that it does not explain the undeniable fact that Adkins, Pratt, and Collins were out at the church that night. Further, had there been evidence of a separate or coordinated attack, it would have been brought out by Murphy and Jones during the second round of trials in Helena.

The affidavit of H. F. Smiddy suggests another scenario. The night of September 29 he had been up with Adkins searching for a man who had allegedly stolen property. He said he was too tired to go out to Hoop Spur with Adkins and Pratt and Collins: "I had supper with Adkins. Afterwards about 9 or 9:15 P.M. they got in an automobile in front of the court house, together with a negro by the name of Kid Collins, and left, and said they were going by Mr. E. J. Weyeth's to get some whiskey. That was the last time I saw them that night." Smiddy's affidavit confirms that Jones got him up and that he went out to Hoop Spur and on to Elaine with Jones and the other men: "About 8 o'clock in the morning Kid Collins, a negro who had come in the car with Atkins [*sic*] and Pratt, came into the church house and I had a conversation with him there. He told me they came down for the purpose of breaking up the meeting; that they stopped there in the road and Mr. Atkins [*sic*] begun shooting. He said that the Negroes returned the fire and the shooting became general."[15]

This statement is impossible to verify. It is noteworthy that Jones does not mention in his affidavit that Smiddy ever told him what Collins had said. Had the Ware cases ever been retried, it would have virtually impossible for Smiddy to satisfactorily explain why he had not told his supervisor something as juicy and important as this. On the other hand, why would Smiddy make this up? One answer would be that he might have made it up to make his role in the affair as important as possible. Certainly, he felt that his word would be accepted over that of a black trusty. It is entirely possible that Adkins and Pratt got liquored up, as the affidavit suggests, and stopped off at the church to fire into it to harass the union. It seems totally unlikely that their automobile broke down or that they stopped to urinate—or whatever explanation they offered to justify how they happened to be in front of the church at that particular moment. There is no hard evidence to suggest that Sheriff Kitchens, whatever his views about blacks, had coordinated with planters an assault on the church in advance. If there had been such a plan, Smiddy or Jones would surely have been privy to it.

Had there been a retrial of the Moore defendants, T. K. Jones's testimony, assuming it followed his affidavit, would have caused some problems for the prosecution, especially in the Clinton Lee case. The prosecution contended that Frank Hicks had fired the shot that killed Lee sitting in a car. Jones's affidavit read, "I didn't go out with any of the parties in search of the negroes. Mr. Sam Austin [the Helena chief of police] and I were left near the Hoop Spur commissary to guard the road across where the public road crosses the railroad with orders to arrest all negroes who came by there armed."[16] He was there from 8:30 to 12:30 and then was told to move down to the McCoy house, about a half-mile away, where an attack was expected. He remained there until three o'clock and encountered no attack. He saw blacks in the vicinity, but none were armed: "I know positively no negro stopped in the road, kneeled, and made a shot or two up the road, because if he had done so I would have seen him as I was looking right at the bunch of negroes that crossed the road."[17]

However, Jones's affidavit makes it difficult to believe that he could be this sure of himself because he admits that he "was not immediately present when Clinton Lee was shot." On the other hand, he also states that he "did not see a single negro with a gun or weapon of any kind during the whole day I was in the country."[18] There would always be the suspicion that Lee had been accidentally killed by cross fire from another white man.

After three o'clock Jones went into Wabash and Elaine, where he stayed until approximately seven o'clock that evening. He gives no details of what occurred there, but as he was riding the train back to Helena, he "passed the Hoop Spur church house. . . . I noticed that it had been burned down sometime during the day."[19] Blacks contended that the church had been burned to destroy evidence.

Jones had been present when James Tappan was mortally wounded. He states, "Lieu. Tappan was brought in a dying condition and I saw him die on the bed in the McCoy house," but gives no further details concerning him.[20]

Jones's strongest testimony involves the torture that took place inside the jail:

> I saw a great many negroes whipped on the third floor of the county jail to compel them to give evidence against themselves and others about the trouble. . . . They were not only whipped but formaldehyde was put to their noses and were stripped naked and put into an electric chair which they had in the room to further frighten and torture them. I not only personally saw a great many negroes whipped with a leather strap that would cut blood at every lick, but I whipped probably two dozen of them myself. I either whipped or helped to whip several of these petitioners. I don't know which, but I do remember that I helped to whip Frank Moore and J. E. Knox. Walter Ward, one of the witnesses against the petitioners was whipped two or three times and put in the electric chair to make him testify against the petitioners.

Col. George Murphy, a one-time Confederate officer who carried his war wounds into the courtroom, was lead attorney for the Elaine 12 until his death in October of 1920. *Courtesy of Butler Center for Arkansas Studies, Central Arkansas Library System.*

Edgar L. McHaney, a law partner of Colonel Murphy, and later Arkansas supreme court justice, proved to be a valuable member of the defense team for the Elaine 12. *Courtesy of Butler Center for Arkansas Studies, Central Arkansas Library System.*

John E. Martineau, Pulaski County chancellor who later became governor and a federal district judge, bent the law to gain time for six of the Elaine 12. *Courtesy of Butler Center for Arkansas Studies, Central Arkansas Library System.*

Judge Jacob Trieber, a brilliant Jewish immigrant from Prussia who eventually settled in Helena, and was appointed federal district judge in Little Rock, signed a writ of habeas corpus for six of the Elaine 12 and then took himself off the cases. *Courtesy of Butler Center for Arkansas Studies, Central Arkansas Library System.*

Scipio A. Jones posing with six members of the Elaine 12 after their release. *Courtesy of Butler Center for Arkansas Studies, Central Arkansas Library System.*

Scipio A. Jones posing with six members of the Elaine 12 after their release. *Courtesy of Butler Center for Arkansas Studies, Central Arkansas Library System.*

Moorfield Storey wrote the brief in *Moore v. Dempsey* which went to the United States Supreme Court in 1923 and eventually resulted in the freedom of six of the Elaine 12 in 1925. *Courtesy of Butler Center for Arkansas Studies, Central Arkansas Library System.*

Death mask of Scipio A. Jones, who died at the age of eighty, his circumstances much reduced. *Courtesy of Butler Center for Arkansas Studies, Central Arkansas Library System.*

Jones said that not all prisoners were whipped but that all saw the whippings. A doctor had to be brought to attend to the injuries. Both Jones and Smiddy implicate others. Jones states: "Those that did the whipping of the negroes in the Phillips County jail other than myself and Mr. Smiddy were Mr. Dick Dazell, Louis Anselman, Charlie Gist, and some others whose name [sic] I do not recall."[21]

Significantly, Jones confirms the mob atmosphere that surrounded the trials: "Large crowds thronged the court house and grounds, all of whom were unfriendly to the defendants, and desired their condemnation and death. The feeling against them was so bitter and so strong and so universal that it was absolutely unanimous and no man could have sat upon a jury in any of these cases and have voted for an acquittal and remained in Helena afterwards."[22] Jones also states that the mob surrounding the jail when the blacks were first brought in would have lynched them had it not been for the presence of the soldiers: "They were told that if the mob would not lynch the negroes that they would be tried and convicted."[23]

As mentioned in chapter 3, H. F. Smiddy had gone out with the posse that morning. They began to arrest blacks, going out to their houses and bringing them into the church at Hoop Spur. Smiddy states:

So far as I know, none of them we found armed that morning. Between nine and ten o'clock on the morning of October 1st a great many people from Helena and other portions of Phillips County, and from other surrounding counties, began coming in, quite a large number of them, several hundred of them, and began to hunt negroes and shooting and killing them as they came to them. The posse I was in was composed of fifty or sixty men. We left the church house and marched down a slough leading off from the church. . . . We began firing into the thicket from both sides thinking possibly there were negroes in the thicket and we could run them out and kill them. As we marched down the thicket to the southwest, I saw about five or six negroes come out unarmed, holding up their hands, and some of them running and trying to get away. They were shot down and killed by members of the posse.

I didn't see a single negro during all the man hunt that was armed, and I didn't see a single negro fire a shot. I was present when Jim Miller was killed and Arthur Washington was killed, and when Milliken [sic] Giles was injured. I shot Milliken [sic] Giles myself.

He was in the edge of the thicket trying to hide. When I shot him he was not trying to shoot anybody and didn't have a gun.[24]

What possessed Smiddy to implicate himself so thoroughly is not known, but his willingness to do so certainly adds to the sense that he was describing precisely what he remembered from that day. In the process he also casts doubt as to who shot James Tappan. There were men on both sides firing into the thicket:

He [Tappan] was on my side of the thicket, which was the east side of the thicket. He had gone down that side of the thicket and when we came to the point we turned around and were going back on the same side of the thicket. At the point where Mr. Tappan was killed the thicket was probably 30 feet wide. I am sure that there were no negroes in the thicket at that point as we searched it thoroughly after the shooting of Tappan and found no negroes near anywhere he was shot.

Mr. Tappan was shot in the left side of the face. . . . He was shot with a load of buck-shot at a short distance. I don't know who killed him, but I feel perfectly sure that he was accidentally killed by a member of our own posse. About the time he was killed somebody hollered from both sides of the thicket, "Look out, we are shooting our own men." I know this is possible because I was shot in the right shoulder by a stray shot of some kind by a member of our posse, and also Mr. Dazell was shot over the left eye.[25]

Smiddy also states that he had not heard Herbert Thompson say that the blacks would be unharmed if they surrendered: "When we started down the thicket it was the understanding of all of us that we would shoot the negroes as we came to them, which we did."[26]

By coincidence Smiddy had also been in the car when Clinton Lee was killed and was nearly wounded himself, the bullet passing through his coat: "I don't know who fired the shot. I didn't see anybody at the time the shot was fired. A short time before the shot, I saw a bunch of Negroes, probably between twenty and thirty, crossing the dirt road about half a mile south of the McCoy house and get into a corn field on the east side of the dirt road. They were running,—seemed to be scared and seemed to be trying to get out of the way of the white folks. I didn't see any negro with a gun in his hand as he crossed the dirt road, although they were in plain view."[27]

Smiddy continues by saying that although an attack was expected on Elaine, none occurred and they found no blacks. Not a shot was fired, so far as he knew. But the attacks on blacks were just beginning: "During that afternoon, October 1st, a crowd of men came into the vicinity of Elaine from Mississippi and began the indiscriminate hunting down and shooting of Negroes. They shot and killed men, women, and children without regard to whether they were guilty or innocent of any connection with the killing of anybody, or whether members of the union or not. Negroes were killed time and time again out in the fields picking cotton, harming nobody. They [sic] next day, October 2nd, the soldiers came there and placed the town of Elaine under martial law."[28]

Neither Smiddy nor Jones mentions any misconduct on the part of the soldiers. Whether they observed any misconduct or not, the soldiers were not a part of the cases. Like T. K. Jones, Smiddy admits that he had taken part in the torture of prisoners: "I personally administered the lash and saw others do it time and time again to a great many Negroes who had been previously whipped. The lash was applied on the old sores made at the first whipping, and usually the second whipping would get the Negro to say what was wanted if he had refused in the first instance. One of the petitioners in this case, Frank Moore, was whipped at least three times to try to compel him to give evidence against himself and the other petitioners, which he never did do. He stated he would rather die in this manner, than to tell something on himself or others that was not true."[29]

Smiddy's affidavit adds detail after detail about the torture. Four black prisoners in the jail who were not among the defendants were ordered to hold the defendants face down on the concrete floor as they were being whipped: "I know that Walter Ward was whipped and compelled to give this testimony, and I furthermore know that George Green and John Jefferson were told that if they didn't give the same evidence they would get what Walter Ward and the others had got. . . . Walter Ward was whipped about three times; had formaldehyde put to his nose; and was put into the electric chair before he agreed to testify to what he did testify to."[30] The only one of the Elaine Twelve who was not whipped was Ed Coleman, who was so old that the authorities were probably afraid he would die of a heart attack or stroke. Smiddy named the same white individuals as Jones had as participating in the torture.

Before Smiddy finished, Jones and McHaney had him get out in the open that he had testified differently at trial to one detail in his affidavit: "I did testify heretofore that I examined the Hoop Spur church house and found no bullet holes in it. This was true so far as it went. The first time I was at the Hoop Spur church house I examined it and it was dark and I was unable to see any bullet holes in the church and didn't find any. The second time I did find them as before stated. Furthermore, I was instructed by those in authority that I should give no testimony of any character favorable to the defendants."[31]

September 1921
Little Rock

On September 21, McRae, as expected, again denied requests for clemency. Nor would he delay the executions. The stage was set for the defendants' entry into federal court, where they expected better treatment. After all, the district judge was Jacob Trieber, a remarkable man and jurist who had long demonstrated his sympathy for the federally protected rights of Delta blacks. In 1904 he had ruled in *United States v. Morris* and *United States v. Hodges*—cases that involved the intimidation and harassment of blacks by "whitecappers" in eastern Arkansas—that "the right to lease lands and to accept employment for hire are fundamental rights, inherent in every free citizen, is indisputable."[32] Though the United States Supreme Court would overrule his interpretation of the Thirteenth Amendment, banning slavery, and of the Civil Rights Acts of 1866 and 1870, Trieber's reasoning would be vindicated by the Supreme Court in 1968. Scipio Jones especially had high expectations. With the help of Hugh Fisher, he had already secured one victory in the Elaine cases in front of Trieber. He had represented V. E. Powell, an associate of Robert Hill, and had won the case without even having had a trial.

Trieber was ideal. The man had come a long way to become a United States district court judge. His family had moved from Prussia to Saint Louis to Helena, which experienced an influx of Jewish families during and after the Civil War. In Helena Jews thrived, and Trieber had thrived along with them. One chronicler of the Jewish experience in Arkansas counted in 1909 "at least twenty-two Jewish businesses in Helena. . . ."[33] Not only did Jewish people excel in the commercial life of the town, they were accepted for the most part as social equals: "Jews were accepted as members of the local country club when it was established in 1916, and some served as its president at various times."[34] Acceptance, however, was not total; Jewish boys could not join high school fraternities.

Jacob Trieber was a phenomenon even among high achievers. Though he had never graduated from college or law school, Trieber, a Republican, became the first Jewish person in the United States ever to be appointed a U.S. district judge, no small feat considering that he had come to the United States as an immigrant at the age of thirteen, had a strong German accent, and had settled in eastern Arkansas. There were times, though, when he wondered at his choice of states. In a letter to a fellow Republican in 1901 he wrote, "People wouldn't know there is anything in Arkansas except murders and demagoguery. . . . This country is growing by leaps and bounds . . . while Arkansas is asleep . . . despite her great natural resources."[35]

Jones and McHaney had been waiting for a judge like Trieber since their experience with Chancellor Martineau. As soon as McRae turned them down again, they filed their action pursuant to the Habeas Corpus Act of 1867, which granted protection to individuals imprisoned in derogation of their constitutional rights. The petition was a collage of their previous arguments, affidavits, and pleadings, accompanied this time also by the affidavits of Jones and Smiddy. The thrust of the petition was that the defendants' Fourteenth Amendment rights to due process of law had been violated. In it they recited their familiar story of peonage, the union's efforts to resist it, the conduct of the trials, and the torture. The petition alleged that "the entire trial, verdict and judgment against them was but an empty ceremony. . . ."[36]

Immediately upon their filing of the petition, two events occurred that no one had predicted. First, though Trieber signed the writ of habeas corpus and granted a hearing, he then recused. He said he couldn't preside over the hearing because of his Helena connections, though by this time he had moved his family to Little Rock. Though the executions had been temporarily halted, a new judge would have to be appointed. Strictly speaking, if Trieber was going to recuse, he should never have even signed the writ of habeas corpus. Still, though he had taken himself out of the case, by granting the hearing he had gotten Jones and McHaney over the first important hurdle.

Second, and most importantly, the state of Arkansas filed a demurrer that meant that the position of the attorney general was that the state was entitled to a dismissal of the habeas corpus petition as a matter of law, without even a trial. On September 26 the visiting federal judge, J. H. Cotteral, from Oklahoma, granted the state's demurrer after a hearing that had taken place the preceding day. On September 27, Judge Cotteral certified that there was "probable cause for appeal."[37] The practical effect of the state's demurrer and Cotteral's decision was to allow the defendants

to appeal the case in a posture favorable to them: for the purpose of deciding the case on the issue of law and avoiding the necessity of a trial, the
Supreme Court was bound to treat the facts alleged by the defendants as
though they were true. However, if it found for the Moore defendants on
their legal arguments (due process claims), the Supreme Court of the
United States could remand the case back to the U.S. district court to
determine whether the allegations of the petition were true. But on appeal
the Court was bound to treat the allegations of torture, mob domination,
and peonage as true. Scipio Jones and Edgar McHaney had to be pleased
once they realized that this would be the best posture for the case when
it went up to the United States Supreme Court.

In the state court arena, the affidavits of Smiddy and Jones were having a greater effect on the prosecution than anticipated. The state of
Arkansas in the Ware cases, set for October, declared that it was not ready
for trial and asked for a continuance. Jackson had been beaten the year
before by E. D. Robertson, who was thought to be better than Jackson
or at least more sympathetic. The cases were passed until the next term
with the consent of the defendants' attorneys. With the reluctance of the
prosecution to try the cases, Scipio Jones and Edgar McHaney may well
have suspected that the Elaine Twelve were now on a slow train to
freedom.

CHAPTER 12

Moore v. Dempsey: A Supreme Victory

I told the Court that conditions had grown up there that were worse than before the Civil War.

> —*Letter from Ulysses Bratton about his oral argument to the Supreme Court, November 1921*

November 1921–March 1923

Governor Brough and the white power structure in Phillips County had bragged that the county had never had a lynching. If it was in fact intact, that record ended in November with two lynchings. On November 18, "a Helena mob of some twenty-five to thirty men shot Will Turner, a black man accused of assaulting a thirteen year old white girl, and burned his body."[1] The girl had been on her way to her job at a telephone exchange. The sheriff claimed he had been trying to get Turner to Marianna when his car had been stopped and Turner taken out and shot. After the ambulance brought him in, it was stopped. "Burn the body!" the crowd chanted. It was stripped naked and set on fire across from the courthouse.

The Wednesday before Thanksgiving there was another lynching, in Lake Village, south of Helena in Chicot County. Robert Hicks, a well-known black man, had written an insulting letter to a white girl who was said to be eighteen years old. Hicks was taken four miles out of town and shot numerous times. The lynching in Lake Village was not reported in the *Arkansas Gazette* until the Saturday after Thanksgiving. The *Gazette* reported that the authorities in Lake Village had tried to suppress the news of it. A coroner's inquest reported that the man "had met death at the hands of unknown persons."[2]

On November 25 the second lynching occurred in Phillips County. "Dallas Knickerson, also black, was shot by whites in Cypert for allegedly assaulting a white girl," reported the *Arkansas Gazette.*[3]

This wave of terror could not have been reassuring to the Ware defendants in the Marianna jail, which was right up the road from Helena.

The authorities in Helena had warned from the beginning that the only reason there hadn't been a lynching was the promise that "justice" would be done. The lynchings were a reminder that given enough rumors and hysteria death could come for any black male at any time, whether he was in police custody or not.

The notice of appeal of Judge Cotteral's decision had been filed by Scipio Jones in October, and the search was on by the NAACP to find a lawyer to argue the case before the Supreme Court. The deal all along with Murphy had been that his firm's responsibility in the cases would not go further than U.S. district court. That did not change with his death.

Picking the right lawyer to argue a case to the United States Supreme Court was not the cottage industry that it has become today, when national advocacy groups will actually pay off local counsel and their clients to keep a bad case from coming up to the high court. The NAACP knew from the beginning who it wanted—its former board president, Moorfield Storey, who had the right stuff as a blue-blood Boston lawyer. From Mary White Ovington's point of view, Storey fairly reeked of the kind of moral rectitude this case demanded. Not only did the patrician Storey number Puritans in his family's lineage, but he also had in fact clerked as a young man for U.S. senator Charles Sumner, whose advocacy on behalf of blacks during Reconstruction had become a legend in the North and a horror story in the South. Not only that, he was an excellent lawyer. Ovington adored him. Her book, *Portraits in Color,* is dedicated to him. The only problem was that Storey was old and trying to wind down his practice. He said he would think about it and at least read the record in the case if some other lawyer did the preliminary work of preparing the appeal. There was no urgency for him to make up his mind. It would be January 1923 before *Moore v. Dempsey* would be orally argued. Though Scipio Jones had advised the NAACP "to find the ablest constitutional lawyer possible," Jones himself would want to be asked to participate in the oral argument, along with whoever was selected.[4] It is every lawyer's dream to argue a case before the highest court in the land. No black lawyer from Arkansas ever had. Jones came a step closer to it when the NAACP hired him to prepare the appeal, which did not include writing the legal brief or orally arguing it to the United States Supreme Court. Storey, who initially suggested that Ulysses Bratton be retained as counsel rather than himself, said he didn't have time to attend to such details.

One reason for Storey not leaping on this case was the Leo Frank case, which stood in the way of the Moore defendants like a huge boulder. Lynching and mob violence were not phenomena limited only to blacks, of course (though blacks were their primary targets). Leo Frank, a Jew, had been charged with killing a thirteen-year-old girl in Atlanta in 1913. Shrieking mobs had surrounded the courthouse, yelling for Frank's blood and the blood of those responsible if he didn't get the death penalty. Inside, the spectators were yelling so loud that the trial judge had difficulty hearing the jurors' guilty verdict as they were polled. The Georgia Supreme Court had no problem affirming such conduct, and the case went up to the United States Supreme Court on a writ of habeas corpus after it had initially refused to hear the case on a writ of error. Frank hadn't been given due process under the Fourteenth Amendment, his lawyers contended. In its decision in *Frank v. Mangrum,* the Court essentially said that the federal courts wouldn't review criminal cases for due process violations if the state court had provided a "corrective process"—and the state of Georgia had. The case had been reviewed on three different occasions by the Georgia Supreme Court, which had concluded each time that there were no due process violations.[5] Frank was going to be a hard case to get around. After all, the Arkansas Supreme Court had reviewed the Moore defendants' due process claims and had found them insufficient.

The tragedy of Leo Frank. He couldn't win for losing. When the governor of Georgia courageously commuted his death sentence, the mob broke into the prison and hung him anyway.[6]

None of this was encouraging to the Elaine Twelve as the calendar turned over to 1922. And if the hostile attitude of the judicial system in the country, both federal and state, weren't bad enough, whites throughout the country, including in the North, seemed to have a need to formalize their prejudices. Not just a Southern phenomenon, the Ku Klux Klan was back and, in this slightly more civilized incarnation, as American as apple pie.

On February 10, 1922, four miles outside of Little Rock, about 650 men ate lamb and barbecued beef in a pasture, passing the time until the ceremony began that would induct them into the "Invisible Empire." The reporter for the *Arkansas Gazette* wrote that among the initiates were "state, county and city officials, preachers, lawyers, doctors, merchants, [and] laborers. . . . There were men who have barely reached their majority, and there were men whose hair is snowy white."[7]

A match was struck at eight o'clock igniting a pile of wood. The initiates "knelt before the cross, kissed a Bible and an American flag . . .

swore absolute fealty to the tenets of the Klan."[8] The Klan would soon become the new bully boy in Arkansas politics. Started in 1915 in Atlanta, this new incarnation was not nearly as violent as the old Reconstruction Klan had been, but it didn't need to be. Blacks in Arkansas were sufficiently cowed as it was. "Arkansas Klansmen only occasionally took action against 'uppity' Negroes. . . . One of the surprising features of Klan history in Arkansas is not that men in white robes beat up a few Negroes, but that, considering the social acceptability of violence against Negroes, only a few were assaulted," writes Charles Alexander, a historian of the Klan.[9]

What Scipio Jones and Edgar McHaney would have to worry about was the effect the Klan would have on Arkansas politics. They couldn't just wash their hands of the governor's office and pretend it didn't exist. After all, the Phillips County defendants were more than the Elaine Twelve. Regardless of what he said, McRae, like every governor, released men from the penitentiary before their sentences were up.

Not a member of the Klan, McRae won the Democratic primary (and thus, for all practical purposes, reelection) in 1922 by a four to one margin. McRae, however, was "reportedly regarded" by the Klan as a "friendly neutral" and received its support. McRae's executive secretary, Clarence Newton, who would go on to become the county judge of Pulaski County, was a Klan member.[10] Pulaski County was becoming a bastion of the Klan, a Mecca of intolerance toward Jews, Catholics, foreigners, and blacks. Jones and McHaney could only hope that if McRae was a "friendly neutral" he wouldn't shift into a higher gear in his second term.

Meanwhile, Smiddy's situation was becoming desperate. Had he known what he would have to go through, there is no doubt that he wouldn't have signed his name to any affidavit. He had lost another railroad job shortly after signing his name to the statement and hadn't worked since. Truly, he was a marked man. He was arrested in Memphis but released because there were no charges against him. There was a federal charge of extortion against him in Little Rock. McHaney and Jones had posted a thousand-dollar bond for him, but now he was in Kansas, which had become an emancipation zone for Arkansans who opposed the state power structure in the Elaine cases. "My wife is worrying herself to death about me and the Four little children we have neither one of the children are big enough to take care of them selves, so you can see I am in A bad shape right now," he wrote Walter White.[11] Smiddy felt that he wasn't being helped enough and resented it: "I'm the Fellow that saved them not no one els, I could not get A nother white man down their to make A affidavit to help save them only A man by the Name of T. K. Jones and he did not want to give the streight facks about it until I got right behind him."[12]

It fell to Scipio Jones to take care of the needs of both Smiddy and T. K. Jones, but nothing he did seemed to be enough. Smiddy even complained to Ulysses Bratton, who, in characteristic fashion, reprimanded Jones. "It is important that he not be permitted to be humiliated and suffer great loss, as a result of giving you the facts. I think that to permit such would indeed be an outrage, for it is undoubtedly too often true that men who dare to have the courage to stand out for what they know to be right are permitted to be humiliated and suffer severe reverses for that reason," Bratton wrote Jones.[13] Bratton was obviously thinking of his own humiliation in being forced to leave Arkansas, but his self-righteous tone could only have irritated Scipio Jones, who had taken on the role of chief Arkansas fundraiser and lawyer. If anybody knew what was at stake, it was Scipio Jones, who wrote Walter White in March that "I have taken care of both Smiddy's and Jones' families for about six months and am still contributing to their support."[14]

The exchanges over money between Smiddy and Scipio Jones provide a window into both men's personalities. Smiddy had confessed to torturing blacks and to having shot at least one defenseless man. Yet in February he was admitting to Walter White that Scipio Jones "balled me out good and plenty about the letter I wrote you several days ago."[15] Scipio Jones had written him that he was "very much surprised at the contents of your letter and regard it as the height of ingratitude on your part."[16] He had just visited Smiddy's family in Memphis and given his wife fifty dollars. In his March letter to Walter White, Jones wrote that he had given the men over eight hundred dollars. The NAACP eventually paid for Smiddy's family to move to Kansas.

At the April term of court in Lee County in 1922, C. E. Yingling, who was John Miller's law partner but also the newly elected prosecutor (prosecuting attorneys could have a private practice), again asked for a continuance. This time defense counsel Burke Mann objected. The team of Mann and Smith was ready for trial. Judge Robertson, who had defeated J. M. Jackson, set the cases over for the October term.

Throughout the summer of 1922 Moorfield Storey was prodded to handle the appeal by the NAACP, which went so far as to announce in July that he had agreed to take the case. Storey reminded James Weldon

Johnson that he had "promised only if after reading the record I found that I had an arguable case. I have never seen the record. Can you get me a copy?"[17] By September, however, he was on board. In a memo written on September 14, Johnson noted that Scipio Jones had called to find out if it had been definitively settled that Storey was going to argue the case. "As the Board knows," Johnson wrote, "it has been arranged that Mr. Jones will be associated with Mr. Storey in the conduct of the cases through the Supreme Court and will give Mr. Storey all the assistance in the preliminary work."[18]

In the same memo Johnson touches on the upcoming second retrial of the Ware defendants in October: "Mr. Jones stated that tremendous support has been given him in these cases by two local firms of attorneys. He felt that such local help was absolutely necessary." He goes on to note that the fee of these firms was "quite a large one—$10,000. Mr. Jones said he had already raised $7,000 of this amount and paid it to these two firms."[19] The money had come from the fraternal organizations that Scipio Jones represented. He wanted the NAACP to raise the other three thousand dollars. Whatever the NAACP could raise to help Jones would be well worth it. Johnson concludes the memo by writing, "Mr. Jones also stated that of the eight-seven [*sic*] who were sentenced to the penitentiary for terms of from three to twenty-one years, he has been able to secure the release of all of them on parole or otherwise excepting fourteen or fifteen, and he is making an effort, through paroles or furloughs, to secure the release of these."[20]

In October Yingling had the Ware cases passed again. In a letter to Walter White, Edgar McHaney reports the astonishing news that the local prosecutor had told him he was not going to retry the Ware defendants. Whether the prosecutor meant this or not, the Ware defendants were not released. The state had opened the door for McHaney and Jones to argue for the men's release because the law required that if two terms of court passed without a trial (with some exceptions), the defendant had to be released. That argument would not be made until the April term in 1923.[21]

Meanwhile, as the deadline for submitting the brief to the United States Supreme Court neared, possibly some jockeying was taking place as to who would conduct the oral argument with Moorfield Storey. At one point the NAACP understood that both Ulysses Bratton and Scipio Jones were going to participate. In a letter to Bratton on December 7, Walter White wrote, "I want to tell you how much we all appreciate your considerateness in agreeing to appear with Mr. Storey and Mr. Jones in these cases."[22] In the meantime, Scipio Jones was trying to keep Bratton's name off the brief. On December 21, he wrote Walter White:

> I fear that you misunderstood my position with reference to Mr. Bratton's name appearing on the brief. If Mr. Bratton's name appears on our printed briefs, when the Attorney General receives his copy of the brief, the newspapers of this City will make capital of the fact that Mr. Bratton was counselor for the Elaine prisoners, which in my opinion, will prejudice the mind of the public against our clients and deprive them of any chance they may have for executive clemency but if he should just appear and participate in the argument, I can say he volunteered and was not selected by the defendants.
>
> I am a friend of Mr. Bratton's and would be glad to help him in any way that I can and do not believe that he will object to the leaving of his name off of the brief. Have Judge Storey to leave Mr. Bratton's name off at my request and I will be personally responsible for a satisfactory explanation to Mr. Bratton.[23]

Bratton's name did not appear on the brief.

Was there some professional jealousy going on here? Perhaps, but if so it was understandable. Scipio Jones had lived and breathed all of the cases since the very beginning. Bratton had been gone for almost two years. As late as January 6, Scipio Jones expected to argue with Storey on January 9. A letter from James Weldon Johnson to a staff member in Washington, D.C., flatly stated, "The cases will be argued for the Association by Mr. Storey and Mr. Jones. We have wired Mr. Jones asking him to let us know the time of his arrival in Washington."[24] It must have been a terrible disappointment for Scipio Jones when Storey, in Washington, D.C., wired Walter White on the morning of January 9, 1923: "Jones not needed here. Case probably argued this afternoon."[25]

It appears that Storey had never wanted Scipio Jones to argue the case with him in the first place but didn't have the integrity to tell him that he wanted Bratton alone. It was not Storey's finest hour. There is no evidence that Scipio Jones expressed resentment to anyone about his shabby treatment, but he would become much more aggressive in the future and would not always wait for direction from the NAACP and the great Moorfield Storey. The Supreme Court of the United States might not be his turf in the Elaine cases, but from now on Arkansas sure as hell would be.

The law had not changed in the almost eight years since the Leo Frank decision, but the composition of the Court had most decidedly been altered. There were only three judges left who had voted in the majority on that decision. There had been two dissents in *Frank,* including a blistering opinion by Oliver Wendell Holmes, who wrote, "[I]t is our duty . . . to declare lynch law as little valid when practiced by a regularly drawn jury as when administered by one elected by a mob intent on death."[26] The judge who had written the majority opinion in *Frank,* Mahon Pitney, had just recently retired, leaving only eight justices to decide the case. The chances for overturning Frank had improved, but it was an open question as to what the Court would do. One of the new justices was the former president of the United States, William Howard Taft, a conservative, but he was balanced by the first Jewish member on the Court, the relatively liberal Louis D. Brandeis.

Bratton and Storey felt the oral argument went well. Only Justice McReynolds had appeared to be against the defendants. Even Taft had jumped on the Arkansas attorney general, Elbert Godwin, who had tried to dispute the allegations of torture and peonage. Taft had cut him down with the retort that he had demurred to the petition. Undoubtedly feeling at last that it had been worth taking on the state of Arkansas, even if that meant being run out of the state, Ulysses Bratton had gotten in his licks on peonage. "I told the Court that conditions had grown up there that were worse than before the Civil War," he wrote Walter White on January 11.[27] The Court heard it all—the violence, the exploitation, the kangaroo justice dealt the defendants.

Back in Arkansas the man who had done much of the work, Scipio Jones, must have had his own moment of satisfaction when he heard the decision that was announced on February 19. The state of Arkansas had not provided a "corrective process" or it would have corrected the decisions of the trials courts in the Elaine cases: "If the case is that the whole proceeding is a mask,—that counsel, jury, and judge were swept away to the fatal end by an irresistible wave of public passion, and that the state courts failed to correct the wrong,—neither perfection in the machinery for correction nor the possibility that the trial court and counsel saw no other way of avoiding an immediate outbreak of the mob can prevent this court from securing to the petitioners their constitutional rights."[28]

There were two dissents. Justice McReynolds, now writing for the minority, argued right past Holmes: "Under the disclosed circumstances I cannot agree that the solemn adjudications by courts of a great state . . .

can be successfully impeached by the mere ex parte affidavits made upon information and belief of interested convicts, joined by two white men,—confessedly atrocious criminals."[29]

McReynolds had a point, of course, but the majority wasn't setting the men free. It was sending the case back to federal district court with instructions to the judge to hold a hearing in which the petitioners would have an opportunity to prove everything they had alleged—a daunting proposition, to say the least.

Though the state's judicial system had been humiliated by the decision, the reaction by the *Arkansas Gazette* was predictable. The U.S. Supreme Court was of course wrong to reverse *Frank*. The effect would be even more delay, and the judicial system was slow enough already: "The Supreme Court has been looked upon as the last bulwark of law and order in the United States, where there is so little law. It is terrifying to contemplate the consequences of this case."[30]

In fact, there was plenty of law but little justice if your skin was black. To the Elaine Twelve, this could only have seemed a paper victory. After all, no one was being released, and in Lee County conditions in the Marianna jail were terrible and not getting any better.

Ed Ware got a letter smuggled out to Scipio Jones in February 1923: "Seems Like i Have Completely Lost My Health. . . . Listen, Mr. Jones, if there is any Way that you can give me some Relief now is the time i Wish you Would if you please Sir Because we is Suffering so much. . . . Here on this Hard concrete floor, and We is kep so confine and is fed so Bad until we are Just about Woe out."[31] At least in "the Walls" they had gotten to walk around occasionally.

In any advocacy organization there is always the temptation to sacrifice individuals to the group's principles. Now, with the great victory in *Moore v. Dempsey*, this urge would soon manifest itself in the NAACP. Scipio Jones had always had only one thing on his mind, and that was to obtain the release of all the men in as short a time as possible. Unlike anyone in the New York office, he had come to know the men as human beings. With the victory in *Moore*, the NAACP would see the defendants as symbols, not as men who were aging rapidly in an Arkansas jail. Apparently without waiting for the NAACP's blessing (not for the last time), Scipio Jones contacted John Miller, whose partner C. E. Yingling was prosecutor in the cases, to see if a deal was possible. On March 24, Miller got back in touch with him and reported back the terms that would be acceptable: "a plea of second degree murder, and a sentence of five years dated from the incarceration of these parties in the Penitentiary."[32]

Scipio Jones would have been delighted at these terms. This meant the men would be out a year from November. Yet this was just the first hurdle. Yingling would have to get the Phillips County authorities to agree. Miller wrote back that he would be in touch as soon as he had anything to report.

Jones's unilateral action touched off a debate over how to proceed with the cases, and it was at this juncture that the personal welfare of the men became less than the primary consideration for Moorfield Storey, who wrote Walter White on May 7, "I should dislike to have the prisoners plead guilty and take a five years' sentence. They had better lie in jail without plea for a year or two than incur a certain imprisonment and discredit all our attempts to save them by pleading guilty."[33] Three months later, James Weldon Johnson would go even further in placing the NAACP's reputation above the Moore defendants' welfare. In a letter to Walter White on August 7, he wrote, "Personally, I should prefer to see the faces [cases] fall out. Even if we lost them and the men were sentenced or executed it would not hurt our record in the fight at all. The reflection would be entirely upon the state of Arkansas and people would know that if the six men who have been released were innocent, that the six men executed were also innocent. On the other hand, of course, the lives and liberty of the six men cannot be disregarded."[34] Johnson did go on to write that "the wiser course" was to have the men plead guilty if they could be pardoned.

For almost four years the men had been characterized as ignorant Southern sharecroppers by the NAACP, their leader Robert Hill too stupid to have masterminded an insurrection. They were part of the "cause," not flesh-and-blood human beings with wives and children. This attitude wasn't going to change now that their freedom was visible. Only one man knew their families and how much they had suffered. Fortunately for the Moore and Ware defendants, Scipio Jones no longer felt bound to do what the NAACP and the New York lawyers wanted. He listened to them, but *only* listened to them, having learned that he couldn't quite trust them. *He* represented the men, not Moorfield Storey or the NAACP.

Further litigation was a difficult call. It was clear that the prosecution did not want to litigate the Moore cases in federal court, but there were

risks for the defendants too. It was not at all certain that they could convince a federal district judge that a mob atmosphere had dominated the
proceedings to the same degree as it had in the Frank case. In *Moore v.
Dempsey,* the Supreme Court had, quite frankly, assumed this on the basis
of general allegations. To prove it would be difficult. Then too, there was
no guarantee that their star witnesses would agree to come to Arkansas
for a hearing. And even if they did, any minimally competent cross-
examination of them would have revealed how much they had been supported by the defense.

April 1923
Lee County

At last the April term of court rolled around, and McHaney and Jones
went over to Marianna for a hearing to present their case that the prosecution had allowed without justification two terms of court to pass without going forward with the trials in Marianna. The transcript shows that
it was Edgar McHaney who handled the hearing for the Ware defendants.
Scipio Jones was present, and so was their old nemesis, Judge Jackson,
who was appearing as a witness for the state of Arkansas.[35] McHaney's
case was direct and to the point. The docket sheets that contained the
entries of the postponements spoke for themselves. The prosecution had
moved for two continuances in April and October 1922 over the objection of the defendants, who had announced themselves ready for trial,
but the court in each instance had put off the cases until the next term.

To rebut this, P. R. Andrews, who had conducted several of the Elaine
cases, argued that the defendants had consented to the postponement of
the trials, which if true would have been sufficient justification not to
order the release of the men. To get around the docket entries, he called
Judge Jackson and asked him about the October 1922 term:

Q: Will you tell the Court . . . if Mr. Mann was present, and if so,
whether or not he consented to the adjourning of court . . . and
for what purpose?

A: Yes, sir. I remember Mr. Mann discussing this matter with me,
among other things, he said that he had not collected his fee,
he and Mr. Smith, and there was a considerable balance due
them at that time.

Q: . . . [H]e consented to the adjournment did he?

A: . . . Yes sir. That was the only purpose of an adjourned term,

and he so understood and other counsel in the case understood it.[36]

Though McHaney tried to cross-examine Jackson, the only way he
could successfully deal with the issue was to call Burke Mann from the
Forrest City firm of McCullough and Mann. It was a ticklish moment,
but Mann didn't back down at all. McHaney called him to the witness
stand and asked him if he had agreed to a continuance:

Q: Are you the attorney that filed the motion requesting the setting
of these cases at the April and October Terms 1922?
A: Yes sir.
Q: You filed them in open court?
A: Yes sir.
Q: Did you at either of those terms consent or agree to a continu-
ance of these cases at any time?
A: I did not.
Q: You heard Judge Jackson testify here that you agreed, in open
court, to a continuance of the cases. . . .
A: Judge is mistaken about that, in his memory, about that,
because I wouldn't have filed a motion to have the cases set
down for trial and then in the next breath agreed to a continu-
ance.[37]

It was a decisive moment, demonstrating that the "good ole boy" system
in the Delta was no longer at work in these cases. Mann went on to testify that he hadn't asked for a continuance from Jackson in any meeting
with him, formally or informally. McHaney then called R. D. Smith from
Marianna to the stand and elicited the same answers from him.

Though Judge Robertson ruled for the prosecution that there hadn't
been sufficient time to try the cases, he found that neither "[t]he defendants, or any one acting for them, consent[ed] to a continuance. . . ."[38]
The stage was set for the third and final appeal of the Ware cases.

While the Ware cases were being briefed (the oral argument would
be heard in June), Jones and McHaney decided to go forward and in May
asked for a hearing in federal district court in the Moore cases. The case
was assigned to U.S. district judge Arba S. Valkenburgh out of Kansas
City, Missouri. Yet Valkenburgh seemed in no hurry to set a hearing date,
obviously knowing that a decision in the Ware cases was imminent, the
result of which might put more pressure on the parties to settle. There
seemed to be little agreement about how the defendants should proceed.

Scipio Jones wanted to bring in outside counsel. The NAACP wanted Storey to try the habeas case, an idea he quickly shot down. He was too old; Arkansas was too hot; it was too far away. Scipio Jones suggested that Storey contact George B. Rose, whose ancestor had begun the state's most prestigious law firm. Despite his earlier statement about allowing the men to linger in prison a while longer, Storey wrote Walter White on May 16 that "Rose told me some time ago that he thought I had rendered the state of Arkansas a great service, and it might be that he would be able to make some suggestions as to the way out of the difficulty. I am sure he does not want these negroes executed."[39]

In his letter to Rose, Storey recalled his visit to Washington and asked Rose to intervene in the case and "bring about some adjustment of the matter which will relieve all parties concerned."[40] The "adjustment" suggested by Storey was of course to drop the habeas proceeding and set the men free. All he could do now was to await a response.

It is impossible to know what influence the United States Supreme Court decision in *Moore v. Dempsey* had on the Arkansas Supreme Court and on their decision in the third appeal of the Ware defendants. Certainly, all members of the Arkansas court would have denied any influence, yet the U.S. Supreme Court had basically announced to the country that the legal proceedings in Helena in November 1919 appeared to have been a travesty of due process and that the Arkansas Supreme Court had turned a blind eye to this. It is one thing for a local newspaper publisher to wring his hands over a decision; it is quite another to know that the highest court in the country is watching your every move, even if you think it is wrong. Whether admitted or not, it has an effect. Perhaps the opinion in *Moore* prompted the majority of the Arkansas Supreme Court to burst forth with its own rhetoric in overruling Judge Robertson. "Justice delayed is justice denied," the majority said, quoting Gladstone in the opinion it announced on June 25. The statute requiring a speedy trial "imposes upon the ministers of justice the obligation not to unnecessarily delay the trial of the charge which the State has lodged against him, and to afford him an opportunity to prove his innocence before he has been compelled to endure a prolonged punishment."[41]

In reality, the cases against the Elaine Twelve had begun to fall apart the day Jones and Smiddy signed their names to affidavits giving a radically different version of what had occurred in October 1919. If Jones and Smiddy were willing to testify, all sorts of unpleasant prospects were suddenly imaginable. In his dissent in *Moore,* Justice McReynolds had called Smiddy and Jones "low criminals." If this was true, they were little different from other white men in Phillips County, who had participated in the torture and the shooting of defenseless blacks. Suddenly, prosecuting the Elaine cases no longer seemed like an urgent matter. The majority in the Ware cases noted that the prosecution "did not name a single witness, nor set up any facts to which any witness would testify to if the cause were continued. They did not designate any place where a single witness could be found."[42] The failure to make even a halfway decent argument that in fact the prosecution was doing all it could to find its witnesses was a neon sign. In fact, the cases were dead in the water. McHaney had been correct when he wrote that the prosecution had said it didn't intend to retry the cases. Yingling was apparently willing to let the defendants rot in the Marianna jail, but he wasn't about to take the cases to trial.

Once again, with the decision announcing their imminent release, what had to be in the minds of the Ware defendants—Ed Ware, Albert Giles, Joe Fox, Alf Banks Jr., William Wardlow, and John Martin—was whether they were now going to be lynched. Lynching was also on the minds of everyone else connected with the cases. Nobody was going to forget what had happened to Leo Frank. Lynching was certainly on the mind of the trial judge who had the duty of releasing the men. Judge Robertson directed the Lee County sheriff on June 25 to transport the six men to the Walls in Little Rock on a train. Accompanied by J. R. Booker, a young black attorney, Scipio Jones, who had worried that the Moore defendants would meet the fate of Leo Frank, met the men at the train depot at eleven o'clock at night to accompany them to the Walls.

The next two hours would be seen as amusing but in fact were quite harrowing. The penitentiary in Little Rock, of course, had no authority to take the men, and Sam Taylor, the night watchman, refused to let them in, refusing again after consulting the warden. The governor and a member of the penitentiary board were called. From a strictly legal standpoint, the men didn't have to be released until the official "mandate" came down from the Arkansas Supreme Court. The prosecution could still ask for a rehearing. But Robertson hadn't been about to give his fellow citizens in the Delta time to mull over the injustice of it all. An hour passed, and Taylor still wouldn't open the gates. Sheriff Calloway had carried out his orders, so he simply shook hands with Taylor and a reporter from the *Arkansas Gazette* and got into a waiting taxi with his deputies and left. Though Ed Ware told the *Gazette* reporter he felt "mighty fine," it was still a dangerous moment. For their own safety, the men couldn't simply be allowed to wander off. The prospect of thousands of angry whites hunting them down the next day was Scipio Jones's worst nightmare, but he agreed to find them temporary housing in Little Rock until the time to ask for a rehearing had passed.

Ed Ware told the reporter that "after consulting God, we made up our minds that if we would have to die in that chair, we would be ready to meet Jesus. We all know that Jesus took care of us."[43] He might better have said, "Jesus and Scipio Jones."

Again, predictably, the *Arkansas Gazette* howled at the scene portrayed by its reporter. The worst incident in the history of the judiciary. "Never before has any one incident so discredited our courts and never before has the public had more just ground for complaints," its editorial read.[44] Judge Robertson claimed he didn't care what anybody thought: "The sheriff carried out his orders exactly. I told him to take the negroes to the penitentiary, and if the warden would not accept them to turn them loose in the warden's presence."[45] He wasn't going to have his jail stormed by a lynch mob. That was going to be the state's responsibility. To protect himself from further criticism, Robertson held Warden Martin in contempt of court for not opening the doors to the Walls and fined him five hundred dollars, a decision that was later overturned by the Arkansas Supreme Court.

Jones and McHaney had done what all the wise heads in New York and Boston had not. Six of the Elaine Twelve were now free. The jubilation was short-lived, however. The fate of the Moore defendants seemed to be in limbo.

CHAPTER 13

Scipio Jones Takes Charge

Anticipate favorable results by tomorrow.
    —Telegram from Scipio Jones the day before the last of the Elaine
    Twelve were released from prison

July 1923
Little Rock

George Rose's letter to John Miller on July 2 was a masterpiece of diplomacy. Rose began by noting that he had no interest in the Elaine cases except as a citizen of Arkansas. But now, since the Arkansas Supreme Court had turned loose six of the men because no case could be made against them, "and in view of the sentiment throughout the country, it seems to me that it would be very unwise to press these cases much further."[1] He did not come out and say there had been no plan to mount an insurrection but said that "if there was a conspiracy, the heads of it, the men who ought really to be punished to the limit of the law, have escaped from our jurisdiction and will not be returned here for trial."[2] He added that he had been out at the Walls some months ago to make a talk to the prisoners and had met the men from Elaine. He had been "convinced that if they were guilty, they were simply farm negroes who had been misled and that there was really no malice in them." Justice would be served, he thought, with a plea of homicide and a sentence "for three or four years and let the sentence date back to the time of their arrest."[3]

Basically, Rose was suggesting that the men be released as soon as they pleaded guilty to second-degree murder. There were imminently practical reasons for disposing of these cases: "Rightly or wrongly, this matter has been taken up by the Northern press, and the conviction is general throughout the country that the prosecutions are unjustified. It would make a good impression everywhere if the course that I suggested were adopted, and it would do something to stop the emigration of the negroes to the North, which is disastrous to many of our Southern planters."[4]

Such was his standing in the Arkansas legal community that both

John Miller and C. E. Yingling wrote Rose the very next day. Miller put in writing what he had told Edgar McHaney months earlier by stating, "I have information to the effect that there will be no further prosecution in the Elaine cases."[5] He went on to defend his prosecution in the Elaine cases, adding that "there is no doubt that a conspiracy existed" but that the real leaders had gotten away.[6]

Yingling's letter distanced him from the previous prosecution of the cases and stated that he "would feel disposed to recommend" the proposal made by Rose. He added, "And in your case, knowing your reputation as to character and standing and your ability as a lawyer, I assure you that I appreciate your interest in this matter."[7]

Although it was now just a matter of time, Scipio Jones did not feel optimistic that Governor McRae would be willing to commute the sentences. He'd had one bad experience with McRae before on this issue, but McRae was nothing if not a shrewd politician who knew how to protect himself politically. On November 3, Scipio Jones telephoned the office of the NAACP to follow up on a telegram he had sent the day before. Here was the offer he had been waiting on for more than four years: the cases of the Moore defendants would be commuted to twelve years in prison, but Jones had been given "assurance sentence will terminate less than a year."[8] For this deal to be legitimate, the governor would have had to have signed off on it. The kicker was that Scipio Jones would have to give one thousand dollars to an unnamed attorney in Phillips County to present the commutation petition, and he wanted immediate authority to make this agreement. Johnson put Jones off by telling him to send a special-delivery letter; the NAACP would decide on Monday and telegram him.

Unwilling to let this opportunity slip away, however, Scipio Jones accepted the proposal that very afternoon. He defended his decision in a letter to Walter White by saying that he "consulted Judge Trieber and two or three other white friends, and I have been satisfactorily assured that a full and complete pardon will be granted to my clients in less than a year, and that reduction of sentences or full pardons will be granted to the 21 year men. . . ."[9]

Though the petition for clemency makes no reference to the unwritten and secret deal that all the men would be released within a year, it is still an extraordinary document. Signed by five of the seven Committee of Seven members—Mort Allen, Sebastian Straub, H. D. Moore, T. W. Keesee, and E. C. Horner (Frank Kitchens had died)—as well as by twelve others—including Joseph Solomon, John Moore, the new mayor, and the new sheriff—it begins by stating that the group of citizens had been informed that the Moore defendants' attorney was now

> willing to abandon any further defense of these negroes, provided their sentences are commuted to second degree murder, and their terms fixed at twelve years in the penitentiary.
>
> In view of the fact that the other six negroes who were equally guilty have escaped all punishment, and that the further prosecution of these negroes would entail on our people a large expense, and considering all the conditions, we hereby petition you to commute the sentences of these negroes to a term of twelve years each in the penitentiary.[10]

The very same afternoon McRae announced that he had granted clemency to the Moore defendants because of the appeal of the Committee of Seven and others from Phillips County.[11] He did not say that within a year he would release the men. This part of the deal was secret, dependent on the integrity of McRae to carry out his word well before he left office in January 1925.

It was a major gamble by Scipio Jones, who now saw himself as *the* attorney for the men in prison. There is no mention of Edgar McHaney's name in any of the correspondence with the NAACP concerning this decision. McHaney's name, in fact, disappears from the cases with the decision in the third Ware case in June 1923. Though Jones may have discussed with him how to proceed with the Moore defendants, McHaney seems not to have been a figure in the cases any longer. As he had his entire professional life, Scipio Jones put his trust in the word of a white governor—but this time one who had gone on record as opposing clemency, pardons, and parole for criminals. It must have been distasteful to McRae to become part of the bargain. Whether he would keep his word remained to be seen.

In New York, the NAACP was unhappy that Jones had acted unilaterally. Five months earlier James Weldon Johnson had written to Walter White that "I think we have to really almost depend entirely upon Jones' judgment regarding the procedure to be followed in the fight of the six. . . ."[12] But Jones was expected to consult with the NAACP before making a decision of such magnitude.

Storey wrote Walter White on November 9 that "our responsibility in the matter is really nonexistent, since Mr. Jones, the counsel of these people, has himself accepted the proposition without waiting for our advice." On the other hand, Storey recognized the difficulties that would have presented themselves had the Moore defendants gone back to federal court, adding: "If they can now get off with a few more months' imprisonment, I think we have accomplished our purpose."[13]

Three days later, Walter White's nose was still out of joint. He wrote James Weldon Johnson that he could not understand how Scipio Jones could expect the NAACP to pay the one thousand dollars that was promised to the attorney (whose name remains a mystery) who prepared the commutation papers. The irritation would eventually dissipate as it began to sink in that the cases seemed to be resolved. If the men were released, it would be a great victory.[14]

1924
Little Rock

There was no real political reason for Thomas McRae to refuse to run for a third term in Arkansas. He was in good health, popular enough with the people, and head and shoulders above the four other Democrats who would make the race. Stubborn as a mule, he had butted heads repeatedly with the legislature, but when his two terms were done he would have accomplished what Brough had not—finding a sensible way to finance desperately needed highway construction in the state. But Arkansas governors, with the exception of Jeff Davis, had always honored the precedent of running for just two terms, and like Brough before him, McRae bowed to tradition and stood aside to allow someone else to assume the mantle of leadership.

Unfortunately, the pickings were slim. The eventual winner, Tom Terral, was so anxious to run for governor as a Klan candidate that "after the Little Rock Klan rejected his application for membership three times and the El Dorado Klan once, Terral joined the Klan in Morehouse Parish, Louisiana. Then he came back to Little Rock and showed his membership card to James Comer, who demanded that he return it. But Terral refused and announced his candidacy for the governorship," writes Charles Alexander, the historian of the Klan in Arkansas.[15] Not everybody was afraid of the Klan. John Martineau, the Pulaski County chancery judge who had granted the writ of habeas corpus to stop the execution of the Moore defendants, entered the race as an anti-Klan candidate. (Though Scipio Jones had gone back to the Republican Party while his friends were becoming Democrats, he is thought to have secretly voted for Martineau.) Nothing, however, was going to stop the Klan in Arkansas in 1924, especially not in central Arkansas, where the sheriff and new U.S. congressman from the Second Congressional District had been elected with Klan support. Edgar McHaney, who had served a single two-year term in the Arkansas House of Representatives beginning in 1922, didn't even bother to run again. With a man like Terral coming into the governor's office, Scipio Jones knew that if McRae didn't keep his promise, the Moore defendants would probably not get out until they had served their full five years. It could even be longer for the men who were still in prison and sentenced to twenty-one years.

But a year had come and gone, and McRae had done nothing. Scipio Jones had to have been wondering whether the political climate in Pulaski County had become so antiblack that McRae would back out on his end of the deal. So far, it had not been a particularly good year for Jones. He had taken on the appeal of a black man sentenced to death for rape and murder and had made exactly the same argument the colonel had made in the first Ware case—that the jury had not specified the degree of murder. In April the decision in *Bettis v. State* had come down. The Arkansas Supreme Court had completely brushed aside his argument, sending his client to die in the electric chair.[16] Then in November, Chester Bush, the son of John Bush, one of the original founders of the Mosaic Templars, had died. People didn't live forever.

It was common practice for Arkansas governors to issue commutations of some prisoners' sentences at Christmas. On December 19 McRae released the remaining eight men who had been given twenty-one-year terms.[17] They didn't receive pardons or paroles. Instead, they were given "indefinite furloughs," making them subject to being returned to the penitentiary almost at will. Still, the practice was that if a man avoided the law, he would not be returned.

One can only imagine Scipio Jones's reaction to the front-page story in the *Arkansas Gazette* on December 20. The paper reported that the sentences of the Moore defendants were not being commuted.[18] No explanation was given. It must have been a long Christmas for the defendants as well as their attorney.

On January 13, the day before McRae went out of office, Scipio Jones met with him. It is not known what he said to the governor, but it is likely that he reminded him of the suffering the six men had already endured. It is unimaginable that Jones told McRae that the men had been racial victims of a social and legal system that was considered barbaric by much of the rest of the country, or told him how reprehensible it was that not a single white man had ever been called to account for his role in the murders of blacks in Phillips County. That wasn't the man's style, nor did he have any leverage except an appeal to McRae's conscience. Probably, Scipio Jones gently reminded McRae of his unfulfilled promise and of the men's good behavior over the last four years and four months. After the meeting with McRae, Jones telegraphed Walter White: "Just completed presentation of our matters, anticipate favorable results by tomorrow."[19]

As one of his last acts in office, McRae signed indefinite furloughs for the six men. He did not in fact honor his commitment completely. There were no pardons. Still, the men were free, and the *Arkansas Gazette* finally acknowledged the achievement without a hint of sarcasm: "After five years' effort, which has taken him into the county, state and federal courts, Scipio Jones, negro attorney, armed with the governors' proclamation, will report at the gates of the Cummins State Farm this morning and obtain the release of five of the negroes. He will then return to Little Rock and report at the penitentiary 'walls' where Paul Hall is incarcerated and obtain his freedom."[20] The long battle was over.

It is not known what happened to the Elaine Twelve. By 1936, the whereabouts of all but four were unknown. Scipio Jones reported that two were still in Arkansas; the other two were living in Chicago.[21]

It was a great victory for the NAACP and for Scipio Jones personally. Invited to speak to the NAACP convention in March, he would be duly honored by the NAACP for his dogged and "brilliant" persistence in the Elaine cases. Yet, as significant as his work in the Elaine cases had been, for the rest of his life he would never forsake his belief that for blacks to survive in Arkansas, certain behavior would be required. Given the unwillingness of the federal government to protect African Americans from white violence during this era (and, indeed, given the government's willingness to act as the perpetrator of such violence), it is difficult to fault his approach, however distasteful it might appear to current sensibilities.

The principal reality of Scipio Jones's life was not litigation but insuring that the African American community survived the violence and discrimination directed against it. Nothing would illustrate his commitment to this goal more than the last lynching that took place in Little Rock.

On April 12, 1927, a twelve-year-old white child named Floella McDonald disappeared from the streets of Little Rock. She had last been seen at the public library. A day earlier another child, Lonnie White, had also vanished. The disappearances were assumed to be connected, and a reward was offered. On April 30, Floella's mutilated body was discovered in the bell tower of the First Presbyterian Church, just blocks east of the public library.[22] The person who found her was the janitor, Frank Dixon. His son, Lonnie Dixon, age fifteen, was soon in police custody along with seven other blacks. The next afternoon, after twenty-four hours of police interrogation, during which Lonnie Dixon did not sleep or eat and was made to stand much of the time, Police Chief Burl C. Rotenberry announced that the boy had confessed to him that he had committed the crime.[23]

The reaction was immediate. Literally thousands of Little Rock residents poured into the streets, demanding that Lonnie Dixon be turned over to them. Rotenberry managed to hide Lonnie Dixon and his father in the rumble seat of a new Studebaker patrol car, which was sneaked past the mob and out of Little Rock. The mob was furious, threatening to kill Rotenberry. It broke through police lines at city hall and surged to the front doors. A delegation was permitted to search the jail with no results, but that made the mob even angrier. By eleven o'clock a contingent of National Guard soldiers arrived, and the show of force dispersed the crowd, but not before a portion of it had descended upon the "the Walls," where the Elaine Twelve had waited to be executed. The gates were broken open, and 150 people poured onto the grounds, where they were faced down by Warden Todhunter, who brandished a six-shooter at them and told them to "get out." Still, Todhunter permitted a delegation of five to search the prison, so it could be satisfied that Dixon wasn't there.[24] To protect himself and his family, Chief Rotenberry had a machine gun set up in his living room and aimed at his front door. He received so many death threats that by May 4 he had taken his family to Memphis to hide as mobs roamed the streets.

The day after Lonnie Dixon gave his confession, Little Rock Mayor Charles Moyer was reported as saying, "I sincerely hope that Little Rock citizens will let the law take the speedy course it has followed so far. *Lonnie will not escape the electric chair. We allow Lonnie's execution to be done according to law.*"[25] The next day the mob atmosphere had receded to the point at which, on May 3, the *Arkansas Gazette* editorialized, "We happily escaped the worst and for that outcome we should thank the authorities and the peace officers to whom it fell to handle a peculiarly difficult situation."[26] But the *Gazette*'s relief was premature. So was that of John Martineau, who had been elected governor and had sent the National Guard to the jail. He left Little Rock to travel to Van Buren in the western part of the state to be the guest of honor at a strawberry festival.

On May 4, at around 10:30 in the morning, a thirty-eight-year-old black man named John Carter assaulted Mrs. B. E. Stewart and her young daughter Glennie outside the city limits of Little Rock. He hit Mrs. Stewart with an iron bar, causing two fractures, but she and her daughter escaped when a passing car frightened him away. Once the news got out that a black man had assaulted two white females, a white mob descended on the wooded area where John Carter was thought to be hiding. Soon it found him and quickly decided it wasn't going to turn him over to the police to be protected. It forced him to jump off a car with a noose around his neck and then riddled his body with over two hundred bullets. The horror was only beginning.[27]

All the pent-up hatred toward African Americans was now unleashed. Mr. B. E. Stewart remembered later that he hollered, "Everybody that want to drag the nigger down Ninth Street and burn him, gimme your right hand."[28] Every hand went up, including those of the policemen present, said Stewart. As the mob knew, Ninth Street was the heart of the African American community. It was time to teach Little Rock blacks a lesson. Carter's body was thrown across a Ford and taken into Little Rock, where at Ringo and Fourteenth Streets it was tied headfirst to another car. There, headed by a motorcyclist, the mob began a procession of vehicles twenty-six blocks long through the heart of the black community.[29]

What Scipio Jones had long feared had come to pass. His triumph in the Elaine cases must have seemed like so many ashes in his mouth. It had been a hard year, anyway. His beloved daughter Hazel had died in Chicago at the age of thirty-five, leaving a husband and three young children, John, Scipio, and Hazel.[30] Now Jones's response was what it had been his entire life when there was racial trouble: "At noon, nine of the city's black leaders, including Scipio A. Jones, called the sheriff to offer their assistance."[31] The offer was refused.

Jones and other black leaders in Little Rock had to be thinking about what had occurred in 1921 in Tulsa because of a similar incident. Just as in Phillips County, some blacks had fought back. The result was that perhaps as many as three hundred blacks had been killed. Thirty blocks of black-owned property had been burned to the ground. One thousand homes had been destroyed.[32]

Instead of resisting, Scipio Jones and his friends saw to it that their community was shut tight as a drum. No blacks were to go out on the streets; no blacks were to fight back. Carter's body was finally dragged past city hall and then south on Broadway. There at 7:00 P.M., between the two most significant landmarks in the black community—Bethel African American Episcopal Church, the largest black church in Little Rock, and the Mosaic Templars Building—a huge bonfire was started on the trolley tracks. To feed it the mob broke into the church and brought out pews. Carter's body was thrown on the fire. A black who wandered by was grabbed up by the mob and beaten unconscious. Amazingly, he survived. For three hours the mob raged at will. Mayor Moyer went into hiding; no one knew where. The police chief was hiding with his family in Memphis, and the governor was in a town not far from the Oklahoma border. J. H. Bilheimer, acting mayor, said later, "I immediately went to Ninth and Broadway when I learned the mob had the body of John Carter. I attempted to stop the disturbance. Thousands of people, mostly armed, were present, and after discussing the situation with some of them, for a moment, I saw that they were in no humor to be argued with, and I left the scene."[33] Two hours into the bonfire on Ninth Street, the city council of Little Rock acted. The council "deemed it best that our small force of men not be sent to the scene of the burning."[34]

An observer from a block away remembered, "I really didn't know what was going on, but I could see the flames leaping high into the sky; and the noise of the running, screaming mob was terrible. I have never seen anything like it before or since."[35]

Finally, Governor Martineau was reached by telephone. He immediately ordered in the National Guard, which proceeded west on Tenth Street from the Arsenal Building in McArthur Park. At Tenth and Broadway, "the first thing they observed was a man from the mob directing traffic with a badly charred arm which had been broken from Carter's body."[36] The troops immediately took control and dispersed the crowd. Patrols throughout the night went into black neighborhoods to prevent further violence. Martineau returned at 4:30 the next morning on a special train. He ordered the troops to shoot if necessary. The mob was finished.

Remarkably, John Carter was the only black person killed during the riot or afterward. No estimate was given as to property damage in the black community, nor typically was there an assessment of psychic damage. However, at least some of the white power structure in Little Rock was genuinely embarrassed by the complete breakdown of law and order. The *Arkansas Gazette* headline on May 5 read: "WITH OFFICERS MAKING NO ATTEMPT AT RESTRAINT MOB BURNS NEGRO'S BODY AND CREATES A

REIGN OF TERROR."[37] Though a grand jury was assembled, there were no indictments returned against any whites for their actions.

The mayor of Little Rock and the sheriff of Pulaski County justified their inaction by saying that the city had been wise to take no measures to stop the mob because it would have only ended up with people getting killed. There was no need to add that the "people" they referred to were white.

Throughout the affair, the legal system in Little Rock performed as poorly as it had in Helena. For good reason, the entire legal community, black and white, was terrified of Lonnie Dixon's case. One hundred and fifty deputies surrounded the courthouse the day of the trial, on May 19.[38] The National Guard was standing by, ready to move in at a moment's notice to keep order. The names of Lonnie Dixon's court-appointed attorneys, Ector Johnson and J. F. Wills, were literally drawn out of a hat on May 17. A rumor made the rounds that if the jury returned a verdict of "not guilty," the courthouse would be blown up. Dixon's attorneys made no motion for a change of venue. Lonnie Dixon took the witness stand during the trial, which lasted five hours.[39] He renounced his confession, implicating a cousin, and stubbornly refused to change his story on cross-examination. The jury was out for seven minutes. There was no appeal. On the day of his execution, June 24, Lonnie Dixon repudiated his courtroom testimony and said he was guilty. Two hours and twelve minutes later he was electrocuted.[40]

It can be argued that Scipio Jones's greatest contribution was not his representation of the Elaine defendants but his willingness to do what was necessary to save his own community from death and destruction.

Scipio Jones lived until 1943. During that period and afterward, until the election of Republican Winthrop Rockefeller in 1966, the state of Arkansas, with few exceptions, remained morally dead to the concerns of its black citizens. For his part, Scipio Jones continued to challenge the absence of African Americans on juries in three criminal cases, but Pulaski County managed to circumvent the law. "Defendant was not entitled to have African-Americans represented on the jury, but only that they not be discriminated against in the jury panel selection," the Arkansas Supreme Court stated.[41]

This kind of smoke-and-mirrors reasoning would continue throughout his career, but it didn't prevent Jones from trying. In 1930, he, John Hibbler, and J. R. Booker sued unsuccessfully to permit blacks to vote in the Democratic primary. Jones died before the completion of a case in federal court, *Morris v. Williams,* which challenged the disparity in pay between black schoolteachers and administrators and their white counterparts. Despite the obvious differences in salaries, the case had to be appealed to the Eighth Circuit Court of Appeals. It was successfully argued by Thurgood Marshall, who would go on in 1954 to argue and win the *Brown* case, which would forever change civil rights history in the country.[42]

Scipio Jones died at eighty, an old man with almost nothing in his estate except his house.[43] The Depression had not been kind to any businesses, especially black enterprises. The Mosaic Templars and Jones's icehouse venture had both collapsed. He had almost outlived his time. Had he lived to see the modern Civil Rights Movement with its protests and civil disobedience, like Thurgood Marshall he would have been appalled at first. But had he lived to see the successes of the movement, he surely would have understood some of its tactics. He had always gone directly to the most powerful whites in Arkansas, just as Martin Luther King Jr. would rely on his relationships with presidents, leaders of Congress, and other important whites.

Did Scipio Jones know that blacks had been slaughtered by the mobs and soldiers in Phillips County in 1919? Of course he knew. Did he know that confronting Brough with that knowledge would have accomplished absolutely nothing except to make him even more defensive? Of course he did. Whatever was needed for the survival of his clients and community, Scipio Jones gave his maximum effort. A new day would dawn in civil rights. It would begin in Arkansas in 1957, when nine black children and their parents—led by Daisy Gatson Bates, Arkansas's most celebrated civil rights activist—would summon the courage to infiltrate the previously all-white Central High School in Little Rock.

What of Charles Hillman Brough, the state's "best and brightest"? With the heady days of being governor behind him, what did he do? As mentioned earlier, always the booster, he worked for a while for a group touting the virtues of the state. He ran an ill-advised race for U.S. senator in 1930, losing badly to the widow of the incumbent. Did Charles Hillman Brough ever have any sleepless nights because of his actions during the Elaine crisis? Most likely not. Whatever he saw personally or was told about the mobs and soldiers he transformed into a version of events that was palatable to him. The honor of the Old South did not jibe with massacres, so something had to go. It was not going to be the honor of the Old South.

Notes

Introduction

1.   Jeannie M. Whayne, "Low Villains and Wickedness in High Places: Race and Class in the Elaine Riots," *Arkansas Historical Quarterly* 58 (1999): 285.

2.   O. A. Rogers Jr., "The Elaine Race Riots of 1919," *Arkansas Historical Quarterly* 19 (1960): 147.

3.   Rogers, "Elaine Race Riots of 1919," 148.

4.   J. W. Butts and Dorothy James, "The Underlying Causes of the Elaine Riot of 1919," *Arkansas Historical Quarterly* 20 (1961): 102.

5.   Peggy Harris, "Elaine Race Riot Revisited," Associated Press, Feb. 4, 2000.

6.   Daniel Goleman, *Vital Lies, Simple Truths: The Psychology of Self-Deception* (New York: Simon and Schuster, 1985), 15.

7.   Goleman, *Vital Lies,* 164.

8.   Whayne, "Low Villains," 295–97. See also Nan Elizabeth Woodruff, "African American Struggles for Citizenship in the Arkansas and Mississippi Deltas in the Age of Jim Crow," *Radical History Review* 55 (1993): 33–51.

9.   Goleman, *Vital Lies,* 188.

10.   Goleman, *Vital Lies,* 188.

11.   Quoted in *Arkansas Gazette,* Mar. 23, 1969, from front-page editorial in Forrest City *Daily Times Herald* (date unknown).

Chapter 1. Charles Hillman Brough's Midnight Train Ride

1.   *Arkansas Gazette,* Oct. 1, 1919.

2.   Tom Dillard, "Scipio A. Jones," *Arkansas Historical Quarterly* 31 (1972): 212.

3.   Quoted in Foy Lisenby, *Charles Hillman Brough: A Biography* (Fayetteville: University of Arkansas Press: 1996), 42.

4.   *Arkansas Gazette,* Sept. 30, 1919.

5.   *Arkansas Gazette,* Sept. 30, 1919.

6.   *Arkansas Gazette,* Sept. 30, 1919.

7.   Charles Hillman Brough, "The Clinton Riot," *Publications of the Mississippi Historical Society* 6 (1902): 61.

8.   Brough, "Clinton Riot," 62.

9.   Brough, "Clinton Riot," 53.

10. Brough, "Clinton Riot," 63.

11. Brough, "Clinton Riot," 63.

12. Quoted in Michael Dugan, *Arkansas Odyssey: The Saga of Arkansas from Prehistoric Times to Present* (Little Rock: Rose Publishing Company, 1993), 313.

13. Quoted in Vincent Vinikas, "Specters in the Past: The Saint Charles, Arkansas, Lynching of 1904 and the Limits of Historical Inquiry," *The Journal of Southern History* 55 (1999): 549.

14. Quoted in Vinikas, "Specters in the Past," 540.

15. Quoted in Vinikas, "Specters in the Past," 553.

16. Quoted in Vinikas, "Specters in the Past," 551.

17. Quoted in Vinikas, "Specters in the Past," 553.

18. Jacqueline Froelich and David Zimmerman, "Total Eclipse: The Destruction of the African American Community of Harrison, Arkansas, in 1905 and 1909," *Arkansas Historical Quarterly* 58 (1999): 158.

19. *Arkansas Gazette,* Oct 1, 1919.

20. Lisenby, *Charles Hillman Brough,* 13.

21. Lisenby, *Charles Hillman Brough,* 28.

22. Price Roark, personal interview with author, Little Rock, Arkansas, 1998.

23. Quoted in Lisenby, *Charles Hillman Brough,* 1.

24. Quoted in Charles Orson Cook, "Arkansas's Charles Hillman Brough, 1876–1935: An Interpretation" (Ph.D. diss., University of Houston, 1980), 71.

25. Quoted in Cook, "Arkansas's Charles Hillman Brough," 81.

26. Quoted in Cook, "Arkansas's Charles Hillman Brough," 81.

27. Lisenby, *Charles Hillman Brough,* 48.

28. Quoted in Cook, "Arkansas's Charles Hillman Brough," 79.

29. Quoted in Cook, "Arkansas's Charles Hillman Brough," 75.

30. Lisenby, *Charles Hillman Brough,* 38.

31. Charles Hillman Brough Papers, Special Collections Division, University of Arkansas Libraries, Fayetteville, Box 2, File 27.

32. Mary L. Demoret Jones, "Elaine, Arkansas," *Phillips County Historical Quarterly* 10 (June 1972): 21.

33. Gerard B. Lambert, *All Out of Step: A Personal Chronicle* (Garden City, N.Y.: Doubleday, 1956), 64.

34. *Arkansas Gazette,* Oct 1, 1919; Oct. 2, 1919.

35. *Arkansas Gazette,* Oct. 2, 1919.

36. Quoted in Ann McMath, *First Ladies of Arkansas: Women of Their Times* (Little Rock: August House, 1989), 135.

37. Lisenby, *Charles Hillman Brough.*

38. Roark, interview.
39. Jacob E. Odle III, "Little Rock in 1919 Post War Southern City," *Pulaski County Historical Review* 22 (1974): 45.
40. Odle, "Little Rock," 48.
41. The Redeemers were Southern loyalists who returned to power with the end of Reconstruction.
42. Starr Michell, personal interview with author, Little Rock, Arkansas, 1999.
43. Ken Story, personal interview with author, Little Rock, Arkansas, 1999.
44. Roger C. Mears Jr., personal interview with author, Little Rock, Arkansas, 1999.
45. James Bratton to *Mountain Wave* (Marshall, Ark.), Aug. 29, 1919.
46. James Bratton to *Mountain Wave.*
47. Willard Gatewood, "Theodore Roosevelt and Arkansas," *Arkansas Historical Quarterly* 32 (1973): 13.
48. Tom Dillard, "To the Back of the Elephant: Racial Conflict in the Arkansas Republican Party," *Arkansas Historical Quarterly* 33 (1974): 3–15.

Chapter 2. The Law of the Delta

1. Willie Mae Countiss Kyte, "Elaine, Arkansas," *Phillips County Historical Quarterly* 23 (spring 1985): 38–59; Frances Keesee, telephone interview with author, Dec. 21, 2000. See also Demoret Jones, "Elaine, Arkansas," 15–30.
2. Quoted in Kieran Taylor, "'We Have Just Begun': Black Organizing and White Response in the Arkansas Delta, 1919," *Arkansas Historical Quarterly* 48 (1999): 268.
3. Lambert, *All Out of Step,* 74.
4. Greenfield Quarles to David Thomas, Jan. 5, 1920, Special Collections Division, University of Arkansas Libraries, Fayetteville, D. Y. Thomas Papers.
5. Ernest D. Justice, "Retrospect and Prospect," *Phillips County Historical Review* 35 (spring 1997): 60.
6. Justice, "Retrospect and Prospect," 60.
7. Quoted in Susan E. C. Huntsman, "Race Relations in Phillips County, 1895–1920" (Student paper, University of Arkansas, 1996), 56. In possession of author.
8. Quoted in Huntsman, "Race Relations," 5.
9. For examples of violence against the African American population in Arkansas, see Tom W. Dillard, "Madness with a Past: An Overview of Race Violence in Arkansas History," *Arkansas Review: A Journal of Delta Studies* 32 (2001): 93–101.

10. Quoted in Fon Louise Gordon, *Caste and Class: The Black Experience in Arkansas, 1880–1920* (Athens: University of Georgia Press, 1995), 10.

11. Quoted in Peggy S. Lloyd, "The Howard County Race Riot of 1883," *Arkansas Historical Quarterly* 49 (2000): 365.

12. Quoted in Lloyd, "Howard County Race Riot," 362.

13. Quoted in Lloyd, "Howard County Race Riot," 357.

14. Quoted in Lloyd, "Howard County Race Riot," 360.

15. Peggy S. Lloyd has noted the relatively better conditions that existed for blacks in some areas of southern Arkansas before the imposition of Jim Crow and how those conditions affected the way racial violence was handled by whites once the judicial system was involved. For example, blacks tried in the old plantation town of Washington in Hempstead County were given bail and were represented aggressively by white attorneys in the area.

16. Quoted in Kenneth C. Barnes, *Who Killed John Clayton? Political Violence and the Emergence of the New South, 1861–1893* (Durham, N.C.: Duke University Press, 1998), 112.

17. William F. Holmes, "The Arkansas Cotton Pickers Strike of 1891 and the Demise of the Colored Farmers Alliance," *Arkansas Historical Quarterly* 32 (1973), 107–19.

18. Quoted in Whayne, "Low Villains," 296.

19. Quoted in Huntsman, "Race Relations," 34.

20. Quoted in Huntsman, "Race Relations," 33, 34.

21. Huntsman, "Race Relations," 34.

22. Huntsman, "Race Relations," 38.

23. Quoted in Huntsman, "Race Relations," 41.

24. Huntsman, "Race Relations," 41.

25. Quoted in Richard C. Cortner, *A Mob Intent on Death: The NAACP and the Arkansas Riot Cases* (Middletown, Conn.: Wesleyan University Press, 1988), 82.

26. *Helena World,* Oct. 7, 1919.

27. Quoted in Cortner, *Mob Intent on Death,* 82.

28. E. M. Allen to William Avery, Nov. 20, 1919, Special Collections Division, University of Arkansas Libraries, Fayetteville, D. Y. Thomas Papers.

29. Quoted in Huntsman, "Race Relations," 16.

30. Quoted in Taylor, "'We Have Just Begun,'" 279.

31. "Why Helena is Your Natural Market." Brochure in possession of author.

32. Taylor, "'We Have Just Begun,'" 279.

33. *Helena World,* Sept. 26, 1919.

34. Arthur I. Waskow, *From Race Riot to Sit-In: 1919 and the 1960s* (New York: Anchor Books, 1967), 122, citing NAACP, "Memoranda on Tenancy in

the Southwestern States" (Extracts from the Final Report of the United States Commission on Industrial Relations, 1916).

35. Quoted in Taylor, "'We Have Just Begun,'" 281.
36. Quoted in Taylor, "'We Have Just Begun,'" 280.
37. Research materials for Butts and James, "Underlying Causes," Charles Straub, interview, Oct. 15, 1960. In possession of Helena Library.
38. Research materials for Butts and James, "Underlying Causes," Lynn Smith, statement, Oct. 28, 1960. In possession of Helena Library.
39. Taylor, "'We Have Just Begun,'" 276.
40. Quoted in Vertie L. Carter, *Dr. E. C. Morris* (Little Rock: VLC Research and Biographical Technical Enterprises, 1999), 105. In possession of author.
41. Quoted in Taylor, "'We Have Just Begun,'" 277.
42. Quoted in Taylor, "'We Have Just Begun,'" 271
43. Quoted in Waskow, *From Race Riot to Sit-In,* 122.
44. Quoted in Bessie Ferguson, "The Elaine Race Riot" (Master's thesis, George Peabody College for Teachers, Nashville, 1927), 31.
45. Robert L. Hill to NAACP, Nov. 26, 1919, NAACP MSS.

Chapter 3. The Boys from Camp Pike

1. Governor Charles Hillman Brough to Commanding General of Camp Pike S. D. Sturgis, Oct. 10, 1919, National Archives, Record Group 407, Box 1229, File "Race Relations At Camp Pike."
2. Brough to Commanding General.
3. L. S. Dunaway, *What a Preacher Saw Through a Keyhole in Arkansas* (Little Rock: Parke-Harper Publishing Company, 1925).
4. *Arkansas Gazette,* Sept. 4, 1959.
5. *Arkansas Gazette,* Sept. 4, 1959.
6. Dunaway, *What a Preacher Saw,* foreword.
7. Dunaway, *What a Preacher Saw,* 12.
8. Dunaway, *What a Preacher Saw,* 102.
9. Dunaway, *What a Preacher Saw,* 109.
10. Dunaway, *What a Preacher Saw,* 109.
11. Dunaway, *What a Preacher Saw,* 102.
12. Dunaway, *What a Preacher Saw,* 109.
13. Dunaway, *What a Preacher Saw,* 101, 102.
14. Dunaway, *What a Preacher Saw,* 109.
15. Dunaway, *What a Preacher Saw,* 109, 110.
16. Waskow, *From Race Riot to Sit-In;* Cortner, *Mob Intent on Death.*
17. B. Boren McCool, *Union, Reaction, and Riot: The Biography of a Rural Race Riot* (Memphis: Memphis State University Press, 1970).

18. Whayne, "Low Villains," 287, n. 5.

19. James Street, *James Street's South* (Garden City, N.Y.: Doubleday and Co. 1955), 227.

20. John E. Miller, interview with Walter Brown, Fort Smith, Arkansas, Mar. 18, 1976, Special Collections Division, University of Arkansas Libraries, Fayetteville, transcript 35, MC 279.

21. Miller, interview, 13.

22. Miller, interview, 14, 15.

23. Roger Mears, personal interview with author, 1999.

24. Ulysses Bratton Jr., telephone interview with James Johnston, 1965. In possession of author.

25. Edward Molitor, telephone interview with author, July 1, 2000.

26. Lambert, *All Out of Step,* 78.

27. Lambert, *All Out of Step,* 77.

28. *State of Arkansas v. Joe Fox and Albert Giles,* Phillips Co. Cir. #4481 (Nov. 4, 1919), T. 33.

29. Quoted in Cortner, *Mob Intent on Death,* 30.

30. Quoted in Cortner, *Mob Intent on Death,* 30.

31. The affidavits of T. K. Jones and H. F. Smiddy can be found in the Abstract and Brief (Record) of the appellants (86–100) in *Moore et al. v. Dempsey,* 261 U.S. 86 (1923). They are also at the University of Arkansas at Little Rock, William H. Bowen School of Law Library/Pulaski County Law Library.

32. *State of Arkansas v. Will Wardlow,* Phillips Co. Cir. #4482 (Nov. 4, 1919), T.12.

33. Quoted in Cortner, *Mob Intent on Death,* 170.

34. Record, *Moore et al. v. Dempsey,* 93.

35. Record, *Moore et al. v. Dempsey,* 93.

36. Record, *Moore et al. v. Dempsey,* 93.

37. Record, *Moore et al. v. Dempsey,* 95.

38. Record, *Moore et al. v. Dempsey,* 88.

39. Record, *Moore et al. v. Dempsey,* 90.

40. While it was Edgar McHaney who obtained the affidavits from Smiddy and Jones, Scipio Jones maintained the crucial personal contact with them to try to insure their presence at trial had it been needed. It is impossible at this date to determine which attorney drafted which specific motions and briefs. Scipio Jones was involved in all phases of the work and, except for the affidavits of Jones and Smiddy, had more contact with the defendants and witnesses than Murphy or McHaney. From the beginning, it was clear to Scipio Jones that the Elaine defendants would fare better if their cases were argued in court by white attorneys.

41. Ferguson, "Elaine Race Riot," 83, 84.

42.   Harry Anderson to Charles Hillman Brough, Oct. 7, 1919, Brough Papers, Box 4, File 89.

43.   Miller, interview, 20, 21.

44.   Ida B. Wells-Barnett, *The Arkansas Race Riot* (Chicago: Hume Job Print, 1920).

45.   Wells-Barnett, *Arkansas Race Riot,* 13.

46.   Wells-Barnett, *Arkansas Race Riot,* 13.

47.   Wells-Barnett, *Arkansas Race Riot,* 13, 14.

48.   Wells-Barnett, *Arkansas Race Riot,* 18.

49.   Miller, interview, 15.

50.   Wells-Barnett, *Arkansas Race Riot,* 14.

51.   Wells-Barnett, *Arkansas Race Riot,* 20.

52.   Wells-Barnett, *Arkansas Race Riot,* 20.

53.   Wells-Barnett, *Arkansas Race Riot,* 20.

54.   Wells-Barnett, *Arkansas Race Riot,* 24.

55.   Otis Howe III, telephone interview with author, Apr. 30, 1999.

56.   Oliver McClintock, telephone interview with author, Apr. 30, 1999.

57.   George Washington Davis to NAACP, n.d., NAACP MSS.

58.   (?) Booker, video interview with Hazel Hubbard and Thelma Bryant, Jan. 1992. In possession of Central High School Library, Helena, Arkansas.

59.   Dunaway, *What a Preacher Saw,* 118.

60.   *Arkansas Gazette,* Oct. 2, 1919.

61.   *Commercial Appeal,* Oct. 2, 1919.

62.   *Daily Graphic,* Oct. 6, 1919.

63.   *Brinkley Argus,* Oct. 2, 1919.

64.   *Arkansas Gazette,* Oct. 2, 1919.

65.   *Memphis News Scimitar,* Oct. 2, 1919.

66.   *Commercial Appeal,* Oct. 2, 1919.

67.   *Arkansas Democrat,* Oct. 2, 1919.

68.   *Arkansas Gazette,* Oct. 2, 1919.

69.   *Tunica Times,* Oct. 4, 1919.

70.   *Tunica Times,* Oct. 4, 1919.

71.   *Helena World,* Oct. 2, 1919.

72.   Goleman, *Vital Lies,* 107.

73.   *Arkansas Gazette,* Oct. 2, 1919.

74.   Goleman, *Vital Lies,* 133.

75.   Goleman, *Vital Lies,* 131.

76.   *Arkansas Gazette,* Oct. 2, 1919.

77.   *Arkansas Gazette,* Oct. 2, 1919.

78.   Ocier Bratton to Ulysses Bratton, Nov. 5, 1919, NAACP MSS.

79.   *Arkansas Democrat,* Oct. 3, 1919.

Chapter 4. A Committee of Seven

1. Quoted in Ralph Desmarais, "Military Intelligence Reports on Arkansas Riots: 1919–1920," *Arkansas Historical Quarterly* 33 (1974): 182.

2. *Arkansas Gazette,* Oct. 3, 1919.

3. Report of Col. Issac Jenks to Commanding General, Camp Pike, Arkansas, Oct. 14, 1919, National Archives, Record Group 407, Box 1229, File "Race Relations at Camp Pike," 1.

4. Report of Col. Issac Jenks, 1.

5. Charles Hillman Brough to Dunbar Rowland, Oct. 3, 1919, Brough Papers, Box 4, File 54.

6. Report of Col. Issac Jenks, 1.

7. *Arkansas Gazette,* Oct. 3, 1919.

8. Quoted in Desmarais, "Military Intelligence Reports," 183.

9. Report of Col. Issac Jenks, 2.

10. Quoted in Desmarais, "Military Intelligence Reports," 183.

11. *Memphis Press,* Oct. 2, 1919, NAACP MSS.

12. *Commercial Appeal,* Oct. 3, 1919.

13. Report of Col. Issac Jenks, 2.

14. Report of Col. Issac Jenks, 2, 3.

15. Report of Col. Issac Jenks, 4.

16. Report of Col. Issac Jenks, 4.

17. Quoted in Desmarais, "Military Intelligence Reports," 184.

18. Quoted in Desmarais, "Military Intelligence Reports," 186.

19. *Arkansas Gazette,* Oct. 3, 1919.

20. Ocier Bratton to Ulysses Bratton.

21. Report of Col. Issac Jenks, 2.

22. Quoted in Desmarais, "Military Intelligence Reports," 185.

23. See chapter 13. One can only speculate as to how much personality has played a role in the actions of Arkansas governors. Though conservative on the issue of race, Thomas McRae, who succeeded Brough, would in the course of his two terms develop the kind of skepticism toward law enforcement that would be needed to prevent lynchings.

24. John Williams Graves has researched the background of some members of the Committee of Seven. T. W. Keesee was the owner of a "2,000 acre plantation and president of the Helena Cotton Exchange and the Helena Compress Company and head of W. W. Keesee and Company cotton factors and shippers." E. C. Horner "was founder and first president of the Business Men's League." See John William Graves, "Protectors or Perpetrators? White Leadership in the Elaine Race Riots." *Arkansas Review: A Journal of Delta Studies* 32 (2001): 139.

25. *Helena World,* Oct. 3, 1919.

26. Goleman, *Vital Lies,* 131.

27.　As Arkansas historian John William Graves writes: "The incident [at Hoop Spur] provided planters with just the rationale they needed to unleash a reign of bloody repression and break the back of Hill's union and the challenge it posed to their traditional authority. To justify their response, planters needed to believe that there had been a conspiracy for planning the mass murder of whites in the neighborhood, and they easily convinced themselves this was so." Graves, "Protectors or Perpetrators?" 138.

28.　*Arkansas Gazette,* Oct. 3, 1919.

29.　*Helena World,* Oct. 1–3, 1919.

30.　*Helena World,* Oct. 2, 1919.

31.　*Helena World,* Oct. 3, 1919.

32.　*Arkansas Gazette,* Oct 4, 1919.

33.　*Arkansas Gazette,* Oct. 6, 1919.

34.　D. Y. Thomas, *Arkansas and Its People: A History, 1541–1930* (New York: The American Historical Society, 1930), 294.

Chapter 5. More Than One Version

1.　*Helena World,* Oct. 3, 1919.

2.　Report of Col. Issac Jenks.

3.　Research materials for Butts and James, "Underlying Causes," E. M. Allen to J. W. Butts, Oct. 13, 1960. In possession of Helena Library.

4.　Quoted in Taylor, "'We Have Just Begun,'" 283; *Greenwood Commonwealth,* Oct. 15, 1919.

5.　Taylor, "'We Have Just Begun,'" 283.

6.　C. Calvin Smith, "Serving the Poorest of the Poor: Black Medical Practitioners in the Arkansas Delta, 1880–1960," *Arkansas Historical Quarterly* 57 (1998): 301.

7.　The last name of the Johnston brothers has been occasionally spelled by other writers as "Johnson" because of various spellings in the papers.

8.　*Helena World,* Oct. 3, 1919.

9.　(Walter White ?), report of shooting of the Johnston brothers, n.d., NAACP MSS.

10.　Wells-Barnett, *Arkansas Race Riot,* 25.

11.　McCool, *Union, Reaction, and Riot,* 31.

12.　McCool, *Union, Reaction, and Riot,* 31. Emphasis original.

13.　Research materials for Butts and James, "Underlying Causes," notes by authors. In possession of Helena Library. Emphasis in original.

14.　James Lilly, quoted in document in possession of author.

15.　James Lilly, personal interview with author, Apr. 5, 2000.

16.　*Arkansas Gazette,* Oct. 4. 1919.

17.　*Arkansas Gazette,* Oct. 4. 1919.

18.   John A. Thompson, "Gentleman Editor: Mr. Heiskell of the Gazette: The Early Years: 1902–1922" (Master's thesis, University of Arkansas, Little Rock, 1983).

19.   *Arkansas Gazette,* Oct. 5, 1919. The editorial writer, undoubtedly Heiskell, suggests a reasonable explanation from the whites' point of view: blacks had erroneously believed themselves to be under attack.

20.   *Helena World,* Oct. 7, 1919.
21.   *Helena World,* Oct. 7, 1919.
22.   *Helena World,* Oct. 7, 1919.
23.   *Helena World,* Oct. 7, 1919.
24.   *Helena World,* Oct. 7, 1919.
25.   *Helena World,* Oct. 7, 1919.
26.   *Helena World,* Oct. 7, 1919.
27.   *Helena World,* Oct. 7, 1919.
28.   *Helena World,* Oct. 7, 1919.
29.   *Helena World,* Oct. 7, 1919.
30.   *Arkansas Gazette,* Oct. 8, 1919.
31.   *Arkansas Gazette,* Oct. 8, 1919.
32.   *Courier Index,* Oct. 24, 1919.

Chapter 6. Little Rock and New York: An Uneasy Alliance

1.   West Law Search—Scipio Jones.

2.   J. H. Carmichael quoted in Octavius Coke, *The Scrapbook of Arkansas Literature* (Little Rock: American Caxton Society Press, 1939), 312.

3.   Todd E Lewis, "Booker T. Washington and His Visits to Arkansas," *Pulaski County Historical Review* 42 (1994): 54–65.

4.   Dillard, "Scipio A. Jones," 215.

5.   *Arkansas Democrat,* May 6, 1909.

6.   Dillard, "Scipio A. Jones," 210.

7.   A. E. Bush and P. L. Dorman, eds., *History of the Mosaic Templars of America: Its Founders and Officials* (Little Rock: Central Printing Company, 1924).

8.   Little Rock and North Little Rock City Directory (Little Rock: Southern Directory Co., 1920), 269.

9.   Dillard, "Scipio A. Jones," 212.

10.   Todd E. Lewis, "Race Relations in Arkansas, 1910–1929" (Ph.D. diss., University of Arkansas, 1995), 274–323.

11.   Dillard, "Scipio A. Jones," 210.

12.   Hazel Adams (granddaughter of Scipio Jones), telephone interview with author, 1999.

13.   Sandford Reamey, May 8, 1999, statement at Scipio Jones High

School reunion, May 8, 1999, North Little Rock. Such is the delicate nature of race.

14.   U.S. Census, 1870.

15.   Dillard, unpublished notes for "Scipio A. Jones," Butler Center for Arkansas Studies, Central Arkansas Library System, Little Rock.

16.   Dillard, "Scipio A. Jones," 212.

17.   Dillard, "Scipio A. Jones," 206.

18.   *Castleberry v. State*, 69 Ark. 346 (Ark. S. Ct. 1901).

19.   Walter White, *A Man Called White* (New York: Viking Press, 1948), 11.

20.   Carolyn Wedin, *Inheritors of the Spirit: Mary White Ovington and the Founding of the NAACP* (New York: Wiley, 1998), 16.

21.   Wedin, *Inheritors of the Spirit,* 107

22.   White, *Man Called White,* 49.

23.   White, *Man Called White,* 51.

24.   White, *Man Called White,* 51.

25.   Quoted in Cortner, *Mob Intent on Death,* 29.

26.   Quoted in Cortner, *Mob Intent on Death,* 46.

27.   Gordon, *Caste and Class,* 111, 112.

28.   Dillard, "Scipio A. Jones," 213.

29.   Ulysses Bratton to Committee of Seven, Oct. 15, 1919, NAACP MSS.

30.   Ocier Bratton was erroneously thought to be a lawyer because of his work for his father. Though he did some work for his father's firm, according to his granddaughter, Thea Crosier, Ocier had been "a supervisor at an electric and water plant" before coming to Little Rock. Thea Crosier, reply to query from author, n.d.

31.   Ocier Bratton to Ulysses Bratton.

32.   *Arkansas Democrat,* Oct. 3, 1919.

33.   *Arkansas Gazette,* Oct. 3, 1919.

34.   *Arkansas Gazette,* Oct. 6, 1919.

35.   Gailon McHaney, biographical sketch of E. L. McHaney (n.p, n.d.). In possession of author.

36.   Cortner, *Mob Intent on Death,* 41.

37.   Guy Bratton to Ulysses Bratton, Nov. 16, 1919, NAACP MSS.

Chapter 7. The Trials Begin

1.   Ocier Bratton to Ulysses Bratton.

2.   Dallas T. Herndon, ed., *Centennial History of Arkansas,* vol 1. (Chicago: S. J. Clarke Pub. Co., 1922), 404.

3.   Ocier Bratton to Ulysses Bratton.

4.   Guy Bratton to Ulysses Bratton, Nov. 9, 1919, NAACP MSS.

5. Quoted in Cortner, *Mob Intent on Death,* 114.

6. *Helena World,* Oct. 31, 1919.

7. Though his claim has never been verified, Robert Hill alleged that the union was active in a number of counties.

8. Quoted in *Bettis v. State,* 164 Ark. 17 (Ark S. Ct. 1924).

9. Though the name of Peter Beasley (one of two black attorneys in Helena) is listed on the transcript as one of the attorneys for Will Wardlow and he apparently sat at counsel table, he did not question any of the prosecution's witnesses and is not mentioned as participating in any way in this trial.

10. *Helena World,* Nov. 3, 1919.

11. *Helena World,* Nov. 3, 1919.

12. *Helena World,* Nov. 3, 1919.

13. *Helena World,* Nov. 3, 1919.

14. *State of Arkansas v. Frank Hicks,* Phillips Co. Cir. # 4509 (Nov. 3, 1919), T. 30, University of Arkansas at Little Rock, William H. Bowen School of Law Library.

15. *State of Arkansas v. Frank Hicks,* T. 33.

16. *State of Arkansas v. Frank Hicks,* T. 37.

17. *State of Arkansas v. Frank Hicks,* T. 38.

18. *State of Arkansas v. Frank Hicks,* T. 39.

19. *State of Arkansas v. Frank Hicks,* T. 41.

20. *State of Arkansas v. Frank Hicks,* T. 42.

21. *State of Arkansas v. Frank Hicks,* T. 52.

22. *Helena World,* Nov. 3, 1919.

23. Transcript of Record, *Frank Moore et al. v. State of Arkansas,* U.S. 955 (1921), T. 10. Special Collections, University of Arkansas at Little Rock, William H. Bowen School of Law Library/Pulaski County Law Library, "Elaine Race Riot" materials.

24. Record, *Moore et al. v. State of Arkansas,* T. 10, 11.

25. Record, *Moore et al. v. State of Arkansas,* T. 12.

26. Record, *Moore et al. v. State of Arkansas,* T. 13, 14.

27. Record, *Moore et al. v. State of Arkansas,* T. 17.

28. Record, *Moore et al. v. State of Arkansas,* T. 17.

29. Record, *Moore et al. v. State of Arkansas,* T. 19

30. Record, *Moore et al. v. State of Arkansas,* T. 20.

31. Record, *Moore et al. v. State of Arkansas,* T. 20, 21.

32. Record, *Moore et al. v. State of Arkansas,* T. 24.

33. *Hicks v. State,* 143 Ark. 158 (Ark. 1920).

34. *Helena World,* Nov. 4, 1919.

35. *State of Arkansas v. John Martin and Alf Banks, Jr.,* Phillips Co. Cir. #4482 (Nov. 4, 1919), T. 9.

36. *State of Arkansas v. John Martin and Alf Banks, Jr.,* T. 21.

37. *State of Arkansas v. John Martin and Alf Banks, Jr.,* T. 30.

38. *State of Arkansas v. John Martin and Alf Banks, Jr.,* T. 41.

39. *State of Arkansas v. John Martin and Alf Banks, Jr.,* T. 44.

40. *Helena World,* Nov. 4, 1919.

41. *State of Arkansas v. Joe Fox and Albert Giles,* T. 9, 10.

42. *State of Arkansas v. Joe Fox and Albert Giles,* T. 14, 15.

43. *State of Arkansas v. Joe Fox and Albert Giles,* T. 14.

44. *State of Arkansas v. Joe Fox and Albert Giles,* T. 16, 17.

45. *State of Arkansas v. Joe Fox and Albert Giles,* T. 18, 19.

46. *State of Arkansas v. Joe Fox and Albert Giles,* T. 26.

47. *State of Arkansas v. Joe Fox and Albert Giles,* T. 27.

48. *State of Arkansas v. Joe Fox and Albert Giles,* T. 30.

49. *Helena World,* Nov. 4, 1921.

50. *State of Arkansas v. Joe Fox and Albert Giles,* T. 32.

51. *State of Arkansas v. Joe Fox and Albert Giles,* T. 32.

52. *State of Arkansas v. Will Wardlow,* T. 10.

53. *State of Arkansas v. Will Wardlow,* T. 18.

54. *State of Arkansas v. Will Wardlow,* T. 20.

55. *State of Arkansas v. Will Wardlow,* T. 22.

56. *State of Arkansas v. Will Wardlow,* T. 24, 25.

57. *State of Arkansas v. Will Wardlow,* T. 26.

58. *Helena World,* Nov. 5, 1919.

59. *Helena World,* Nov. 5, 1919.

60. *Helena World,* Nov. 5, 1919.

61. *Helena World,* Nov. 5, 1919.

62. *Helena World,* Nov. 5, 1919.

63. *Helena World,* Nov. 6, 1919.

64. *Helena World,* Nov. 17, 1919.

65. *Arkansas Democrat,* Oct. 2, 1919.

66. *Helena World,* Nov. 17, 1919.

67. *Helena World,* Nov. 17, 1919.

68. *Helena World,* Nov. 17, 1919.

69. *Helena World,* Nov. 17, 1919.

70. *Helena World,* Nov. 17, 1919.

Chapter 8. Colonel Murphy for the Defense

1. Quoted in Wedin, *Inheritors of the Spirit,* 191.

2. Ulysses Bratton to Department of Justice, Nov. 6, 1919, NAACP MS.

3. Ulysses Bratton to Department of Justice.

4. Arthur Henderson to Ulysses Bratton, Aug. 30, 1919, exhibit 2 of Ulysses Bratton to Department of Justice.

5. Ferguson, "Elaine Race Riot," 17.

6. Cortner, *Mob Intent on Death*, 42.

7. Cortner, *Mob Intent on Death*, 43.

8. Ulysses Bratton to John Shillady, Aug. 15, 1919, NAACP MSS.

9. Cortner, *Mob Intent on Death*, 44.

10. Quoted in Cortner, *Mob Intent on Death*, 29.

11. James Weldon Johnson to Robert R. Church, Dec. 2, 1919, NAACP MSS.

12. Johnson to Church.

13. Johnson to Church.

14. Quoted in Cortner, *Mob Intent on Death*, 49.

15. Ulysses Bratton to Mary White Ovington, n.d., NAACP MSS.

16. Cortner, *Mob Intent on Death*, 50.

17. Ulysses Bratton to Ovington, n.d.

18. Quoted in Lewis, *Race Relations,* 247.

19. *Arkansas Gazette,* Nov. 24, 1919.

20. *Arkansas Gazette,* Nov. 25, 1919.

21. *Arkansas Gazette,* Nov. 25, 1919.

22. *Arkansas Gazette,* Nov. 25, 1919.

23. Goleman, *Vital Lies,* 164.

24. James Monroe Cox to William Pickins, Feb. 13, 1920, NAACP MSS.

25. *Arkansas Gazette,* Dec. 1, 1919.

26. Quoted in Cortner, *Mob Intent on Death*, 48.

27. Ulysses Bratton to Mary White Ovington, Dec. 5, 1919, NAACP MSS.

28. *Quapaw Quarter Newsletter,* n.d., Rozelle-Murphy File, Quapaw Quarter Association, Little Rock, Arkansas.

29. Quoted in Cortner, *Mob Intent on Death*, 53. Emphasis added.

30. *State of Arkansas v. Frank Hicks,* Phillips Co. Cir. # 4509, T. 64.

31. *State of Arkansas v. Frank Hicks,* T. 63, 64.

32. *State of Arkansas v. Frank Hicks,* T. 69.

33. *State of Arkansas v. Frank Hicks,* T. 65.

Chapter 9. The Retrials of the Ware Defendants

1. *Arkansas Gazette,* Nov. 14, 1919.

2. *Arkansas Gazette,* Nov. 14, 1919.

3. Clare Kennemore, "11 Negroes to Pay for Greed of One," *New York World,* Nov. 16, 1919. Reprinted in NAACP MSS.

4. Kennemore, "11 Negroes to Pay."

5. Kennemore, "11 Negroes to Pay."

6. Kennemore, "11 Negroes to Pay."

7. Kennemore, "11 Negroes to Pay."
8. *Arkansas Gazette,* Dec. 1, 1919.
9. Robert Hill to NAACP, Nov. 26, 1919, NAACP MSS.
10. Quoted in Cortner, *Mob Intent on Death,* 57.
11. Cortner, *Mob Intent on Death,* 55–83.
12. Cortner, *Mob Intent on Death,* 61.
13. Ulysses Bratton to Senator Dillingham, Feb. 21, 1920, NAACP MSS.
14. Telegram from Ulysses Bratton to John Shillady, May 11, 1920, NAACP MSS.
15. Hugh Fisher to John Shillady, Feb. 10, 1919, NAACP MSS.
16. Hugh Fisher to John Shillady, Feb. 13, 1919, NAACP MSS.
17. Cortner, *Mob Intent on Death,* 69
18. Quoted in Cortner, *Mob Intent on Death,* 62.
19. Quoted in Cortner, *Mob Intent on Death,* 63.
20. Quoted in Cortner, *Mob Intent on Death,* 62.
21. James Monroe Cox to William Pickins, Feb. 12, 1920, NAACP MS.
22. Cox to Pickins, Feb. 12, 1920.
23. Cox to Pickins, Feb. 12, 1920.
24. Cox to Pickins, Feb. 12, 1920.
25. Hugh Fisher to John Shillady, Mar. 24, 1920, NAACP MSS.
26. Fisher to Shillady, Mar. 24, 1920.
27. *Arkansas Gazette,* Mar. 16, 1920.
28. Cortner, *Mob Intent on Death,* 70.
29. Quoted in Cortner, *Mob Intent on Death,* 71.
30. Quoted in Cortner, *Mob Intent on Death,* 72.
31. Quoted in Cortner, *Mob Intent on Death,* 72.
32. Quoted in Cortner, *Mob Intent on Death,* 73.
33. *Hicks v. State,* 143 Ark. 158, 162 (Ark. 1920).
34. *Banks v. State,* 143 Ark. 158, 158 (Ark. 1920). By taking on the defense of all twelve of the convicted men, Murphy and Jones were inevitably risking conflicts of interest, as is apparent in the briefs. This is demonstrated, for example, in the legal arguments on behalf of Frank Hicks and the five of the defendants who were alleged to have "aided and abetted" him in the death of Clinton Lee. The recognition of these conflicts possibly accounts for the reliance in the briefs on technical arguments rather than involved discussions of the evidence. Whatever the explanation, the arguments in the briefs are short and generalized.
35. Quoted in Cortner, *Mob Intent on Death,* 76.
36. Monroe N. Work to John R. Shillady, Apr. 19, 1920, NAACP MSS.
37. Cortner, *Mob Intent on Death,* 91, 92.
38. Quoted in Lewis, *Race Relations,* 367.
39. Quoted in Lewis, *Race Relations,* 368.

40.   Mary White Ovington, *Portraits in Color* (Hallandale, Fla.: New World Book Manufacturing Co., 1927; reprint, New York: Viking Press, 1971), 98, 99.

41.   *Helena World,* May 4, 1919.

42.   Appellants' Brief and Abstract, *Ware et al. v. State of Arkansas* (Ark S. Ct. 1920), Butler Center for Arkansas Studies, Little Rock, Ark., 30. The brief and abstract in the retrials of the Ware defendants bear no case number nor specific date.

43.   Brief and Abstract, *Ware et al. v. State,* 137.

44.   Brief and Abstract, *Ware et al. v. State,* 33.

45.   Brief and Abstract, *Ware et al. v. State,* 34.

46.   Brief and Abstract, *Ware et al. v. State,* 34.

47.   Brief and Abstract, *Ware et al. v. State,* 35.

48.   Lewis, *Race Relations,* 483–84.

49.   Brief and Abstract, *Ware et al. v. State,* 36.

50.   Brief and Abstract, *Ware et al. v. State,* 36.

51.   W. K. Monroe, a civil engineer, had testified that he had come along the same road at midnight and had been wounded.

52.   Eric M. Freedman, "Milestones in Habeas Corpus—Part II: Leo Frank Lives: Untangling the Historical Roots of Meaningful Federal Habeas Corpus Review of State Convictions," *University of Alabama Law Review* 51 (2000): 1502, n. 138.

53.   Brief and Abstract, *Ware et al. v. State,* 141.

54.   Brief and Abstract, *Ware et al. v. State,* 25–28.

55.   Brief and Abstract, *Ware et al. v. State,* 24.

56.   Brief and Abstract, *Ware et al. v. State,* 2.

57.   Brief and Abstract, *Ware et al. v. State,* 49.

58.   Brief and Abstract, *Ware et al. v. State,* 56.

59.   McCool, *Union, Reaction, and Riot,* 53.

60.   Brief and Abstract, *Ware et al. v. State,* 85.

61.   Brief and Abstract, *Ware et al. v. State,* 84.

62.   Brief and Abstract, *Ware et al. v. State,* 93.

63.   Brief and Abstract, *Ware et al. v. State,* 96.

64.   Brief and Abstract, *Ware et al. v. State,* 94.

65.   Brief and Abstract, *Ware et al. v. State,* 94.

66.   Brief and Abstract, *Ware et al. v. State,* 70.

67.   Brief and Abstract, *Ware et al. v. State,* 104.

68.   Brief and Abstract, *Ware et al. v. State,* 107.

69.   Brief and Abstract, *Ware et al. v. State,* 105.

70.   Brief and Abstract, *Ware et al. v. State,* 107.

71.   Brief and Abstract, *Ware et al. v. State,* 107.

72.   Brief and Abstract, *Ware et al. v. State,* 109.

73. Brief and Abstract, *Ware et al. v. State,* 113.
74. Brief and Abstract, *Ware et al. v. State,* 117.
75. Brief and Abstract, *Ware et al. v. State,* 118.
76. Brief and Abstract, *Ware et al. v. State,* 118.
77. Brief and Abstract, *Ware et al. v. State,* 119.
78. Brief and Abstract, *Ware et al. v. State,* 120.
79. Brief and Abstract, *Ware et al. v. State,* 120.
80. Brief and Abstract, *Ware et al. v. State,* 122.
81. Brief and Abstract, *Ware et al. v. State,* 122.
82. Brief and Abstract, *Ware et al. v. State,* 122.
83. Brief and Abstract, *Ware et al. v. State,* 123.
84. Brief and Abstract, *Ware et al. v. State,* 123.
85. Brief and Abstract, *Ware et al. v. State,* 119.
86. Brief and Abstract, *Ware et al. v. State,* 123.
87. Brief and Abstract, *Ware et al. v. State,* 108.
88. For a summary of this chapter, see Griffin J. Stockley, "The Legal Proceedings of the Arkansas Race Massacres of 1919 and the Evidence of the Plot to Kill Planters," *Arkansas Review: A Journal of Delta Studies* 32 (2001): 141–48.
89. *Arkansas Gazette,* May 19, 1919.
90. Quoted in Cortner, *Mob Intent on Death,* 93.
91. Ulysses Bratton to NAACP, Aug. 15, 1920, NAACP MSS.
92. Quoted in Cortner, *Mob Intent on Death,* 95.

Chapter 10. The Changing of the Guard

1. Quoted in Cortner, *Mob Intent on Death,* 94.
2. Walter White to James Weldon Johnson, NAACP MSS.
3. See, for example, Wedin, *Inheritors of the Spirit,* 192: "Murphy's law firm demanded exorbitant fees, and when the NAACP did not produce them, the firm resigned from the case."
4. Lisenby, *Charles Hillman Brough,* 46.
5. Cortner, *Mob Intent on Death,* 98.
6. Resolution from Richard L. Kitchens Post No. 41 to Governor Brough, Oct. 19, 1920, NAACP MSS.
7. Quoted in Cortner, *Mob Intent on Death,* 98.
8. Quoted in Cortner, *Mob Intent on Death,* 99.
9. Quoted in Cortner, *Mob Intent on Death,* 100.
10. Quoted in Cortner, *Mob Intent on Death,* 100.
11. Quoted in Cortner, *Mob Intent on Death,* 101.
12. *Ware v. State,* 146 Ark. 321, 335 (Ark. 1920).
13. Quoted in Cortner, *Mob Intent on Death,* 101.

14. Lewis, *Race Relations*, 281.

15. Quoted in Cortner, *Mob Intent on Death*, 105.

16. McMath, *First Ladies*, 150.

17. Fay Williams and C. C. Allard, *Arkansans of the Years,* vol. 2 (Little Rock: Democrat Printing and Lithographing Company, 1922), 247. Articles contained in this publication were originally printed in the *Arkansas Democrat Sunday Magazine.*

18. Calvin J. Ledbetter Jr., "Thomas C. McRae: National Forests, Education, Highways, and *Brickhouse v. Hill,*" *Arkansas Historical Quarterly* 59 (2000): 1–29.

19. Charles C. Alexander, "White-Robed Reformers: The Ku Klux Klan Comes to Arkansas," *Arkansas Historical Quarterly* 22 (1963): 17.

20. Quoted in Lewis, *Race Relations*, 283.

21. Lewis, *Race Relations*, 283.

22. *Arkansas Democrat,* Mar. 19, 1921.

23. Lewis, *Race Relations*, 286.

24. *Arkansas Democrat,* Mar. 19, 1921.

25. *Arkansas Democrat,* Apr. 9, 1921.

26. Walter White to Scipio Jones, Mar. 8, 1921, NAACP MS.

27. Quoted in Cortner, *Mob Intent on Death*, 109.

28. Quoted in Cortner, *Mob Intent on Death*, 110.

29. Quoted in Cortner, *Mob Intent on Death*, 112.

30. Cortner, *Mob Intent on Death*, 109.

31. Ledbetter, "Thomas C. McRae."

32. Quoted in Cortner, *Mob Intent on Death*, 113.

33. Quoted in Cortner, *Mob Intent on Death*, 113.

34. Quoted in Cortner, *Mob Intent on Death*, 114.

35. Quoted in Cortner, *Mob Intent on Death*, 114.

36. Quoted in Cortner, *Mob Intent on Death*, 114.

37. Miller, interview, 11.

38. Miller, interview, 19.

39. Miller, interview, 11.

40. Miller, interview, 23.

41. Miller, interview, 21.

42. Williams and Allard, *Arkansans of the Years*, 213.

43. McMath, *First Ladies*, 156.

44. Williams and Allard, *Arkansans of the Years*, 209.

45. *Ferguson v. Martineau*, 115 Ark. 317 (Ark. 1914).

46. Williams and Allard, *Arkansans of the Years*, 211.

47. Williams and Allard, *Arkansans of the Years*, 214.

48. Quoted in Cortner, *Mob Intent on Death*, 117.

49. Quoted in Cortner, *Mob Intent on Death*, 117.

50.   *State v. Martineau,* 149 Ark. 237, 244, 245 (Ark. 1921). J. H. Carmichael, dean of the University of Arkansas Law School, was listed as counsel with Jones and McHaney.

Chapter 11. Affidavits from Unlikely Sources
1.   Freedman, "Milestones," 1514.
2.   Edgar McHaney to Mary White Ovington, Aug. 30, 1921, NAACP MSS.
3.   Quoted in Cortner, *Mob Intent on Death,* 133.
4.   Conference of Mr. Scipio A Jones with the Secretary—Re. Arkansas Cases, Sept. 14, 1922, NAACP MSS.
5.   Cortner, *Mob Intent on Death,* 121
6.   McHaney to Ovington.
7.   Quoted in Cortner, *Mob Intent on Death,* 170.
8.   Record, *Moore et al. v. Dempsey,* 86.
9.   Record, *Moore et al. v. Dempsey,* 86.
10.   Record, *Moore et al. v. Dempsey,* 86.
11.   Record, *Moore et al. v. Dempsey,* 86.
12.   Record, *Moore et al. v. Dempsey,* 86.
13.   Record, *Moore et al. v. Dempsey,* 86.
14.   S. H. Tarbet to NAACP, NAACP MSS; Scipio Jones, reply, NAACP MS.
15.   Record, *Moore et al. v. Dempsey,* 92.
16.   Record, *Moore et al. v. Dempsey,* 88.
17.   Record, *Moore et al. v. Dempsey,* 17.
18.   Record, *Moore et al. v. Dempsey,* 88.
19.   Record, *Moore et al. v. Dempsey,* 92.
20.   Record, *Moore et al. v. Dempsey,* 88.
21.   Record, *Moore et al. v. Dempsey,* 89, 90.
22.   Record, *Moore et al. v. Dempsey,* 90.
23.   Record, *Moore et al. v. Dempsey,* 90.
24.   Record, *Moore et al. v. Dempsey,* 93.
25.   Record, *Moore et al. v. Dempsey,* 94.
26.   Record, *Moore et al. v. Dempsey,* 94.
27.   Record, *Moore et al. v. Dempsey,* 95.
28.   Record, *Moore et al. v. Dempsey,* 95.
29.   Record, *Moore et al. v. Dempsey,* 96.
30.   Record, *Moore et al. v. Dempsey,* 97.
31.   Record, *Moore et al. v. Dempsey,* 99.
32.   Gerald W. Heaney, "Jacob Trieber: Lawyer, Politician, Judge," *University of Arkansas at Little Rock Law Journal* 8 (1985–86): 421.

33.   Carolyn Gray LeMaster, *A Corner of the Tapestry: A History of the Jewish Experience in Arkansas, 1820s-1890s* (Fayetteville: University of Arkansas Press, 1994), 99.

34.   LeMaster, *Corner of the Tapestry,* 99.

35.   Quoted in McHaney, biographical sketch, 440.

36.   Quoted in Cortner, *Mob Intent on Death,* 128.

37.   *Hicks v. Dempsey,* # 6247 U.S. Dist. Ct. (n.d.). Interestingly, Judge Trieber wrote the formal order granting the hearing for the habeas corpus in longhand. He signed no formal order of recusal. On September 23, 1921, the *Arkansas Gazette* reported his announcement that he was withdrawing from the case because he was formerly a resident of Phillips County.

Chapter 12. *Moore v. Dempsey:* A Supreme Victory

1.   Lewis, *Race Relations,* 274.

2.   Quoted in Lewis, *Race Relations,* 274.

3.   Quoted in Lewis, *Race Relations,* 274.

4.   Quoted in Cortner, *Mob Intent on Death,* 134.

5.   *Frank v. Mangrum,* 237 U.S. 309 (1915).

6.   Joel Williamson, *The Crucible of Race: Black-White Relations in the American South since Emancipation* (New York: Oxford University Press, 1984), 468–72.

7.   Quoted in Alexander, "White Robed Reformers," 9.

8.   Quoted in Alexander, "White Robed Reformers," 9.

9.   Alexander, "White Robed Reformers," 16.

10.   Charles C. Alexander, "White Robes in Politics: The Ku Klux Klan in Arkansas, 1922–1924," *Arkansas Historical Quarterly* 22 (1963): 205.

11.   H. F. Smiddy to Walter White, Feb. 15, 1922, NAACP Papers, D-42, Library of Congress.

12.   Smiddy to White.

13.   Quoted in Cortner, *Mob Intent on Death,* 171.

14.   Scipio Jones to Walter White, Mar. 31, 1922, NAACP Papers, G-12, Library of Congress.

15.   Jones to White, Mar. 31, 1922. See also Smiddy to White.

16.   Quoted in Cortner, *Mob Intent on Death,* 169.

17.   Quoted in Cortner, *Mob Intent on Death,* 136.

18.   Conference of Mr. Scipio A Jones.

19.   Conference of Mr. Scipio A Jones.

20.   Conference of Mr. Scipio A Jones.

21.   Cortner, *Mob Intent on Death,* 161.

22.   Walter White to Ulysses Bratton, Dec. 7, 1922, NAACP MSS.

23.   Scipio Jones to Walter White, Dec. 21, 1922, NAACP MSS.

24. James Weldon Johnson to Shelby J. Davidson, Jan. 9, 1922, NAACP MSS.

25. Telegram from Moorfield Storey to Walter White, Jan. 9, 1923, NAACP MSS.

26. Quoted in Cortner, *Mob Intent on Death,* 144.

27. Quoted in Cortner, *Mob Intent on Death,* 153.

28. Quoted in Cortner, *Mob Intent on Death,* 155

29. Quoted in Cortner, *Mob Intent on Death,* 156.

30. Quoted in Cortner, *Mob Intent on Death,* 160.

31. Quoted in Cortner, *Mob Intent on Death,* 161.

32. Quoted in Cortner, *Mob Intent on Death,* 175.

33. Moorfield Story to Walter White, May 7, 1923, NAACP MSS.

34. James Weldon Johnson to Walter White, Aug. 3, 1923, NAACP MSS.

35. *State of Arkansas v. Albert Giles et al.,* Lee Co. Cir. #4050–4052. (Oct. 20, 1923), Special Collections, University of Arkansas at Little Rock, William H. Bowen School of Law Library/Pulaski County Law Library.

36. *State of Arkansas v. Albert Giles et al.,* R. 21–22.

37. *State of Arkansas v. Albert Giles et al.,* R. 26.

38. *State of Arkansas v. Albert Giles et al.,* R. 14.

39. Moorefield Storey to Walter White, May 16, 1923, NAACP MSS.

40. Storey to White, May 16, 1923.

41. *Ware v. State,* 159 Ark. 540, 553 (Ark. 1923).

42. *Ware v. State,* 159 Ark. 560 (Ark. 1923).

43. Quoted in Cortner, *Mob Intent on Death,* 164.

44. Quoted in Cortner, *Mob Intent on Death,* 166.

45. Quoted in Cortner, *Mob Intent on Death,* 165.

Chapter 13. Scipio Jones Takes Charge

1. G. B. Rose to John E. Miller, Searcy, Ark., July 2, 1923, NAACP MSS.

2. Rose to Miller.

3. Rose to Miller.

4. Rose to Miller.

5. John E. Miller to G. B. Rose, Little Rock, Ark., July 3, 1923, NAACP MSS.

6. Miller to Rose.

7. C. E. Yingling to G. B. Rose, Little Rock, Ark., July 3, 1923, NAACP MSS.

8. Memorandum re. Arkansas cases from James Weldon Johnson, Nov. 3, 1923, NAACP MSS.

9. Scipio Jones to Walter White, Nov. 3, 1923, NAACP MSS.

10.   Copy of Petition to Hon. T. C. McRae, Governor, Little Rock, Ark. By Committee of Seven, etc., In re Elaine Negro Defendants, NAACP MSS.

11.   *Arkansas Gazette,* Nov. 4, 1923.

12.   Johnson to White.

13.   Moorfield Storey to Walter White, Nov. 9, 1923, NAACP MSS.

14.   Walter White to James Weldon Johnson, NAACP MSS.

15.   Charles C. Alexander, "Defeat, Decline, Disintegration: The Ku Klux Klan in Arkansas," *Arkansas Historical Quarterly* 22 (1963): 317.

16.   *Bettis v. State.*

17.   *Arkansas Gazette,* Dec. 19, 1924.

18.   *Arkansas Gazette,* Dec. 19, 1924; Dec. 20, 1924.

19.   Scipio Jones to Walter White, Jan. 13, 1924, NAACP MSS.

20.   *Arkansas Gazette,* Jan. 14, 1925.

21.   Cortner, *Mob Intent on Death,* 197.

22.   Marcet Haldeman-Julius, *The Story of a Lynching: An Exploration of Southern Psychology* (Girard, Kan.: Haldeman-Julius Publications, 1927), 6, 16.

23.   Haldeman-Julius, *Story of a Lynching,* 9–10.

24.   Haldeman-Julius, *Story of a Lynching,* 22.

25.   Quoted in Haldeman-Julius, *Story of a Lynching,* 12. Emphasis original.

26.   Quoted in James Reed Eison, "Dead, But She was in a Good Place, a Church," *Pulaski County Historical Review* 30 (1982): 34–35.

27.   Haldeman-Julius, *Story of a Lynching,* 40–41.

28.   Quoted in Haldeman-Julius, *Story of a Lynching,* 43.

29.   Haldeman-Julius, *Story of a Lynching,* 50.

30.   Adams, interview.

31.   Quoted in Brian Greer, "The Last Lynching," *Arkansas Times,* Aug. 4, 2000.

32.   *Los Angeles Times,* Oct. 23, 1999.

33.   Quoted in Haldeman-Julius, *Story of a Lynching,* 52.

34.   Quoted in Haldeman-Julius, *Story of a Lynching,* 53.

35.   Quoted in Eison, "Dead," 37.

36.   Eison, "Dead," 37.

37.   *Arkansas Gazette,* May 5, 1927.

38.   Eison, "Dead," 39.

39.   Eison, "Dead," 39.

40.   Eison, "Dead," 39–40.

41.   Judith Kilpatrick, "(Extra)Ordinary Men: African-American Lawyers and Civil Rights in Arkansas before 1950," *Arkansas Law Review* 53 (2000): 389, n. 678.

42.   Kilpatrick, "(Extra)Ordinary Men," 391.

43.   Dillard, "Scipio A. Jones," 210.

A Note on Sources

Richard C. Cortner, author of the constitutional study *A Mob Intent on Death: The NAACP and the Arkansas Riot Cases,* has explained in his work that much of the original source material relating to the Elaine massacres has been lost. Thus, many of the original NAACP papers on this subject at the Library of Congress are not available to researchers. However, as Cortner notes, Arthur I. Waskow prepared verbatim transcriptions of much of the original material for his 1966 book entitled, *From Race Riot to Sit-In, 1919 and the 1960's.* These documents, in addition to Waskow's notes, are located in the Wisconsin State Historical Society on the campus of the University of Wisconsin, Madison. They are designated as Accession M76–358. When citing these materials, I note them as "NAACP MSS."

The University of Arkansas at Little Rock, William H. Bowen School of Law Library/Pulaski County Law Library retains the original transcripts of the first trials of the Elaine Twelve in November 1920 with the exception of the transcript of Ed Ware (which has been lost) and the transcript of the hearing for the Ware defendants in Lee County in April 1923. This library has also recently acquired a number of documents relating to the federal litigation that has become known as *Moore v. Dempsey.* The transcripts of the retrials of the six Ware defendants of the Elaine Twelve in May 1920 are also lost. The Butler Center for Arkansas Studies, a part of the Central Arkansas Library System in Little Rock, is the repository for the only copy located by the author of the abstract and brief of the May 1920 retrials of the Ware defendants. For a discussion of the location of other trial documents of the cases that went to the U.S. Supreme Court in *Moore v. Dempsey,* see Eric M. Freedman, "Milestones in Habeas Corpus—Part II: Leo Frank Lives: Untangling the Historical Roots of Meaningful Federal Habeas Corpus Review of State Convictions," *University of Alabama Law Review* 51 (2000): 1502, n. 138.

Index

Adkins, W. A., xvii, xxiii, 11, 76, 120, 121, 128, 129, 137, 166, 168
Alderman, K. P., 113, 114
Allen, E. M. "Mort," 19, 20, 27, 33
    background of, 10, 19, 20
    and Committee of Seven, 72, 77, 80, 87, 88, 89, 224
Allen, Henry J., xxviii, 154, 155, 159, 161, 162
Andrews, P. R., 110, 111, 112, 137, 218
Arbuckle, John D., 154, 159
Archer, Dave, 119, 120
Arkansas Democrat, xxix, 56, 59, 87, 132, 176, 179, 183, 190
Arkansas Gazette, xxxii, 4, 6, 11, 55, 56, 59, 78, 87, 89, 90, 95, 145, 151, 165, 176, 180, 216, 221, 222, 227, 228, 229
Arkansas legislature, 3, 21
Arkansas Supreme Court, xxxi, 120, 160, 161, 179

Banks, Alf, Jr., xxvii, 120, 121, 122, 124, 125, 126, 127, 128, 165, 170
    affidavit of, 149, 150
Barton, Eugene, 66
Bilheimer, J. H., 231
Blount, Josiah H., 163, 179
Bolsheviks, 4
Bond, Scott, 146
Bondsman, Suggs, xxvii, xxviii, 132, 165, 172, 173
Booker, Joseph A., xxvi, xxviii, 54, 146
    leadership role of in black community, 99, 100
    and urging extradition of Robert Hill, 156, 157
Booker, J. R., xxvii, 158, 169, 221
Bratton, Benjamin, Sr., 16, 17

Bratton, Guy, 11, 18, 176
    letter of to father, 104, 105
Bratton, Mattie, 102
Bratton, Nora, 102
Bratton, Ocier S., 11, 59, 76, 102, 103
    arrest of, xxiii, 106
    background of, 102
    letter of to father, 66, 102, 103, 106
    release of, 103
Bratton, Ulysses S., xix, xxvii, xxviii, xxxi, 101, 102, 103, 104, 105, 143, 144
    background of, 11, 16, 17, 18
    on Col. George Murphy, 142, 175
    on Edgar McHaney, 175, 176
    on Governor Brough, 147
    and James Bratton, 17
    leaving Arkansas, 155
    in New York, 138
    on peonage, 17, 138, 139, 140, 141
    oral argument of before Supreme Court, 215
    relationship with Scipio Jones, 212
    and Republican Party, 17, 18
    threats against, 155
    and U. S. Bratton Jr., 42
    and Walter White, 141
Brinkley Argus, 55
Brough, Anne Roark
    background of, 8, 12, 13
    and governor's mansion, 14, 15
    and suffrage, 13
Brough, Charles Hillman, xii, xxiii, xxiv, xxv, xxvii, xxix, 150, 158, 174, 184
    and Anne Roark Brough, 8
    background of, 5, 6, 7, 8, 13, 15
    and Business Men's League, 10, 27, 28

and *Chicago Defender* and *Crisis,* 151
and clemency, 144, 177, 178, 179
and Committee of Seven, 76, 77, 78
and explanation of causes of massacre, 85, 86, 145
Governor Allen's refusal to extradite Hill, 159, 160, 161
military support of, 34, 63, 64, 67, 68, 72, 75
position on blacks, 8, 9, 15, 157
record as governor, 3
support of by blacks, xix, 146, 147, 157
Brown, Walter Lee, 40, 51
Burke, J. Graham, 119, 122, 167
Bush, Chester E., 96, 227
Bush, John E., 93
Butts, J. W., xvi, xxiii, 29, 84, 169

Callen, Major, 62, 64, 65
Campbell, R. B., 131
Camp Pike, xvi, 4, 15, 28
Carmichael, J. H., 92
Carter, John, 230, 231
Casey, G. R., 18, 110
Chicago Defender, xxvi, 149, 156
Coleman, Ed, xxvii, 115, 116, 117, 118, 119, 120, 178
Collins, Robert "Kid," 11, 76, 168, 171
Commercial Appeal, xx, 55, 58, 65, 90, 91
Committee of Seven, xxv, 29, 72, 76, 77, 81, 224
Conner, Bishop J. M., xxvi, xxviii, 99, 146, 147, 156, 157, 163
Conway County, Ark., 23
Cortner, Richard C., 39, 154
Cotteral, J. H, xxx, 206, 207
Countiss, J. M., 114, 132
Courier Index, 90, 91
Cox, J. M., xxvi, xxviii, 99, 146, 156, 157
Crisis, xxvi, 32, 83
Crow, J. C., 114
Culpepper, Rev. Burke, 25

Curry, Will, 173

Daily Graphic, 55
Davis, George Washington, 53
Davis, Jeff, 6, 35, 36
Dazell, J. R. "Dick," 47, 59, 170, 202
Dempsey, E. H., 190
Dinning, W. G., 121, 122
Dixon, Frank, 229
Dixon, Lonnie, 229, 230, 232
Du Bois, W. E. B., 83, 97
Dunaway, Louis Sharpe, xxv, 35, 36, 37, 38, 62
background of, 36

Earles, Cpl. Luther C., 35, 64, 131
Elaine, Ark., xii, xvi, xxiii, 10
conference on massacres, xv, xx
Ellis, Dr. J. B., 123

Faulkner, Tom, 114
Ferguson, Bessie, 47, 48, 141
Fink, Jacob, 111, 112, 113, 114
Fiser, Mary Louise Demoret, xvi, xvii, xviii
Fisher, Hugh, 154, 155, 156, 160
Forrest City, Ark., xxi
Fox, Joe, 122, 124, 125, 126, 127, 165, 169, 170
Fox, Sykes, 122, 130, 167
Frank, Leo, 210

Garland, Augustus H., 22
Gay, Sgt. Pearl, 64
Giles, Albert, xxvii, 43, 44, 122, 124, 125, 126, 127, 129, 165, 169, 170
Giles, Milliken, 123, 129, 170
Godwin, Elbert, 215
Goleman, Daniel, xviii
psychology of self-deception, xviii, xix, 58, 59, 73, 74
Grand Jury of Phillips County, 109
Green, George, 112, 130
Greenwood Commonwealth, 81

Hall, Paul, xxvii, 115, 116, 117, 118, 120, 178

Harrison, Ark., 7
Hays, Dave, 127, 172
Heiskell, J. N., 86
Helena, Ark., 10, 26, 27, 77
Helena American Legion Post, xxiii, 76, 178
Helena World, xxv, 21, 55, 57, 73, 76, 77, 80, 82, 87, 110, 111, 120, 126, 127, 129, 130, 131, 132, 137, 164, 168
Hibbler, John A., xxvii, 158, 232
Hicks, Ed, xxvii, 115, 117, 119, 120
Hicks, Frank, xxvi, xxvii, 111, 112, 114, 115, 149
Hill, Robert L., xxiv, xxix, 31, 121, 154, 155, 156, 157, 158, 159, 160, 176
    as fugitive, 153
    as labor organizer, 32, 33
    letters from, 31, 32, 152, 153
Hodges, Earle W., 8, 9
Holmes, Oliver Wendell, Jr., 215, 216
Hoop Spur, xvii, xxiv, 11
    Hoop Spur Lodge, xvi
Horner, E. C., 72
Howard County, Ark., 22, 23
Howe, Otis, II, 52, 53
Howe, Otis, III, 52

Jackson, J. M., xxiv, xxvi, 127, 129, 130, 131, 137, 164
    appointment of counsel in November trials, 110
    assistance to Ocier Bratton, 106, 107
    background of, 106, 107
    defeat of, 206
    and denial of motion for new trial, 150
    as witness in *Ware* cases, 218
Jarmon, Amos, 168
Jefferson John, 113, 114, 130
Jenks, Col. Issac C., xxiv
    background of, 16
    military report of, 62, 63, 64, 65, 66, 78
Jim Crow, xv, xix, xxi, 21
Johnson, James Weldon, 42, 155, 177,

217, 224, 226
Johnston, D. A. E., xxiv, 76, 82, 83, 84, 151
    background of brothers, 82
Jones, Scipio Africanus, xxvi, xxvii, xxviii, xxix, xxx, xxxi, xxxii
    actions of during last lynching in Little Rock, 230, 231, 232, 233
    aggressiveness after decision of *Moore v. Dempsey,* 216, 217, 219, 224, 228
    assistance to Smiddy, 211, 212
    background of, 92, 93, 94, 95, 100
    and clemency meeting with Brough, 144
    and clemency meeting with McRae, 227
    death of, 233
    experience of as businessman, 93
    experience of as lawyer, 92, 95, 96, 148
    and extradition of Robert Hill, 158
    and federal petition for writ of habeas corpus, 206
    and freedom of Ware defendants, 228
    fundraising efforts of, 3, 213
    in Helena for second round of trials, 164, 170, 173, 175
    in Marianna, Ark., 218
    and motion for new trials, 148, 149, 150
    in New York, 174
    and representation of V. E. Powell, 205
    and work on *Moore v. Dempsey* appeal, 209, 213, 214
    relationships: with Brough, 3, 94, 99, 179, 180; with McHaney, 177; with NAACP, 93, 95, 101, 143, 144, 162, 183, 184; with Republican Party of Arkansas, 163, 164; with Ulysses Bratton, 213, 214; with Walter White, 92; with whites generally, 4, 91, 92, 93, 94, 101, 157, 158, 182, 183
Jones, T. K., xxx, 45

affidavit of, 46, 47, 193, 194, 195, 196, 197, 202, 204
background of, 46

Keesee, T. W., 27, 72, 109
Kelley, Harry, 19
Kennemore, Clare, 152
Kerlin, Robert, 184, 185
Kirby, W. S., 7
Kitchens, F. F., 11, 48, 72, 80, 98
Knight, J. C., 5, 72, 80
Knox, Joe, xxvii, 115, 116, 117, 118, 119, 120, 178
Ku Klux Klan, xxxi, 210, 211, 226

labor problems
in Lee County, 23
in Phillips County, 23, 24, 27, 28, 31
Lambert, Gerard, 11, 20, 42, 43
Lambrook operation, 11, 19, 20
Lee, Clinton, xxiv, xxvi, 76, 111, 112, 114
Lee County, Ark., xx, 23
Lilly, James, xxiv, 84
Lilly, O. R., 76
Lions Club in Helena, 178
lynchings, xv, 110
in Arkansas, 6, 94, 180, 181, 182, 183, 208
in Little Rock, xxxii, 230, 231
in Phillips County, xxxi, 208
in United States, 4

Machon (Michon), Joe, 171, 172
Mann, Burke, xxxi, 193, 194, 218, 219
Marianna, Ark., 41, 180, 192, 193, 208, 218, 219
Marshall, Thurgood, 233
Martin, John, xxvii, 120, 121, 122, 124, 128, 165, 166, 167, 168
Martineau, John E., xxix, xxxii
action as governor during last lynching in Little Rock, 229, 230, 231
background of, 188, 189, 190
as foe of Ku Klux Klan, 226

and issue of writ of habeas corpus, 190, 191
Marvell, Ark., xx
massacres, xviii, 46
McAdoo, William Gibbs, 3
McClintock, Oliver, 53
McCool, B. Boren, 39, 84, 169
McCulloch, Edgar A., 191
McDonald, Floella, 228, 229
McHaney, Edgar L., xxvi, xxix, xxx, 47
affidavits obtained by, 193
appointment to Arkansas Supreme Court, 189
in Arkansas House of Representatives, 227
background of, 103, 104
Bratton on, 175
and dispute on fees, 175
in Marianna, Ark., 192, 218
in New York, 174
and petition for federal writ of habeas corpus, 206
and petition for state court writ of habeas corpus filed by, 190, 191
and threatened resignation, 192, 193
McRae, Thomas C., xxix, xxx, 179, 191, 192, 226
attitude toward Ku Klux Klan, 211
background of, 180, 181
and meeting with Scipio Jones on last day as governor, 227, 228
position on clemency for Moore defendants, 184, 185, 186, 188, 205, 224, 225
position on lynching, 182
McReynolds, James C., 215
Mears, Roger C., 15, 16
Memphis News Scimitar, 56
Memphis Press, xxiii, 41, 64, 182
Meyers, Joseph, 28, 29, 84
Millar, A. C., 151
Miller, Jim, 124, 125, 126
Miller, John E., xxvi, xxxi, xxxii, 115, 117
background of, 40, 107
and dismissal of charges against defendants during grand jury

proceedings, 109
as intermediary for plea bargain
with Moore defendants in 1923,
216, 217, 223, 224
interview with, 40, 41, 49
and opposition to clemency for
Moore defendants in 1921, 186,
187, 188
and plea bargains with Elaine
defendants, 129, 130, 131
as prosecuting attorney during trials, 108, 109, 123, 129
Monroe, W. K., 168
Moore, Frank, 115, 116, 117, 118,
119, 120
Moore, H. D., 72
Moore, J. N., 132
Moore, John I., 115, 225
Moore v. Dempsey, 215, 216
Morgan, Cornelius, 131
Morris, E. C., 30, 77, 100, 145, 163
background of, 30
and philosophy of race relations,
30, 31, 92
Mosaic Templars of America, 3, 93, 94
Moseby, J. R., 131, 168
Moyer, Charles, 229, 231
Murphy, George W., xxviii, xxix, 164,
165, 166
background of, 141, 142, 148
and brief to Arkansas Supreme
Court, 160, 165
conflict of interest in re-trials of
Ware defendants, 168
death of, 176
and illness during trial, 169
and motion for new trial, 148, 149,
150
NAACP hires as counsel, 142, 143

NAACP, xxvi, xxxi, xxxii, 44, 45, 97,
162, 183, 217, 220, 224, 225,
226
assistance of during attempted
extradition of Robert Hill, 154,
155, 156
and distrust of black lawyers, 142,
143, 162

financial agreements with Murphy,
McHaney, and Jones, 192
James Weldon Johnson and, 97,
143, 217, 224
John Shillady and, 97
Mary White Ovington and, 97
Moorfield Story and, 212, 213,
214, 217, 220
visit by U. S. Bratton, 141
Walter White and, 97
W. E. B. Du Bois and, 97
William H. Pickens and, 97, 156
Newton, C. P., 181

Ovington, Mary White, 97, 138, 141

Parker, Dr. O., 123
Passailaigue, Edward, 61, 64, 65, 66,
67
Phillips County, Ark., xii, xxi, 10, 23
racial attitudes of, 24, 25, 26
Pratt, Charles W., 11, 76, 121, 127,
137, 168, 171
Price, Thomas J., xxvii, 100, 142, 143,
144, 157
Proctor, Ira, 129
Progressive Farmers and Household
Union of America, xxiii, 29, 32,
158

Quarles, Greenfield, 20, 21, 115, 123

race riots, 4
racial cleansing, 7
Ratliff, John, 121, 122, 130, 167, 171
Reamey, Sanford, 95
Remmel, A. C., 163
Republican Party of Arkansas, 163,
164
Robertson, E. D., xxxii, 207, 212,
219, 220, 221, 222
Rogers, O. A., Jr., xvi, xvii
Rose, George B., xxxii, 220, 223, 224
Rotary Club in Helena, 178
Rotenberry, Burl C., 182, 229

Saint Charles, Ark., 6
Semmes, L. A., 137

sharecroppers, 23, 26, 31, 32, 33, 49, 86
Shillady, John, 142, 154, 162
Simmons, Lit, 166, 168, 170
slavery, xv, xix
Smiddy, H. F., xxix, 45, 168
   affidavit of, 46, 170, 193, 194, 195, 196, 202, 203, 204, 205
   Jones's financial assistance to, 211, 212
Smith, R. D., 193, 212, 219
Solomon, Joseph, 225
Stewart, Glennie, 230
Stewart, Mr. B. E., 230
Stewart, Mrs. B. E., 230
Stokes, Sid, 3, 10, 114, 119, 132
Storey, Moorfield, xxxi, xxxii
   background of, 204
   comment on decision of Jones to settle cases by, 225
   George B. Rose and, 220
   hiring of, 209, 212, 213
   and objection to release of *Moore* defendants, 217
   oral argument by, 214
Straub, Charles, 29
Straub, Sebastian, 28, 29, 30, 76, 109
Street, James, 39, 62
Sturgis, S. D., 63

Tappan, James, xxiv, 76, 122, 123, 125, 126, 129, 165, 169, 170
Terral, Tom J., 226, 227
Thomas, D. Y., 78, 79
Thompson, Herbert, 123
Trieber, Jacob, xxx, 188, 205, 206, 224
Tunica Times, 57

U.S. military, xv, xxiii, 4, 36, 37, 38, 43, 44, 62

U.S. Supreme Court, xxxi, 192

Valkenburgh, Arba S., 219

Walker, Sam, 166
Ward, Walter, 118, 130
War Department, U.S., xii
Wardlow, William, 120, 127, 128, 129, 149, 168, 169
Ware, Ed, xxvii, 50, 51 131, 165, 170, 171, 172, 173, 174, 216, 221
Ware, Lula, 52
Washington, Arthur, 124
Washington, Booker T., 93
Waskow, Arthur, 38
Wells-Barnett, Ida B., xvi, 49, 50, 52, 97
West, Emmanuel, 182, 183
Whayne, Jeannie M., xv, xviii, 39
White, Walter F., xxvi, 44, 45, 176, 226
   background of, 96, 97
   Bratton's meeting with, 97
   Brough interviewed by, 97
   on escape from Helena, 97
   on financial report by Scipio Jones, 184
   on number of blacks killed and version of events, 99
Wilson, Sam, 131
Wilson, Woodrow, 3, 4
Wordlow, William, 120, 127, 128, 129, 168
Work, Monroe N., 162
Wright, Lizzie, 165
Wright, Richard, 20

Yingling, C. E., xxxi, 212, 216, 217, 221, 224